CHARLES DICKENS

Some books by
STEPHEN LEACOCK

The Greatest Pages of Charles Dickens
Charles Dickens
Wet Wit and Dry Humour
Laugh with Leacock
Afternoons in Utopia
Back to Prosperity
Economic Prosperity in the British Empire
The Iron Man and the Tin Woman
Short Circuits
Winnowed Wisdom
The Garden Folly
College Days
Over the Footlights
My Discovery of England
Winsome Winnie
The Unresolved Riddle of Social Justice
Frenzied Fiction
The Hohenzollerns in America
Further Foolishness
Essays and Literary Studies
Moonbeams from the Larger Lunacy
Arcadian Adventures with the Idle Rich
Behind the Beyond
Sunshine Sketches of a Little Town
Nonsense Novels
Literary Lapses
Elements of Political Science

CHARLES DICKENS

His Life and His Work

by

Stephen Leacock

Fitzhenry & Whiteside

In Canada
Fitzhenry & Whiteside Limited
195 Allstate Parkway
Markham, Ontario L3R 4T8

In the United States
Fitzhenry & Whiteside Limited
121 Harvard Avenue, Suite 2
Allston, Massachusetts 02134

www.fitzhenry.ca godwit@fitzhenry.ca

National Library of Canada Cataloguing in Publication
Leacock, Stephen, 1869-1944
Charles Dickens : his life and work / Stephen Leacock.

ISBN 1-55041-767-3
1. Dickens, Charles, 1812-1870. 2. Novelists, English–19th century–Biography. I. Title.
PR4581.L4 2003 823'.8 C2003-903432-1

Publisher Cataloging-in-Publication Data (U.S.)
Leacock, Stephen.
Charles Dickens : his life and work / Stephen Leacock.
[320] p. : cm.
Includes index.
Originally published, 1934.
Summary: This biography explores the humor as well as the morality of Dickens' novels.
ISBN 1-55041-767-3 (pbk.)
1. Dickens, Charles, 1812-1870. 2. Novelists, English – 19th century – Biography. I. Title.
823/.8 B 21 PR4581.L43 2003

Fitzhenry & Whiteside acknowledges with thanks the Canada Council for the Arts, the Government of Canada through its Book Publishing Industry Development Program, and the Ontario Arts Council for their support of our publishing program.

Many of the illustrations in this volume, especially the ones depicting rare pages of Dickens manuscripts and letters, are reproduced through the courtesy of Dr. A.W.W. Rosenbach, of the Rosenbach Company, New York and Philadelphia.

Certain other Dickens illustrations are through the courtesy of James F. Drake, Inc., Culver Service, and The New York Public Library.

This reprinted edition of *Charles Dickens, His Life and Work,* has not been edited, updated or revised to correct typographical errors or omissions found in the original version, published by Doubleday, Doran & Company, Inc., 1933, 1934.

Cover Image Credit: © Bettmann/CORBIS/MAGMA
Cover Design: Darrell McCalla
Interior Layout: Karen Petherick

Printed in Canada

CONTENTS

ILLUSTRATIONS

CHARLES DICKENS

Chapter One

CHILDHOOD AND YOUTH OF DICKENS

Poverty, Debt, and Debtors' Prison – The Sweet Uses of Adversity

PEOPLE READING DICKENS – ALL OVER THE WORLD for a hundred years, almost, there have been people reading Dickens. In town and in country, at home and abroad, in winter with the candles lighted and the outside world forgotten, in summer beneath a shadowing tree or in a sheltered corner of the beach, in garret bedrooms, in frontier cabins, in the light of the camp fire, and in the long vigil of the sick-room – people reading Dickens.

And everywhere the mind enthralled, absorbed, uplifted, the anxieties of life, the grind of poverty, the loneliness of bereavement, and the longings of exile, forgotten, conjured away as there rises from the magic page the inner vision of the lanes and fields of England, and on the ear the murmured sounds of London, the tide washing up the Thames, and the fog falling upon Lincoln's Inn.

And of all the people who have thus read Dickens, hardly any have read for an ulterior purpose and with an artificial aim. Other writers are read as a task, are read for self-improvement, for the pedantry and for the vainglory of scholarship. Not so Charles Dickens. His books from first to last have been read for their own sake. The written word has of itself called forth that laughter that lay among the lines, and for its own sake the tears that have fallen upon the page.

One stands appalled at the majesty of such an achievement. In the sheer comprehensiveness of it, no writer in all the world has ever equalled or approached it. None ever will. The time is past.

There are many younger people now, so we are told, who do not read Dickens. Nor is it to be wondered at. We live in a badly damaged world. It is a world of flickering shadows, tossed by electric currents, of a babel of voices on the harassed air, a world of inconceivable rapidity, of instantaneous effects, of sudden laughter and momentary tragedy, where every sensation is made and electrocuted in a second and passes into oblivion. It is a world in which nothing lives. Art itself is as old as man, and as immortal. But the form and fashion of it change. Dickens lived and wrote in a world that is visibly passing, the age of individual eminence that is giving place to the world of universal competence.

If early adversity is what is needed to bring out latent genius, Charles Dickens had a rare chance. He was born in a shabby second-rate home and spent his childhood in a series of homes each as shabby and as second rate as the last. For a time the "home" of his impecunious father was a debtors' prison. At the best it rose only to the level of what might be called respectability.

Of school he had but little; of college none at all. The early flowering of his boyish genius received neither encouragement nor recognition. If he was precocious, there was none to know it. A little boy reading in an attic his tattered books – who cared for that? A child in an agony of humiliation at his lot as a little working drudge – who was there to notice that? In all the pictures drawn by Dickens of the pathos of neglected or suffering childhood, there is none more poignant than the picture of little Dickens himself. The pathos of little Oliver, of Tiny Tim, and little Paul is drawn with a sympathy that sprang from the childhood experiences of Charles Dickens.

It is the wont of biographers to ramble through details of ancestry as tedious as they are remote. Fortunately nothing of that sort is needed in the case of Dickens. He came of a family on both sides and in all branches as utterly undistinguished as those of all the rest of us: a fact which helped perhaps to implant in Dickens's mind a contempt for ancestry in general and for descent at large. The queer opening chapter of *Martin Chuzzlewit* with the biography of the Chuzzlewits from the crusades down may well combine something of personal bitterness in its burlesque. The thousand and one references to dead-and-gone dullness, the contempt for the arrogant solemnity of ancient nobility, and the wooden immobility of the landed gentry of the old school, remind us that all that was a world to which Dickens was born a stranger and which he never entered nor coveted. There is no man living who can overcome the ingrained prejudice of social disadvantages. Yet it was on the basis of these disadvantages, without opportunity, without encouragement, that Charles Dickens achieved his unrivalled success in the world of imaginative literature.

He was born on February 7, 1812, in a house in what was then Landport, Portsea, and which still stands as No. 387 Mile End Terrace, Portsmouth. He was christened Charles John Huffham. His father was John Dickens and his mother, in her maiden name, Elizabeth Barrow – both entirely undistinguished people until their gifted son raised them above distinction to immortality as Mr. Micawber and Mrs. Nickleby.

Dickens was born in war-time, and his father, John Dickens, was a clerk in the Navy Pay Office whose duties placed him at the time beside the great seaport of Portsmouth of which Portsea was a suburb. Readers of *David Copperfield* will recall Mr. Micawber, whose name has become almost a part of the English language; will recall his shiftless life, in and out of luck, in and out of a debtors' prison, waiting for something to turn up, and mingling heroic tears with rapid returns of cheerfulness over a pot of porter. This was, it seems, quite literally John Dickens. His job was small, his family was large, and he shifted from one shabby home to another with the ease of impecuniosity, enveloped always in a cloud of debt. He was at Portsea till the peace of 1814, then in London lodgings (Norfolk Street) for two years, after which the Lords of the Admiralty sent him to Chatham (1816-21) and then placed him again in London, where he lived on the ragged edge of penury till he subsided into the debtors' prison of the Marshalsea in 1822. Yet brains he must have had, and a queerly radiant mind, full of bright fancies and self-deceptions and ability, since his ill-fortunes ended later with his accession to the post of a shorthand reporter in the gallery of the old House of Commons.

His helpmate bore him many children and shared his ill-luck with what grace and cheerfulness we do not know. One child, Fanny Dickens, came before Charles, and after him six other children, of whom two died in childhood. After the fashion of those unsanitary days, death took its easy and accustomed toll.

The precocious intellect of little Charles enabled him dimly to recall even the Portsea home, and to retain vague memories of the first lodgment in London. But the house at Chatham (in St. Mary's Place) was his first truly remembered home. He was a frail child, debarred from rough play. Books were his earliest world. His father numbered among his Chatham possessions a few books grandiloquently called by him his "library." Dickens has told us what these books meant to him. Among them were *Roderick Random*, *Peregrine Pickle*, *Humphrey Clinker*, *Tom Jones*, *The Vicar of Wakefield*, *Don Quixote*, *Gil Blas*, and *Robinson Crusoe*. "They came out," he wrote (pretending that he was David Copperfield), "a glorious host to keep me company. They kept alive my fancy and my hope of something beyond that place and time, they and the *Arabian Nights* and the *Tales of the Genii*, – and did me no harm. For whatever harm was in some of them was not there for me: I knew nothing of it."

People who seek for the literary background on which

Dickens's work was based will find it partly in the books he read thus for himself as a child: these books, and presently the streets and sounds of London and the glittering gaslight of the cheap London stage. But the real basis and background was his instinctive observation and interpretation of the life about him. This was born in him, not made. There is no need to quote Latin over a thing so obvious.

Of instruction Dickens never had very much. At Chatham he went to a dame's school and attended, at the age of eight and nine, something like a real school kept by a William Giles, a Baptist minister. The Chatham of those days was still a sort of country place with the fields in easy reach with Rochester Cathedral near at hand (waiting for Edwin Drood). The town was rendered bright and romantic by the presence of the military, with the spectacles of sham fights (such as the one that overwhelmed Mr. Pickwick). Beside it the Medway opened to a view of the tall ships out at sea. In spite of isolation and neglect, little Dickens was happy there.

But fortune darkened over his head. His unlucky father, still wrapped in his cloud of debt, was moved by the Lords of the Admiralty to work in London. The journey in a stagecoach from Chatham up to London (the year was 1821) lived in the memory of his son as his first acquaintance with those pictures of highways and coaches, gabled inns and quaint villages, and guards blowing on key bugles, and galloping horses clattering on the frosty road, which live forever in his works. Later on, when Tom Pinch sat staring in the coach, lost in a new world of wonder on his journey from Salisbury up to London, he had been preceded in reality by a little boy of nine who journeyed up from Chatham.

With London came the darkest period of Dickens's childhood, one may say of his whole life. It would be difficult indeed to imagine a childhood of deeper shadow and greater pathos. The family lived in a succession of mean homes and in an atmosphere of sordid makeshift and continual debt. Their first abode was a little house in Baynham Street, Camden Town – a poor suburb in those days – somewhere just below the level of respectability. A washerwoman lived next door, a Bow Street runner over the way. Little Charles, occupying a back garret looking out on a squalid court, wept for even his humble home at Chatham, his lessons, and the little life of romance that he had built about him. In Baynham Street there was nothing. Lessons had stopped. There were no playmates, and at home nothing but neglect, penury, and the shadow of a coming disaster. Most of all, and hardest for the child to bear, was the fact that nobody seemed to care what might become of him. "Many times," writes his intimate friend and biographer John Forster, "had he spoken to me of this and how he seemed at once to fall into a solitary condition apart from all other boys of his own age and to sink into a neglected state at home which had always been unaccountable to him."

It is indeed hard to account for it. There was nothing vicious or cruel about the parents of little Dickens. His father was proud of the boy's talents, would have him up on a chair to sing or recite for his friends: from first to last there was great affection between them, and Charles Dickens wrote of him afterward in the highest terms. "I know my father," he said, "to be as kind-hearted and generous a man as ever lived in the world. Every thing that I can remember of his conduct to his wife or children, or friends, in sickness or affliction, is beyond all praise. By me, as a sick child, he has watched night and day, unweariedly and patiently many nights and days. He never undertook any business, charge or trust that he did not zealously, conscientiously, punctually, honorably discharge. But in the ease of his temper and the straightness of his means, he appeared to have utterly lost at this time the idea of educating me at all."

The truth is, the elder Dickens was a man of easy temperament. He saw only what he had to see. Living in financial embarrassment, the cloud of debt threatening to burst over his head, he preferred, no doubt, to fancy to himself that all was well with the beautiful and gifted boy moping his heart out in an attic.

Of his mother we know less. Her domestic cares must have been great. But if there was any realization in her mind of the genius and suffering of her son during these times and the still darker hours of his childhood that followed, at least the evidence of it is hard to find.

Yet Mrs. Dickens made an effort to get the family out of the rising tide of debt. It was a characteristic effort. She plunged in more deeply still – *sauter pour mieux reculer*, as it were. She moved into a larger house, in Gower Street North, and indicated that it had become a young ladies' school by having a brass plate put on the door with the legend *Mrs. Dickens's Establishment*. It was confidently expected by the family that the influx of young ladies – especially of rich Creoles from across the sea, attracted somehow by the process of paying His Majesty's navy – would restore the family fortunes. It was characteristic of Dickens's parents that even in the lowest stage of their adversity a mirage of prosperity haunted their imaginations; even in the desert march they pictured the oasis which must lie before them. Thus might Mr. Micawber have opened a school on borrowed money and engaged Mrs. Nickleby to conduct it.

No pupils came – not one. Credit failed. Even the brass plate ceased to inspire confidence. There were an unpaid landlord, an indignant butcher, and a baker whose patience was exhausted. The rigour of the law accorded them a remedy since forgotten. John Dickens was arrested, and the doors of the Marshalsea prison shut him in.

The old King's Bench prison of the Marshalsea has long since vanished from the earth. It stood south of the Thames in Southwark, dated back to Plantagenet times, and took its name from the Marshal of the King's House, among whose functions was the custody of debtors. Prisoners for debt, under the law of England of Dickens's day, were not under the conditions of incarceration imposed upon criminals. Within the precincts of the "prison" they maintained their liberty. If they had money, they could spend it within the prison itself on the purchase of extra food, or more comfortable quarters than the vile diet and squalid accommodation afforded by the government. Beer flowed freely; bad gin and dubious wines were sold to the prisoners by the turnkeys themselves. Visitors came and went. There were a perpetual noise and clatter and the false merriment that for shame's sake covers misfortune with the mimic bravery of laughter. And side by side with it the listless despair and dull stagnation of those whose imprisonment ran back into uncounted years, and forward, it might be, to the grave. Among these scenes of disgrace and misery, of carouse and apathy, there lived and moved the wives and children of the debtors. For a small fee these were accommodated within the prison itself, which thus became the "home" of little children reared in the shadow. Human progress is slow, but we have, in England and in America at least, passed this milestone forever. But let those who wish to see a picture of the prison life of the debtor open again the pages of their Pickwick and recall the incarceration of that eminent man in the Fleet. What seems perhaps at first sight a merry caricature becomes on reflection a simple statement of fact, no feature of it exaggeration, no word of it untrue.

Charles Dickens had reason to know all about it. For many months the Marshalsea prison was all the "home" he had. His mother, when her husband was taken for debt, made a feeble attempt at maintaining the family outside. The Gower Street furniture was sold, item by item, to the pawnshops. Thither little Charles himself carried his beloved books of his father's pretentious library. At last there was nothing left. Then Mrs. Dickens and the younger children moved into the prison. Money was found to place the elder daughter Fanny in a school. Charles had a humble lodging outside, at Lant Street in the Borough, from which he came each morning early to wait till the Marshalsea gates were open so that he might go in and get breakfast with his mother and father. From the prison, when the gates shut at night, the little boy – he was ten years old – took his solitary way to the garret room where he slept.

Dickens always looked back to the memory of these days with feelings too deep for casual expression. To his own family he never spoke of them: even to John Forster, scarcely at all; and to the world at large, never. But it seems to have been his intention to set down some day for all the world to read the whole story of his life. This design he never fulfilled. What should have been the autobiography of Charles Dickens became presently the fictitious biography of David Copperfield. It reappears here and there in his books in indirect form; and the prison life of his father is reflected in the incarceration of Mr. Pickwick and the shadowed tragedy of Edward Dorrit.

But some part of the earlier story of Dickens's life is preserved for us as he first wrote it and as confided to Forster. Here he has given us an account of his father's entry to the debtors' prison more grim and more pathetic than his fiction itself.

"My father was waiting for me in the lodge," he writes, "and we went up to his room (on the top story but one) and cried very much. And he told me, I remember, to take warning by the Marshalsea, and to observe that if a man had twenty pounds a year and spent nineteen pounds, nineteen shillings and sixpence, he would be happy: but that a shilling spent the other way would make him wretched. I see the fire we sat before, now; with two bricks inside the rusted grate, one on each side, to prevent its burning too many coals. ... I really believed at this time," said Dickens, "that they had broken my heart."

But even more bitter to him in later years than the recollection of the prison was his remembrance of his life outside. Some relative of the family, with the consent of his father and mother, found work for little Charles in a blacking warehouse at No. 30 Hungerford Stairs, Strand, a "crazy tumbled down old house abutting on the river and literally overrun with rats." Here the boy worked with two or three others, pasting labels on pots of blacking. The other boys were of the commonest sort; the work was mean and monotonous; the whole surroundings sordid to a degree. "No words can express," wrote Dickens, "the secret agony of my soul as I sunk into this companionship: compared these every-day associates with those of my happier childhood: and felt my early hopes of growing up to be a learned and distinguished man, crushed in my breast. The deep remembrance of the sense I had of being utterly neglected and hopeless: of the shame I felt in my position: at the misery it was to my young heart to believe that, day by day, what I had learned, and thought, and delighted in, and raised my fancy and my emulation up by, was passing away from me never to be brought back any more; cannot be written."

The child meantime lived (during this working period) as a lodger in Little College Street, Camden Town, with a lady in reduced circumstances who "took in children to board." Dickens and two other boys slept in the same room. Charles bought his own supplies, a penny loaf and a pennyworth of milk and a quarter of a pound of cheese being stored in his cupboard as the breakfast and supper for the days when he did not walk to the prison. His dinner he carried with him to Hungerford Stairs or bought in a near-by shop. "It was generally," he tells us, "a fourpenny plate of beef from a workshop: sometimes a plate of bread and cheese and a glass of beer from a miserable old public house across the way." On Sundays Charles and his sister Fanny spent their day in the Marshalsea. Such was the boy's life. And through it all, from week-end to week-end, he had, so he tells us himself, "no advice, no counsel, no encouragement, no consolation, no support from anyone I can call to mind, so help me God."

In time the pathos of it seems to have reached even the easy-going intelligence of the imprisoned father. The child pleaded to be removed from his sordid lodgings, and his father, giving way to the plea, got him another room – a back attic that looked out over a timber yard – into which was sent a mattress with some bedding and a bed made up on the floor. The place, all his own, seemed to little Dickens, so he tells us, "like a paradise." It was here, in this very lodging, transferred to the pages of fiction and enlarged, that there lived the merry medico, Mr. Bob Sawyer, and it was up these stairs to the attic that Mr. Pickwick and his friends found their way to Mr. Sawyer's ill-fated party.

After this the little boy could take his breakfast and his supper in the prison every day.

A further chance came. Dickens Senior had a quarrel with the relative by whom his son was employed and with characteristic hauteur removed him from his service. No doubt by this time his genuinely kind nature had awaked to the facts. But it is sad to relate that the mother saw it in a different light. She was all for composing the quarrel and letting her son return to this unhappy situation. "My father," so writes Dickens, "said I should go back no more and should go to school. I do not write resentfully or angrily: for I know how all these things have worked together to make me what I am. But I never afterwards forgot; I shall never forget, I can never forget, that my mother was warm for my being sent back."

There are many of us, no doubt, who can share, even after the lapse of a century, this indignation, and who feel that we want to know nothing more of Mrs. John Dickens than just that.

At last the clouds lifted. John Dickens, like Mr. Micawber, was always waiting for something to turn up. Something did. A miraculous legacy of several hundred pounds carried John Dickens out of prison on a temporary tide of affluence. The small pension which he drew from a grateful country, even while it held him in prison for debt, added to the legacy, and supplemented presently by general earnings, removed the elder Dickens henceforth from the penury into which he had sunk. The family had a home again, or, rather, a series of homes. Mr. and Mrs. Dickens moved so often that it would puzzle a research student to follow the dates and details of their migrations. They were in lodgings in Little College Street, then at No. 13 Johnson Street, then at the Polygon, Somers Town, then in Fitzroy Street, Fitzroy Square, then at 18 Bentinck Street, Cavendish Square. These are at least some of the places where John Dickens lived.

Meantime little Charles was at last able, from the age of twelve to the age of fourteen, to attend a school – this time a real school. It was quite a pretentious one in its way – Wellington House Academy in the Hampstead Road, a spacious building with quite a staff of masters and a real playground, though the playground and a good part of the house were later on ignominiously shovelled away to make room for the Birmingham Railway. It exists still in a rather glorified form as David Copperfield's school of Salem House and in "Our School" as described in *Household Words*. But little Dickens was never really head boy of it, as David was, and most likely never learned the Latin and such with which he endowed David. But he recaptured, at any rate, the cheery happiness of a child's life, denied to him in the shadows of the prison and the factory.

"He was a healthy-looking boy," wrote one of his schoolfellows long afterward, "small, but well built, with a more than usual flow of spirits inducing to harmless fun, seldom if ever to mischief, I cannot recall then that he indicated that he would hereafter become a literary celebrity." "I do not remember," wrote another classmate, "that Dickens distinguished himself in any way or carried off any prizes. My belief is that he did not learn Latin and Greek there, and you will remember that there is no allusion to the classics in any of his writings. He was a handsome, curly-headed lad, full of animation and animal spirits." All of those who have described the youthful Dickens from boyhood to adolescence have spoken of the singular animation of his look, the arresting power of his eye, the impression of a "mesmeric" personality. As to " allusions to the classics," we have at least Dr. Blimber of *Dombey* to the contrary. But no doubt the writer meant "quotations."

The schooling was but brief. Charles Dickens was never educated, or rather, as his father once grandiloquently phrased it, "he may be said to have educated himself." At fourteen the little boy passed on to the status of an attorney's clerk – not an articled clerk, but what would now be called an office boy – with a Mr. Edward Blackmore of Gray's Inn. This was from May, 1827, to November, 1829. Here began for Dickens that profound knowledge of the forms and surroundings of the law and that profound contempt for it which never left him; here were laid the first foundations of the jurisprudence of Bardell vs. Pickwick: here begin the long series of the Dodson and Foggs, the Vholeses, the Parkers, and the Tulkinghorns, who embody forever in the paper of Dickens's books the figures and the figments of the Victorian bar and bench. Throughout his life Charles Dickens saw little but the comic side of law and government. Politics to him was humbug, the cabinet system a delirious piece of nonsense, and a political party a delightful make-believe. He saw either this or the tragic side – the tyranny and oppression of the strong, the law's injustice, and the heartbreak of the delays of the chancery. Living in the solid security of Victorian England, with peace and property and stability, the very firmness of the ground concealed from him the basis on which it rested. Once or twice only he stood on other ground, as when he depicted the Gordon Riots in *Barnaby Rudge* or the flames of the French Revolution. But it did not occur to him that perhaps the existence of "Doodle and Coodle," alternating in the cabinet with "Noodle and Foodie," and of the wooden magistrates and even the solemn nincompoops of the circumlocution office, had something to do with the unbroken life of peace and security which he himself enjoyed. To the simplest of us now, law, politics, and government have become a life-and-death matter. Not so to Dickens. He saw only the joke of it. No doubt it was better so.

At this time Dickens the elder, with a characteristic change of fortune, converted himself into a reporter working for a London newspaper in the press gallery of the Commons. There is something queer and appealing about John Dickens, alternating from the desk of the pay office and from the tears and the pewter pots of the debtors' prison to the swift efficiency of the shorthand expert in the world's greatest legislature.

"Shorthand" at that time was a rising art. Cultivated in one shape or another since ancient times, it had, like so many other things, made enormous advances in England in the eighteenth century. It had learned to follow sounds, not letters. It had caught up with the ordinary pace of human speech. It had been immensely stimulated by the licensed publication of debates, the steam press, and the rapid carriage of newspapers by the "flying coaches" of the days of William IV. How old Dickens learned it, we do not know. But young Dickens threw himself into the study of the mystic art with ardour and passion. His inimitable description of David Copperfield (that non-existent and unconvincing personage) learning shorthand describes his own efforts and his own success. But access to the parliamentary gallery was not to be had at once, even for so expert a writer as Charles Dickens rapidly became. He got employment as a reporter in one of the offices of Doctors' Commons. This quaint and ancient institution, which has charmed and mystified the readers of Dickens for over half a century, was from the days of Queen Elizabeth till 1857 a society of lawyers concerned with cases of Church jurisdiction, and with such matters as wills and testaments, marriage and divorce, as have, or once had, a ghostly connotation. They were incorporated as the "College of Law Exercent in the Ecclesiastical and Admiralty Courts." The thirty-four "proctors" of the college – as who should say, the solicitors, ground the grist in the mills of the probate, divorce, and admiralty courts. Among these lived and moved the Mr. Spenlow and the "inexorable" Mr. Jorkins of *David Copperfield.* And in the office of one of them laboured as a reporter for two years the youth Charles Dickens.

Dickens, when he reported at Doctors' Commons, was aged eighteen – nineteen when he left it. The law itself as a career meant nothing to him: his work was a task and nothing more, but illuminated and relieved his abiding appreciation of the comic side of anything serious. But life was opening in front of him. He lived, still with his parents, at No. 18 Bentinck Street, had many friends and acquaintances, and went out and about in what was not society with a capital S, but was at any rate social company. It was not unfitting that later on Dickens should have made David Copperfield's Dora (famous among the heroines of fiction) the daughter of Mr. Spenlow of Doctors' Commons. For it was in his days at the Commons that he met his own Dora and fell as immediately and as hopelessly in love as David did. Of this "Dora" one must speak in a later chapter. Suffice it for the moment to say that she was separated in station from young Charles by one of those nice gradations of social status familiar in England – in the England that was – but indistinguishable from a distance. The shabby-genteel status of the Dickens family, their lack of prospects, and their want of "class," put them a cut below the Beadnells. Young Maria's family saw to it that Dickens was not encouraged; and that a little later, absence and distance should terminate the whole connection. Henceforth, for twenty years, Maria was to Dickens like the lost Annabel Lee to Edgar Allan

Poe. Pity that she didn't stay lost. The history of literature would have been spared one of its meanest episodes.

But not even a broken heart can check the ardour of a body of nineteen. Dickens, after all, had the sharp spur of necessity, and with that, plenty of other interests. The "self-improvement" idea had struck him hard. He read and studied in the British Museum. And, more than all, there dawned upon his impressionable mind the glittering of the stage. From youth to age everything dramatic fascinated Charles Dickens. From his boyhood he haunted the cheap and popular theatres of the London of that day. Even in his Wellington House days he took the lead in getting up amateur theatricals a pursuit and a hobby of which he never tired. Had he not turned into a writer, he would inevitably have become an actor. His public "readings," later on, were largely histrionic performances, which held his audiences gripped by the mesmeric power of the presentation. As Dickens "read," the audience saw, not Charles Dickens beside a desk, but the crouching figure of the murderer Bill Sikes, or the glorious comicality of Mr. Weller.

The theatre (not the classic stage of Shakespeare and Racine) left a deep mark on the thought and the work of Dickens – and not all for their good. "The popular drama of that time," writes Mr. Robert Blachford, looking back in, and over, his *Eighty Years*, "would be derided today as wild absurdity. … The audience (at the little London theatre called the Bower) had a robust taste. They demanded ghosts and pirates, smugglers and slave drivers. Jack Tars and brigands; combats, abductions, love, treachery, battle, murder and blue fire, – and they got them. … I have witnessed," continues the same writer, "a soul stirring combat between one seaman and sixteen smugglers. Jack always fought two handed but before he drew his swords he would knock down a pair of pirates with his fists, disable another with his quid, stop a fourth with his hat, and then, putting the muslin-clad damsel in distress behind him, he would get to the business of the evening."

This is the stage which Dickens has portrayed in *Nicholas Nickleby*, the stage of the inimitable but actual Mr. Vincent Crummels, and the stage from which Dickens drew the melodramatic language of his characters and the delirious coincidence of his plots. "Open the door of some place," says the murderer Sikes to his associates, "where I can lock *this screeching Hell Babe*." Just so: right out of the Bower theatre.

Throughout his Doctors' Commons days Dickens's mind was constantly on the stage. "He went to the theatre almost every night for a long time," wrote John Forster, his biographer, "he studied and practised himself in parts and finally resolved to make his first plunge." It was just at the beginning of the year 1831 when he wrote to a Covent Garden manager, received an encouraging reply and an appointment, and then, by one of his own vital coincidences, had a severe earache and couldn't go." And when his ear was well, and the next chance came, other gates had opened for him on wider prospects, and Charles Dickens, the actor that might have been, was converted into "Boz," the writer that actually was. The penury, the servitude, and the apprenticeship were over. Charles Dickens was coming into his own.

Chapter Two

MR. PICKWICK TAKES THE WORLD BY STORM

Dickens as a Reporter – "Sketches by Boz" – "The Pickwick Papers"

CHARLES DICKENS WAS ADMITTED TO THE GALLERY of the old House of Commons – the unreformed and unburned House of 1831 – at the age of nineteen years. He had made himself, even in the merely mechanical sense, a marvellous reporter. He had conquered the system of shorthand as then dispensed at ten and sixpence by a Mr. Gurney. He could write it with singular speed and accuracy, and write it, apparently, sitting or standing, moving or at rest, and – what is the really harder thing to do with shorthand – read it again and transcribe it without a missing word. Thirty years later Dickens once told an admiring company what reporting meant in the days when the stagecoach was and the telegraph was not. "I have often," he said, "transcribed for the printer from my shorthand notes important public speeches in which the strictest accuracy was required, and a mistake in which would have been to a young man severely compromising, – writing on the palm of my hand by the light of a dark lantern in a post chaise and four, galloping through a wild country, through the dead of night, at the then surprising rate of fifteen miles an hour. … I have worn my knees by writing on them in the old back row of the old gallery of the old House of Commons; and I have worn my feet by standing to write in a preposterous pen in the old House of Lords where we used to be huddled like so many sheep. … I have been in my time belated on miry by-roads towards the small hours, forty or fifty miles from London, in a rickety carriage, with exhausted horses and drunken postboys and got back in time for publication."

From such memories as these, Dickens was to draw later on those wonderful scenes of coaching days and coaching nights that adorn so many pages of his books; the flight of Mr. Jingle and the maiden aunt; the moonlight journey of Tom Pinch, and the mail coach on the Dover Road on a heavy November night in the scene that opens the immortal *Tale of Two Cities.*

But meantime Dickens, while still reporting, had begun to "write." It seems that from his childhood he had always made up in his head imaginary tales and sketched imaginary characters. He had even written them down. At school he had improvised dramas and made up a sort of mimic language for himself and his schoolfellows. Now he began in earnest, writing stories, and at length, greatly daring, he sent one by post to a magazine. Every book on Dickens has quoted the passage in which he has himself described his sensations at his first literary success. He had dropped his first manuscript into a letter box, posting it after dark with stealth and fear. Then in due course he saw himself in all the majesty of print. "On which occasion," he says, "I walked down to Westminster Hall and turned into it for half an hour, because my eyes were so dimmed with joy and pride that they could not bear the street and were not fit to be seen there." The magazine to which he sent the story was the *Old Monthly Magazine* published by a Captain Holland, and the story was entitled *A Dinner at Poplar Walk,* afterwards published under the name of *Mr. Minns and His Cousin.* It appeared in December of 1833 and was followed by nine other sketches in the same magazine. The sketch of August, 1834, was the first to be signed with the pen name "Boz." This was the nickname of Dickens's youngest brother, Augustus, and was a sort of nursery adaptation of Moses.

The young author received no pay, the editor of the struggling publication being utterly unable to give him any. So the contributions came to an end. But by good luck a new opening appeared just at the right moment. The *Morning Chronicle*, for which young Dickens worked as a reporter at a salary of five guineas a week, was about to add an evening edition of a special nature. Dickens proposed to the organizing editor, a Mr. Hogarth, that he should contribute sketches to the evening paper and receive an award of extra pay. The arrangement was made. Indeed, everyone on the *Chronicle*, and most of all John Black, the editor, seem to have been immensely impressed with Dickens from start to finish. The extra two guineas a week added to his salary was a further proof of it. Henceforth the sketches flowed in a stream from Dickens's easy pen. The name "Boz" became well known, not to the work at large, but at least to the newspaper world of London. When the sketches had sufficiently accumulated, a publisher (John Macrone) was found who offered a hundred and fifty pounds for the copyright. In due time the *Sketches by Boz* (2 volumes, 1836) appeared as Dickens's first work. The volumes were illustrated by the well known George Cruikshank. Thenceforth and for many years Dickens was "Boz" to those who read him. The *Pickwick Papers* in their first dress bore the legend, "Edited by Boz," *Oliver Twist* as a serial was signed by "Boz," and it was "Boz" who edited the *Memoirs of Grimaldi* in 1838. But *Pickwick* as a book (1837) and *Oliver Twist* as a book (1838) were signed by Charles Dickens. After that the name disappeared, but the public both in England and in America went on using the name at least as an affectionate term for Dickens for many years. It was never, however, a question of hiding a real name behind an anonymity. At first people knew who "Boz" was and were no wiser if told that his real name was Dickens. In time the name wore out, fortunately enough, for it lacked dignity and seriousness, being after all more fit for a dog or a clown or a patent medicine than for a writer. The wonder is that it clung so long. The Americans of the 'forties all welcomed Dickens as "Boz"; old-fashioned people kept it up for a long time. Mr. Percy Fitzgerald, writing his book on Dickens in 1905, "bozzes" him perpetually and apologizes for it, as a reminiscence not shaken off in old age. "Time was," he says, "when it was in everybody's mouth, and it conveyed a great deal more than it does now,...a pleasant tone of affectionate interest."

It is difficult at this date to estimate the literary value of the *Sketches by Boz.* On the one hand they belong to a bygone time. The passage of a hundred years (it is, one notes, exactly a hundred years since they were written) has greatly changed the form of our thought, the fashion of our literature, and the character and cast of our humour. Since they were written, a million writers, great and small, have chronicled their impression of "everyday life and everyday people." In this, as in all else, we stand on the shoulders of those who went before us, albeit that in imaginary literature the position is different from the rising steps of science, and the footing is infinitely harder to keep. It would be silly to say that all writers now are better than any writers then. But at least all now share in the legacy they left then.

On the other hand, and working in the other direction, is the fact that the *Sketches by Boz* were written by Charles Dickens and that when we read them we know who wrote them. This gives them something of the sacred quality which surrounds the quaint incompetence of a primitive artist and opens the way to much the same conventional admiration.

The *Sketches* made no pretense of being on a lofty plane or of opening a tragic depth. They are just light pictures of ordinary people and ordinary happenings. The aim is to interest and amuse. The humour is distinctly in advance of most that had preceded it. Humour in its expression in literature has passed through various stages. There is the humour of primitive literature, reproduced in the nursery as "Jack, the Giant Killer," and such; there is the Gargantuan and grotesque humour of the Middle Ages; the eighteenth-century humour of horseplay and the practical joke; and this we see here passing into the humour of discomfiture and comic misadventure. This became *par excellence* the humour of the early Victorian England and is only now passing to its rest. From the volumes of Dickens it is never quite absent, and it was at least intended as the primary inspiration of *Pickwick.* This mode of

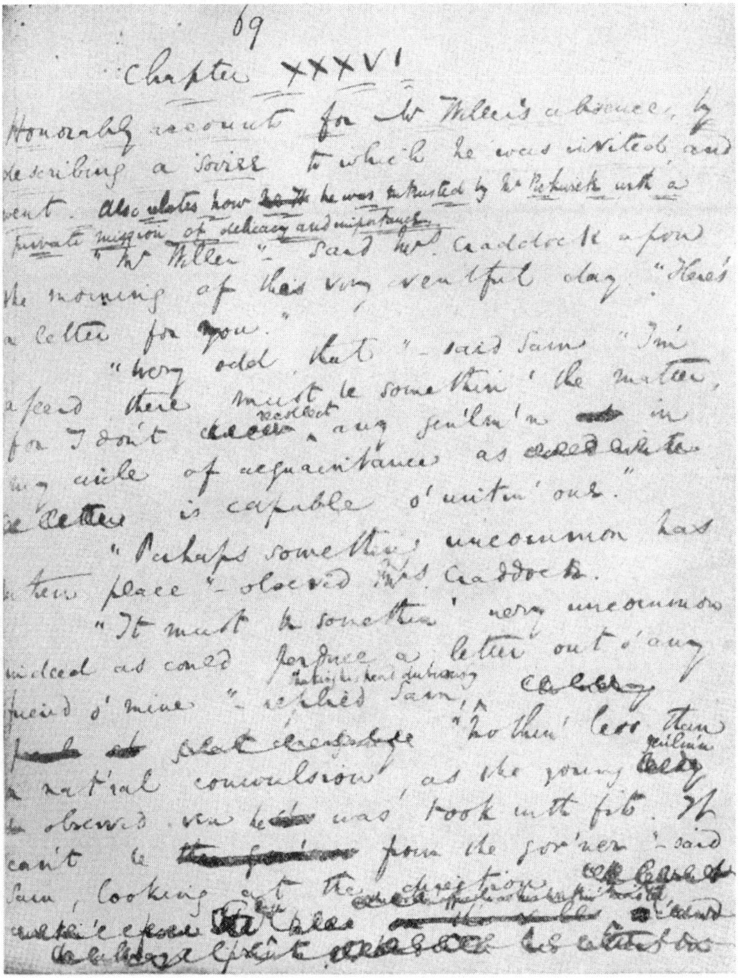

69

Chapter XXXVI

Honorably accounts for Mr Weller's absence, by describing a soirée to which he was invited and went. Also relates how he was entrusted by Mr Pickwick with a private mission of delicacy and importance.

"Mr Weller," said Mrs. Craddock upon the morning of this very eventful day. "Here's a letter for you."

"Very odd that," said Sam. "I'm afeard there must be somethin' the matter, for I don't recollect any gen'l'm'n in my circle of acquaintance as is capable o' writin' one."

"Perhaps something uncommon has taken place," observed Mrs. Craddock.

"It must be somethin' wery uncommon indeed as could produce a letter out o' any friend o' mine," replied Sam, "nothin' less than a nat'ral convulsion, as the young gen'l'm'n observed ven he was took with fits. It can't be from the gov'ner," said Sam, looking at the direction.

The Pickwick Papers
Page from the original manuscript of *The Pickwick Papers,*
mentioning Sam Weller.

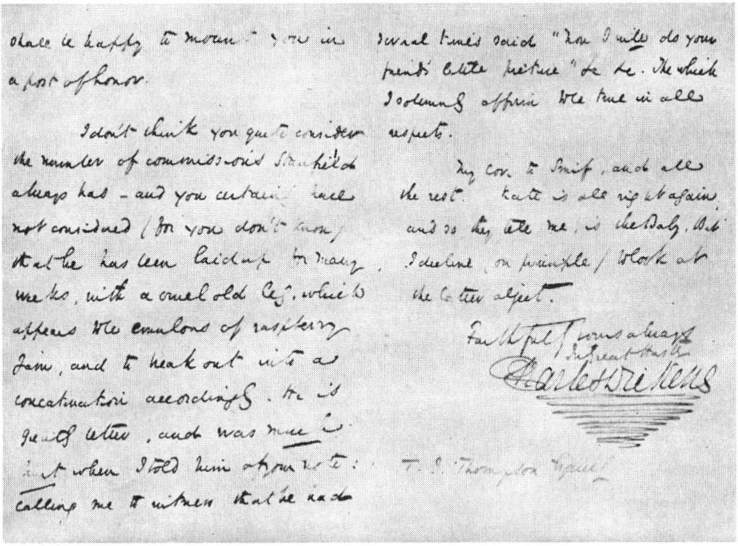

shall be happy to mount you in a post of honor.

I don't think you quite consider the number of commissions Stanfield always has — and you certainly have not considered (for you don't know) that he has been laid up for many weeks, with a cruel old leg, which appears the emulous of raspberry jam, and to break out into an eruption accordingly. He is greatly better, and was much [illegible] when I told him of your note: calling me to witness that he had several times said "how I wish do your friend's little picture" &c &c. Which I solemnly affirm to be true in all respects.

My love to Smif, and all the rest. Kate is all right again, and so they tell me, is the Baby. But I decline, on principle, to look at the latter object.

Faithfully Yours always
[illegible]
Charles Dickens

T. S. Thompson Esquire

Autographed Letter

A letter to William Henry Kolle, the most intimate friend of Charles Dickens's youth. It mentions Maria Beadnell, his earliest love.

humour appears as the main current of Dickens's first story, *Mr. Minns and His Cousin.* Mr. Minns, a precise, trim little old bachelor, is visited by a loud-voiced vulgarian cousin who eats a lion's share of his breakfast, cuts his ham the wrong way, and whose dog chaws up Mr. Minns's curtains. Invited to dinner by the cousin, Mr. Minns is delayed by the coach, choked by the dinner, bored by the company, kicked in the shin by the cousin's awful child (his godson), and, brought to a collapse by having to make a speech, misses the home coach, walks till three in the morning – and as a result cuts the awful child out of his will.

But there is much more in the *Sketches* than the mere humour of misadventure. That alone could never have floated them so long and so high. There is a power of description, or rather of observation, quite out of the common; and that easy and extraordinary command of language to match the observation which came to Dickens as a birthright. But the quite moderate success of the *Sketches by Boz* was soon to be entirely absorbed by the colossal, the phenomenal success that was so rapidly to follow.

Before, however, the sun of Mr. Pickwick appeared over the horizon, an even greater illumination, in the personal sense, was breaking upon Dickens's life. He was rushing headlong toward marriage. The Mr. Hogarth who had come down from Scotland to work on the *Morning Chronicle* was a man of cultivation and culture, possessed of a comfortable home, adorned by a bevy of three charming daughters, each as beautiful as the others. Young Dickens, talented and brilliant, was taken into the bosom of the family, and took the girls, all of them, to his heart. No doubt it was a wonderful experience for him, after his nondescript upbringing, to find himself the welcome guest of a normal and comfortable home, the idol of an admiring circle of pretty sisters. Charles ended by marrying one, and one only, of the Hogarth girls, in as much as the law of the land would not allow him more than one. But he fell in love with them collectively, and those who know the sequel may still wonder where his final preference lay. All were young. Catherine, the eldest, when Charles Dickens became engaged to her, was only twenty years old. Below her was Mary

Hogarth, a beautiful girl of sixteen, the joy of the household, beside whose chair there stood already the unseen figure of Death. The youngest was Georgina, whose later fate it was to share his home for nearly thirty years.

In those days the youth of Catherine, the inexperience of Charles, and the uncertainties of the future were no bar to marriage. It was the fashion then to marry early, just as it is the fashion now to marry often. Aspiring brides of eighteen and nineteen dashed off to Gretna Green, pursued by pink-and-white parents of eight-and-thirty. An unmarried female of twenty-five was an old maid, and Cupid closed his ledgers, apart from his comic supplement, well below forty. Readers of Dickens's books do not need to be told that with him a woman over forty was either a saint, a freak, or a joke.

Meantime young Dickens, in the process of blossoming forth, had left the parental roof and set up quarters of his own in Furnival's Inn – not a tavern but a set of chambers – a quite pretentious place in Holborn with a sort of terrace effect and a spacious colonnaded portico. Here, for example, he was seen and described by that once famous American writer Nathaniel P. Willis, who was at this time in London putting together the notes for a book on England. He speaks of an "uncarpeted and bleak-looking room with a deal table, two or three chairs, and a few books." He describes young Dickens as showing an "English obsequiousness" to the publisher who introduced the American to the youthful Boz – a statement which John Forster charmingly describes as "garbage."

It was to this Inn that Dickens a short time later was to bring his bride. But that was not till the marriage had been rendered feasible by the "tempting emolument" of fifteen guineas a month – the dazzling bait which lured him to the writing of *Pickwick*. Indeed, the wedding and the appearance of *Pickwick* took place almost simultaneously. The 31st of March, 1836, saw the publication of the first month's number of the *Posthumous Papers of the Pickwick Club, containing a Faithful Record of the Perambulations, Perils, Travel Adventures and Sporting Transactions of the Corresponding*

Members, edited by "Boz." The 2d of April of 1836 witnessed the marriage of Charles John Huffam Dickens to Catherine Thomson Hogarth. (He had dropped the "h" of his baptismal name.) The honeymoon was spent at Chalk, on the Dover Road close to Rochester in that part of Kent with which the life and works of Dickens were so closely associated. Then the young couple returned to take up their quarters in London at Furnival's Inn, and then at 48 Doughty Street, with all the world, and all that is best in it, before them.

Happily and auspiciously began the married life whose hearth, thus brightly illuminated, was to burn to dead, cold ashes.

But meantime Mr. Pickwick waits.

Just before his marriage, while young Dickens was enjoying the rapture of courtship and engagement and tasting the first delights of literary success, the fates were preparing for him a sudden and astounding rise to eminence unparalleled at any time in the history of letters. The "origin" of the *Pickwick Papers* has been the subject of so much controversy, so much vituperation, and of so much anger on the part of Dickens himself, that it is well to proceed step by step, moving on assured ground.

There was in London at this date (the close of the year 1835) a new and enterprising firm of publishers, by name Chapman and Hall. Dickens had acquired a certain connection with them, having contributed to their *Library of Humour* a story called "The Tuggs's at Ramsgate," afterwards included in the *Sketches by Boz.* There was in London also a caricature artist called Robert Seymour. He also had worked with Chapman and Hall, having drawn the plates for their *Squib Annual* which came out in November, 1835. Seymour made a suggestion to Mr. Chapman which Mr. Chapman (thirteen years later, at the request of Dickens for a statement as to the origin of the *Pickwick Papers*) explained as follows: "He said he would like to do a series of cockney sporting plates of a superior sort to those he had already published. I said they might do if accompanied by letter-press and published in monthly parts." Mr. Hall, the other member of the firm, then called on Dickens to invite him to undertake the work.

"The idea propounded to me," explained Dickens afterwards, "was that the monthly something should be a vehicle for certain plates to be executed by Mr. Seymour. And there was a notion on the part of either that admirable humorous artist or my visitor that a Nimrod Club, the members of which were to go out shooting, fishing, and so forth and getting themselves into difficulty through their want of dexterity, would be the best means of introducing these." Dickens adds that, as he "was no great sportsman except in regards to all kinds of locomotion," he asked permission to take his own way with a freer range of English scenes and people. He adds in a sentence that deserves an abiding place in the history of literature:

"My views being deferred to, *I thought of Mr. Pickwick*, and wrote the first number from the proof sheets of which Mr. Seymour made his drawings of the club and his happy portrait of its founder."

Seymour drew also the well known cover of the first number of *The Posthumous Papers of the Pickwick Club*. It carries at the top the picture of a very clumsy marksman firing at a very saucy bird; at the bottom, the picture of a middle-aged gentleman fishing in a punt – fast asleep; at the sides, guns, fishing rods, landing nets, and the bows and arrows of genteel archery. This is Seymour's Nimrod Club right enough, with Mr. Winkle specially designed for membership in it, and Mr. Pickwick destined to rise to glory out of it.

Seymour did three pictures for the next number, and then – it is too far away now to inquire why – died by his own hand. Later on the claim was made by his widow and his family that Seymour was the real creator of Pickwick, that Dickens had practically appropriated, one might almost say stolen, his idea. The family even put in a claim for legal compensation. The whole contention was ludicrous. Dickens owed nothing to Seymour except the accident of a start – from somewhere to anywhere. Mr. Pickwick could just as well have begun on board a ship, or at the battle of Waterloo, as in a punt. Dickens would have got him straight presently – by inspiration and by instinct. Seymour's plan had really nothing to do with Dickens's book. Pickwick got out of it, not into it. The serial papers of Pickwick never succeeded, indeed were a flat failure, till they got clean away from Seymour's misadventures into the larger atmosphere of the White Hart Inn and the larger companionship of Mr. Weller. There was nothing new in cockney sportsmen. They were already as old as gunfire. The novelty, the merit, the genius of the book were all Dickens's, and none of it Seymour's. Dickens should have passed over the criticism with a kindly laugh, with a gentle word for the merits of a fellow craftsman dead and gone, with a kindly donation from a flowing purse. He could have even said, "I owe it all to Seymour," and no one would have believed him. But Dickens was not like that. From first to last he was as sensitive, as jealous of his work as any third-rate actor or any unprinted author. An ignoramus could hurt his feelings; a fool could strike him to the heart. He *must* have homage; he must have recognition. Everyone, every single person, must admit that all that he did was wonderful. He knew that he had created Pickwick, and he could not tolerate denial. As late as the year 1866 he wrote to the *Athenæum* an angry letter in regard to something written by Seymour's son.

"Mr. Seymour the artist," he wrote, "never originated, suggested, or in any way had to do with, save as illustrator of what I devised, an incident, a character (except the sporting taste of Mr. Winkle), a name, a phrase, or a word, to be found in the *Pickwick Papers.* I never saw Mr. Seymour's handwriting in my life. I never even saw Mr. Seymour but once in my life."

This, from a man crowned with thirty years of unparalleled success, with honour, fortune, and acclaim, sounds – sounds just what it is: petty, ungenerous, and unnecessary. The whole episode is of interest now only as it illustrates the smaller sides of great men. The extension of human genius in one direction involves perhaps its contraction in another.

In any case, as already said, the *Pickwick Papers*, as they appeared first in monthly parts beginning in April, 1836, were not a success; indeed, were something very like a flat failure. Only four hundred copies of Part I (there were to be twenty-four altogether) were put out, and even that at first seemed too many. Dickens, in fact, seems to have groped his way into the book as Mark Twain did into *Huckleberry Finn*, the prospect opening before him as he moved on. It was only as he shook off all trace of the Seymour stuff that the book seemed to gather inspiration. The first chapter opens with the proceedings of the Pickwick Club, an institution which somehow vanishes into nothing as the book goes on and is painlessly dissolved in the last chapter. The club is a sort of burlesque of Charles Dickens's recollections as a reporter of parliaments, committees, and elections. It is a first indication of his abiding conviction of the comic nature of British government and British politics. Then follow the "Seymour" scenes of the misadventures of Pickwick and Winkle and the rest. But for most of us the *Pickwick Papers* really begin with Mr. Alfred Jingle, or, at any rate, with Mr. Jingle at the cricket match. At once we are lifted into an atmosphere of exhilaration, not alone for Jingle himself, but for the new light thus thrown on Mr. Pickwick. It is perhaps with Jingle that Dickens first really finds himself: that extraordinary magic by which he turns a cheat and a crook into a charming character, a criminal impostor into a thing of delight – that is Dickens, and that is no one else. Jingle is the first of the long line of these amazing creatures. It is as if the world itself were transformed and its worst sins seen in the light of a kindly and amused tolerance that is higher than humanity itself. This is the highest quality of Dickens's work; beside this, all his comic humour, his melodramatic climax, and his fountain of tears are as nothing.

Not that even Jingle (who appears first in chapter II) was enough alone to carry the *Pickwick Papers*. The publishers seriously considered abandoning the enterprise and almost did so, when on the publication of the fifth number the circulation went up by leaps and bounds. This marks the appearance of the immortal Samuel Weller as first seen cleaning boots in the yard of the White Hart Inn. Lord Macaulay, not really himself a comic genius, chron-

The Dying Clown

Original Drawing by Robert Seymour for Dickens's *Pickwick Papers.* Seymour committed suicide just after correcting the proof of this drawing.

icled the fact that it seemed to him that with Samuel Weller something new and great had come into English literature. This was apparently the view of thousands of lesser people. From this point on, the "papers" move with an accelerated power and interest. The Homeric episode of Bardell *vs.* Pickwick gathers on the horizon. The vast gigantic satire upon the law and lawyers, law courts and justice, with the tragic background of the debtors' prison, lifts the *Pickwick Papers* from the hit-and-run of the Nimrods to the proportion of the grand Romance. From this point on a breathless interest followed each successive number. The sales before the end rose to 40,000 copies per number: the publishers' profits were more than £20,000; and the young author, in addition to his "tempting emolument" of fifteen guineas a number, received by the generous foresight of his publishers no less than £2,500 for the serial numbers, and a share in the copyright.

Quite apart from any vain pretension of or for the dead-and-gone Seymour, one may well speculate as to what literary people would call the "genesis" of Mr. Pickwick. Where did he come from? The "genesis" of the *Pickwick Papers* as a publication begins, of course, not with Dickens but with the artist Seymour and with the publishers Chapman and Hall; and before them with the many writers and artists who had dealt in random misadventures and the mishaps of sportsmen. The idea goes back at least to Apuleius, and survives in the perennial "hunt pictures" of Mr. Punch. The name "Pickwick" is probably taken from the sign of a coachmaker at Bath. But Mr. Pickwick? "I thought of Mr. Pickwick," says Dickens, with the sublime brevity of genius. Seymour the artist made, as his first suggestion, the picture of a tall thin man. Chapman the publisher, writing on the subject about thirteen years later, said that he himself suggested to Seymour to change his Pickwick into the stout and comfortable gentleman who sits fishing, asleep, in a punt on the cover of the priceless Part I. "He made the drawing," wrote Chapman," from my description of a friend of mine at Richmond, a fat old beau who *would* wear, in spite of the ladies' protests, drab tights and black gaiters." We are not informed why the ladies protested. But whatever this recollection amounts to, whether or not Chapman saw for himself from the written words the type that Dickens meant, or gathered it from Dickens's talk, is of no consequence. Mr. Pickwick, mind and gaiters, belongs to Dickens alone. One may imagine that Mr. Pickwick came into the world head first, like the Cheshire Cat in *Alice in Wonderland.* The first thought would be a vague notion of a set of qualities, a conception of amiable incompetence. This would demand and shape itself to middle age, a certain dignity, a comfortable port, and sufficient affluence to set aside all question of finance. The resulting figure of Pickwick seems as inevitable as a proposition in Euclid. Later on, the completed character with its necessary relationship to other people and to the world at large would all lock into its place, item by item.

The book was written, as everyone knows, without forethought and prearrangement. Dickens himself had no idea of what was going to happen. The original idea of Chapman and Hall and Seymour – the banging guns of the rook shooting, the baulking horses, and the awkward riders – was utterly forgotten and left behind. Mr. Pickwick and his friends are carried away on the flood tide of life. Dickens himself was afterwards savagely sensitive upon the point. He fiercely challenged the claim that Seymour originated Pickwick. He bitterly resented the accusation or the assertion that the character of Pickwick changes in the book from that of an amiable nincompoop, an easy mark for cheap deception, to that of a hero, or even, as Sam Weller called him towards the end, "an angel in gaiters."

"It has been observed of Mr. Pickwick, that there is a decided change in his character, as these pages proceed, and that he becomes more good and more sensible. I do not think this change will appear forced or unnatural to my readers, if they will reflect that in real life the peculiarities and oddities of a man who has anything whimsical about him, generally impress us first, and that it is not until we are better acquainted with him that we usually begin to look below these superficial traits, and to know the better part of him."

This is very characteristic of Dickens. Of course Pickwick changes. But Dickens could not bear to admit.

Many things in regard to the *Pickwick Papers* seem amazing when we look back upon them. The notion of publishing a huge story in monthly issues spread over two years would appear ghastly in the world of today. It suggests those Chinese dramas which are said to go on night after night for a month. Yet Dickens not only "got away with it" but made it his familiar and expected method of entertaining his readers. The same plan, varied with serial weekly publication, was followed from *Pickwick* to *Edwin Drood.* As each novel was published as a book after coming out in numbers, the scheme represents financially an excellent receipt for eating a cake and still having it.

So terrific was the interest in Mr. Pickwick that he had to go upon the stage before even Dickens had finished with him, or before the public yet knew how the great case of Bardell *vs.* Pickwick would end. A playwright of the hour, a versatile Mr. Moncrieff, put on a Pickwick play in which the dénouement is perhaps – if such a heresy may be hinted – more ingenious than the author's own ending. In this noble drama, entitled *Sam Weller or the Pickwickians,* Mr. Alfred Jingle turns out to be the missing Mr. Bardell, who had not been killed with a pewter pot. Mrs. Bardell is saved only by the generosity of Pickwick from a trial for bigamy. The weak spot of the idea is that not even the alchemy of Dickens would have turned Mrs. Bardell into a real Mrs. Jingle or converted Mr. Jingle back to a Mr. Bardell.

In many respects the peculiar nature of the success of *Pickwick* was as amusing as the book itself. It broke out into a sort of "boom." Men blossomed forth in "Pickwick" coats of dark green or plum colour with large brass and horn buttons; there were "Pickwick" hats copied from the one worn by Mr. Pickwick in the punt, "Pickwick" canes and "Pickwick" gaiters; and most noticeable of all was the famous cigar, the "Penny Pickwick," very long and very thin and named on the Latin principle of *lucus a non lucendo.* In short, the success of the *Pickwick Papers* was entirely Pickwickian.

One tragic and devastating episode occurred to mar the happiness of Dickens's life and work. Mary Hogarth, his sister-in-law, died with appalling suddenness while he was engaged on the *Pickwick Papers.* Dickens was prostrated with grief. Work was impossible even at such an important juncture. The publication of the current number had to be postponed. "Young, beautiful and good" – so wrote Dickens, characteristically, as the epitaph for the girl's gravestone. "God numbered her among his angels at the early age of seventeen." He never forgot her. Her memory often came back to him as he wrote: and once, years afterwards in Italy, she came to him as a vision of the night, so lifelike that he could hardly call it a dream.

Chapter Three

"BOZ" CONQUERS ENGLAND

The Rise of a Rocket – "Oliver Twist" – "Nicholas Nickleby" – Master Humphrey's Clock Bursts Its Case

IT WAS, AS SEEN, IN THE YEAR 1836 THAT CHARLES Dickens, newly married and busily engaged on the *Pickwick Papers*, settled down with his young bride in their chambers in Furnival's Inn. Within the next four years not only in London and in England but in all the English-speaking world he rose to a towering literary eminence as "Boz." The success of Pickwick once assured, book followed book, the new ones beginning while the old ones still ran their course. The busy pen rushed over the paper. Work, to Dickens, was but as play, and his play was as energetic as his work. All this time and throughout his life he was, if there can be such a thing, a "passionate walker." To him a tramp of ten miles was only a start: a real walk meant about twenty. To fatigue he was impervious. Weariness of mind or body in those golden days he never knew. Boredom had no meaning for him and the "blues" was only a name for other people's states of mind.

If literary genius is built on melancholy, indigestion, and cynicism, Dickens never had any. He was blessed by nature with a happy moderation of appetite. He sang the glory of the flowing bowl, but he sang it from the rim only, not from the bottom. Tobacco meant so little to him that the characters in his books, through his negligence, never get a fair share of it, let alone an excess, or they get it only in the form of a "foul pipe" as one of the adjuncts of villainy.

His home was at this time a happy one. He widened the sides of it till it took in fathers, mothers, sisters, brothers, immediate and -in-law – anyone a relative to him. For his own father and mother he presently – as early as 1839 – bought a house, where "Mr. Micawber" lived out his life in comfort on the generosity of his son. When he and his wife took a little cottage at Twickenham for the summer of 1838 it fairly overflowed with the family and the guests. And the family itself increased; for among the many blessings of life enjoyed by Dickens was that of a full cradle. His son and heir, Charles Dickens Junior, was born in January, 1837. A daughter, Mary (Mamie), followed in March, 1838; and a third child, the daughter Kate, in October of 1839. A boy, christened Walter Landor, arrived in February, 1841, and completed the babbling nursery of four which Dickens left behind when he sailed for America. After that even Dickens himself more or less lost count: certain it is that he refers in a letter of a few years later to the latest baby as "it": when a father does this he is pretty far along.

Round the family circle was added a ring of friendships of men rising like himself in life, or risen, and like himself moving on the floodtide of activity, energy, and success.

Of these there was – first, last, and always – John Forster, who made his acquaintance in the Pickwick days, and who became his devoted adherent, his satellite, his proof reader, his rock of refuge, his executor, his biographer. The friendship was so one-sided that nothing could break it. Then there was his legal friend Sergeant Talfourd, the Tommy Traddles of *David Copperfield*; there was Maclise of the Royal Academy; Landseer and other artists; there was Harrison Ainsworth, the novelist of *Old Saint Paul's*, and such; and in a lesser degree Thackeray, his only real rival in the contemporary fiction of his day.

One may read in Forster's biography of the endless walks and rides, visits, dinners, and celebrations, that marked his friendships: dinners for the happy ending of *Pickwick*, for the beginning of this, or the end of that, or for nothing or anything. And with it all never a hint of excess. Dickens's pleasure did not impede, it animated all his work.

Charles Dickens never moved in society with a large S, or appeared in it except at times as a captured star. Nor did he have any contact with public life or politics. The old gallery days had cured him of that. For him public life, like Einstein's space, had a twist in it. It seemed always either comic or crooked, never real. To him members of Parliament and justices of the peace were funny people. His queer, imperfect judgments on democracy in America are based on his equally imperfect judgments of aristocracy in England. His public functions were limited to taking the chair at public benevolent meetings and such things as that. It never occurred to him to take part in politics. It was not a matter of time. If it had suited him he would easily have found time for it. He found time for much more piffling things than that. Throughout his life he was endlessly editing and correcting all sorts of manuscripts of people not worth editing or correcting: carrying on a mass of needless correspondence, explaining, fuming, fussing over trifles. So much so that he never found time to read the great works and the great thoughts of the world he lived in. He visited France and never saw it: only a comic-romantic effect of vineyards, peasants, and bright colours: of people called Monsieur and Madame whose queer speech made for literary effect. But no doubt all this was just as well. Charles Dickens had to lead his life in his own way or not lead it at all. People in America who still dimly resent his picture of their country must remember that France and Italy "got theirs" too.

Thus moved Dickens in a roseate cloud of gathering celebrity. This period of which we are speaking was the real morning of his life. It was the childhood that he had never had before.

Looking back at these years one can realize how full and ample and eager had become the life of Dickens. It seemed as if everything were coming to him at once. Within the space of a few months he seemed to be, indeed he was, passing from poverty to affluence. He had married on the strength of having received

£150 for the copyright of the *Sketches by Boz*, together with two instalments (thirty guineas) advanced on the *Pickwick Papers* before they came out. But the whole situation changed like a transformation scene. The fifteen guineas per number promised by Messrs. Chapman and Hall proved to be but a small part of the gains from *Pickwick*. After the sixth number the circulation rose every month till it went well beyond forty thousand copies per number. The publishers found themselves making net profit that would run to £20,000 with the book still to come. Generosity and self-interest alike led them, as already seen, to give a share of this to the young author whose name was already a byword and whose talent a gold mine.

Dickens rose from the ranks of the poor to the ranks of what plain people call rich in a single bound. If he ever needed money again or wanted still more of it, it was only because of the many claims upon his income, the generosity of his disposition, and because he took over with his riches in some measure the sorrows of the rich. The rich are always more concerned over money than the poor.

Meantime the writing of *Pickwick* itself had become only a part of his labours. With fame came abundant offers of further literary work, and Dickens, making hay while the sun shone, accepted it eagerly. Indeed, far too eagerly: for he took on more work than he could do, and for sums which would have seemed fabulous two years before, but which presently appeared inadequate. While *Pickwick* was only just well started, he undertook (August, 1836) to edit for the publisher Richard Bentley a new monthly magazine to be called *Bentley's Miscellany*. For the next two years a good part of his time was devoted to this work. The contract included the writing of a serial story which presently began to appear as *Oliver Twist*. The publication of *Oliver* began in January, 1837, and the story was therefore actually running at the same time that the *Pickwick Papers* were coming out each month. Dickens finished the story in September of 1838, and *Oliver Twist* appeared as a book in a three-volume edition, illustrated by George Cruikshank, three or four months before it ended as a serial.

Strangely enough, the talented illustrator made the same kind of claim and accusation against Dickens as was made by the widow, and later by the son, of Seymour. He claimed, in the press and in a pamphlet written in his old age (1872) after Dickens was dead, that he was the real originator of the character of Fagin the Jew, the outstanding personage, next to little Oliver himself, of the book *Oliver Twist.* Cruikshank was of a different rank from Seymour. He was, and is still, in memory and by reputation, one of the world's greatest "caricaturists" or "comic artists." (There is no true name for what he was, but everybody knows what is meant.) He was twenty years older than Charles Dickens and was at this time at the height of his success. Apart from his political caricatures, he had made a name by his depiction of city types of humble and low life. If he didn't invent Fagin, he at least could have. His claim was that he told Dickens about a certain Jew, a receiver of stolen goods, and had not only described him but given a sort of pantomime depiction of him. Dickens's faithful and admiring biographer, as touchy on such a point as Dickens himself, dismisses all this as a "marvellous fable." But it may well be quite true, and it would make no difference if it was. When books are written, as Dickens's early books were, in parts and sections, with discussions of plans of illustrations, with no clear idea of the future course or end of the story, such an infiltration of other people's ideas would be inevitable. Even the lion in the fable had its assistant mouse. A man does not "originate" *Oliver Twist* by suggesting that a thieves' den would be an interesting spot for a story. General Sherman did not "originate" Dante's Inferno by saying that "war is hell." Too much is made in literary post-mortem discussion of this "suggestion" business. The point is not who can suggest a story but who can write it.

The story of *Oliver Twist* – or at least the idea of *Oliver Twist* – has become a part of the literary heritage of England and America. No one needs to be told who Oliver Twist was. Everyone has at least a half-idea of the pathetic little orphan boy, tiny and frail, cast into the care of the workhouse; beaten and ill-treated; half starved, along with other little famished creatures who shared his lot; and daring, for himself and his fellows, to "ask for more" – like a child martyr walking first to his fate.

This, one would say, is a story for tears, for anger, for hands clenched in righteous indignation. But Dickens saw fit to write this poignant story, and especially the opening scenes of it, in a way peculiarly his own. The manner of relation carries with it a sort of running amusement, as if the whole retrospect of Oliver's fate had in it something almost laughable. At the famous scene where Oliver Twist "asks for more," the fun gets almost hilarious. Take the following skeleton quotations to indicate the current of the story:

Oliver Twist's ninth birthday found him a pale thin child, somewhat diminutive in stature, and decidedly small in circumference.

"It *was* his ninth birthday; and he was keeping it in the coal-cellar with a select party of two other young gentlemen, who, after participating with him in a sound thrashing, had been locked up for atrociously presuming to be hungry. …

"Oliver, having had by this time as much of the outer coat of dirt which encrusted his face and hands, removed, as could be scrubbed off in one washing, was led into the room by his benevolent protectress. …

"Oliver was then led away by Mr. Bumble from the wretched home where one kind word or look had never lighted the gloom of his infant years. And yet he burst into an agony of childish grief, as the cottage gate closed after him. …

"He had no time to think about the matter, however; for Mr. Bumble gave him a tap on the head, with his cane, to wake him up: and another on the back to make him lively. …

"Oliver was frightened at the sight of so many gentlemen, which made him tremble: and the beadle gave him another tap behind which made him cry. …

"Child as he was, he was desperate with hunger and reckless with misery. He rose from the table and advancing to the master, basin and spoon in hand, said: somewhat alarmed at his own temerity:

Oliver Twist

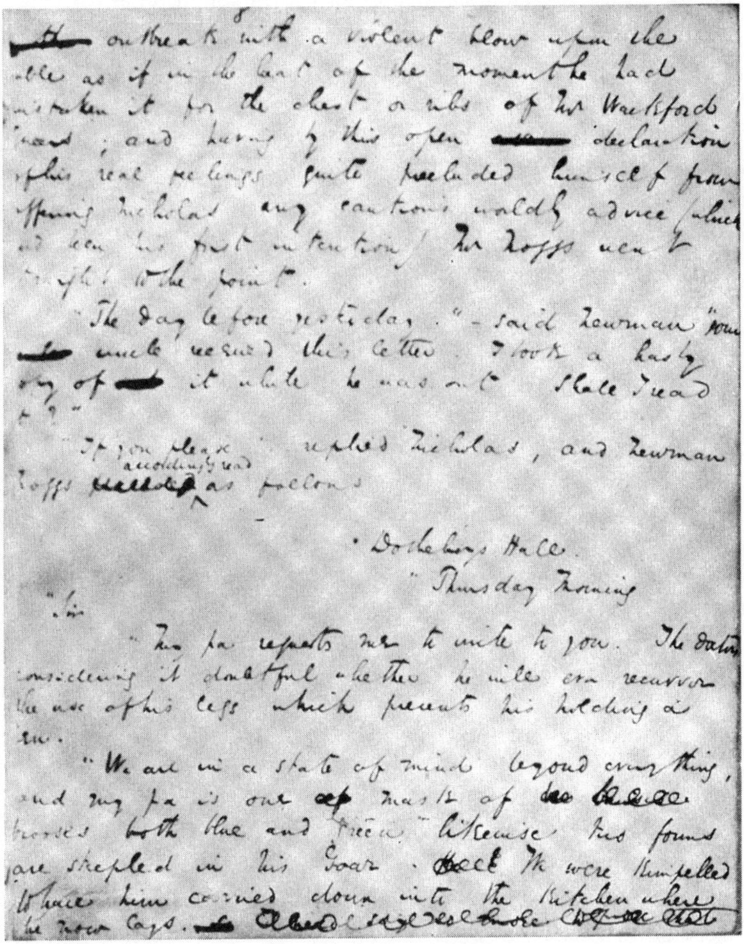
outbreak with a violent blow upon the
able as if in the heat of the moment he had
mistaken it for the chest or ribs of Mr Wackford
Squeers; and having by this open declaration
of his real feelings quite precluded himself from
offering Nicholas any cautious worldly advice (which
had been his first intention) Mr Noggs went
straight to the point.
"The day before yesterday" – said Newman "your
uncle received this letter. I took a hasty
copy of it while he was out. Shall I read
it?"
"If you please" replied Nicholas, and Newman
Noggs accordingly read as follows
"Dotheboys Hall.
"Thursday Morning
"Sir
"My pa requests me to write to you. The doctors
considering it doubtful whether he will ever recuver
the use of his legs which prevents his holding a
pen.
"We are in a state of mind beyond everything,
and my pa is one mask of
brooses both blue and green likewise two forms
are steepled in his Goar. We were kimpelled
to have him carried down into the kitchen where
he now lays.

Nicholas Nickleby
A page from the original manuscript

"'Please, sir, I want some more.'

"The master was a fat healthy man; but he turned very pale. He gazed in stupefied astonishment on the small rebel for some seconds, and then clung for support to the copper. The assistants were paralyzed with wonder; the boys with fear.

"'What!' said the master at length, in a faint voice.

"'Please, sir,' replied Oliver, 'I want some more.'

"The master aimed a blow at Oliver's head with the ladle; pinioned him in his arms; and shrieked aloud for the beadle."

One may comment upon this style of narration without undertaking to approve or to condemn. There are some of us, perhaps, to whom the suffering of little Oliver Twist is too poignant, too harrowing for amusement; who might think, perhaps, that in this method of narration, even from the voice and hand of an inspired genius, the tone in such passages is false, the touch is hard.

But perhaps if Dickens had written it up in a different way the emotion would have broken with its own weight. Compare such a passage as what follows, in which the sentiment becomes overwhelming and its expression beyond all boundaries of truth. Little Dick, a pauper child, Oliver's fellow sufferer, is dying. His face is "earnest" and "wan," and he wants to send a message. "'I should like to leave my dear love to Oliver Twist, and to let him know how often I have sat by myself and cried to think of his wandering about in the dark nights with nobody to help him. And I should like to tell him,' said the child pressing his small hands together and speaking with great fervour, … 'that I was glad to die when I was very young; for, perhaps, if I had lived to be a man, and had grown old, my little sister who is in Heaven, might forget me, or be unlike me; and it would be so much happier if we were both children there together.'"

But let the reader note how the narrative goes on. The tone changes at once again to the comic.

"Mr. Bumble surveyed the little speaker, from head to foot, with indescribable astonishment; and, turning to his companion, said, 'They're all in one story, Mrs. Mann. That out-dacious Oliver has demogalized them all!'

"'I couldn't have believed it, sir!' said Mrs. Mann, holding up her hands and looking malignantly at Dick. 'I never see such a hardened little wretch!'

"'Take him away, ma'am!' said Mr. Bumble imperiously. This must be stated to the board, Mrs. Mann.'"

In other words, the peculiar tone of *Oliver Twist*, the distinctive style of narration, is something like the "comic relief" of the melodrama, with which Dickens was only too well acquainted. Here the audience were saved from the humiliation of tears by the reappearance of the comic character of the play. In melodrama the hysteria of tears heightens the hysteria of laughter, each sentiment reacts upon the other. But everyone knows that the effect is inartistic and unworthy. It is a nice point to decide how far such a method of narration may be carried.

But, in any case, Dickens found plenty of readers to like the story. Such criticisms as were offered against it turned rather upon the fact that it dealt with "low life," a subject of which people of the better classes preferred to know nothing. That it was, in part, at least, oversentimental was an objection not raised in an oversentimental age. Readers of the period, grown-up readers, even such hardened people as lawyers, were not ashamed to read a book in a flood of tears. Looking back now on what we think of as Victorian sentimentality we are apt to see only its feebler aspects, its maudlin exaggeration, its joy in tears, its lack of restraint and reserve. But in its day the tears were as much needed to break down the cruelty and hardness of a preceding age as the soft rains of April to break the ice of winter. These were the days of the unreformed factories, of the "cry of the children," of the little lives worn out unheeded; the days of the grim shelter of the Union and the starvation of the "hungry 'forties," the darkest hour of English industrial history.

And here Dickens "finds himself" again. It is no longer the genial satire of the Boz of the *Sketches*, no longer the uproarious fun, the blazing fires, and the wide humanity of the *Pickwick Papers*. Here begins Charles Dickens the social reformer, driving home with fierce invective and with sardonic humour his protest against the evils of the day – against the cruelty to children, the oppression of the poor, the law's delay, the insolence of office, and the brutality of class indifference which were the besetting sins of the England of a hundred years ago. Tears for imaginary children were to save the lives of real ones.

In these *Pickwick-Oliver Twist* days the activities of Dickens were so eager and so multifarious that it is difficult to chronicle all that he did without sinking to the level of a publisher's catalogue. Among other things, he was now able to give expression to his love of the theatre. While still engaged on Pickwick he seems to have put together no less than four little plays, of which three were put upon the stage. *The Village Coquette* was acted at the St. James's Theatre, December 3, 1836. It was described on the bills as a "burletta" of which the dialogue and the words of the songs were written by Boz. It was followed early in the next year at the same theatre by *Is She His Wife?* or *Something Singular* (presumably by Dickens), by a musical recitation by a local comedian (Mr. Harley) in the character of Pickwick – words by "his biographer Boz" – and a little play called *The Strange Gentleman.* The manuscripts of these dramatic efforts were not preserved, a fact for which Dickens afterwards expressed his profound gratitude.

To acting was added editing. Dickens undertook for Bentley to edit the "memoirs" of Joseph Grimaldi, a once famous clown who had recently gone where all clowns go. Dickens had never seen Grimaldi, but he sorted out the "twaddle," as he called the autobiographical notes given to him, and wrote a preface for the book.

Over and above Grimaldi, Dickens did for Bentley various short sketches later gathered together as the *Mudfog Papers,* and found as such in his complete works as published today. Here belong also the *Sketches of Young Couples,* a series of papers which Dickens scratched off with no particular inspiration to be published without his name. It is no wonder that the *Quarterly Magazine* of October, 1837, in reviewing the completed *Pickwick*

Papers, said, "Mr. Dickens writes too often and too fast; on the principle, we presume, of making hay whilst the sun shines, he seems to have accepted at once all engagements that were offered to him, and the consequence is, that in too many instances he has been compelled to

'*forestall the blighted harvest of the brain,*'

and put forth, in their crude, unfinished, undigested state, thoughts, feeling, observations, and plans which it required time and study to mature – or supply the allotted number of pages with original matter of the most common-place description, or hints caught from others and diluted to make them pass for his own. If he persists much longer in this course, it requires no gift of prophecy to foretell his fate – he has risen like a rocket, and he will come down like the stick."

Three generations of students of our literature have laughed at this prophecy. But in a sense it is true. Dickens did write too fast. It was all very well when he had the superabundant energy of youth as the driving power of the high speed. It was not so well in later years, when he still drove his pen ahead with a tired brain and an exhausted imagination that substituted mechanism for inspiration. In this sense the "rocket" is Mr. Pickwick of 1836, and the "stick" fell in 1865 as *Our Mutual Friend.*

Dickens was amazed and mystified to find that Bentley, the publisher, sold 1,700 copies of *Grimaldi* within a week. We can thus understand the point when the "old gentleman" says to Oliver Twist, "What! You wouldn't like to be a book writer?" and Oliver answered that he should think it would be a much better thing to be a bookseller.

Indeed, Dickens at this period was becoming somewhat obsessed with the idea that the booksellers were making too good a thing out of him. Thus he writes to Forster (in January, 1839) to speak of "the immense profit which *Oliver* had realised to its publisher and is still realising, the paltry wretched miserable sum it brought to me … and the consciousness that I have still the slavery and drudgery of another book on the same journeyman terms: the consciousness that my books are enriching everybody connected with them but myself, and that I, with such a popularity as I have acquired am struggling in old toils, am wasting my energies in the very height and freshness of my fame and the best part of my life to fill the pockets of others while for those who are nearest and dearest to me I can realise little more than a genteel subsistence."

All this is hardly fair. Indeed, it is a foretaste of the impatient and imperious temper into which Charles Dickens was presently to be ground by hard work. It was not the fault of the publishers if the copyrights turned into gold in their hands. When Macrone paid £150 for the full copyright of the *Sketches by Boz*, he paid a fair enough market price for a book of moderate merit by an unknown young man. He could not see that the unknown young man would turn out to be Charles Dickens. When he sold back the copyright to Chapman & Hall and Dickens for ten times as much, Dickens thought him a rogue. But if Macrone had lost on the bargain, would Dickens have considered that he owed a debt? Not very likely.

In any case the "genteel subsistence" is certainly drawing a long bow. When Dickens wrote this his income was rolling in so fast that he could hardly count it; he and his wife moved this same year into a beautiful big house with a garden on Devonshire Terrace; he made the purchase of a charming little country house (at Alphington, near Exeter) for his father and mother, and was living, apart from industry, like a lord.

Part of the trouble arose, no doubt, from the vagueness with which Dickens seems to have made his arrangements with his publishers. He promised to Bentley more than he could possibly write, and at prices which soon looked unfair. *Pickwick* was published by Chapman & Hall on a sort of "gentleman's agreement," and Chapman & Hall acted like gentlemen. But as they expected a new book as part of the understanding, Dickens had to hold off Bentley as best he could. Thus his energy seemed to force him into a sort of race with himself, which gave the impression of slavery and drudgery to a task in reality congenial beyond words. So it came about that the "slavery and drudgery" for the publishers next took the form of a third book (not counting the sketches) that appeared, or rather began to appear, as it ran in serial numbers, in April, 1838, as the *Life and Adventures of Nicholas Nickleby*. It opened up with a sale of fifty thousand copies. Dickens had arrived indeed. *Nickleby* was a great success. Here again were the Dickens atmosphere, the Dickens characters, the inimitable Mrs. Nickleby – a delight in fiction, a trial in real life. And here again Dickens is the social reformer, with the immortal creation of Mr. Wackford Squeers, whose imaginary personality did more to reform the gross incompetence and brutality of English people's schools than volumes of inspectors' reports. For this, Dickens worked up deliberately the local colour; made a trip to Yorkshire before he began the book, to see on the spot whether the schools were as evil as painted; and took with him Hablôt Browne, who was henceforth, with the signature of "Phiz," the illustrator of a series of his books.

But even such wide and constant activities as those described, left Dickens, like Oliver Twist, still "asking for more." He began to plan something more comprehensive than a single story, some sort of general repository, or storehouse, out of which might come not one story but a dozen. Dickens at this day had a sort of liking for "wheels within wheels," for stories told inside other stories – as witness the interpolated tales in *Pickwick*.

This design presently took shape in *Master Humphrey's Clock*, a publication which Chapman & Hall issued in weekly numbers, eighty-eight in all, in 1840 and 1841. The design is in reality a "mess." Old Master Humphrey is supposed to be one of those quaint characters, odd and recluse, dear to Dickens's heart. He possesses an old clock case that is filled up with manuscripts, which he hauls out at intervals and reads to his friends and visitors. Thus Master Humphrey becomes a sort of magazine with a connecting thread of interest, or supposed interest, in the way in which the stories come to light. Here, for example, as listening visitors, dragged back from immortality, are Mr. Pickwick and Sam Weller! It seems awful that Dickens could have done it; that to supply interest for lesser things he could take another round out of Mr. Pickwick. But youth adventures all things. And, in any case, the unhappy Mr. Pickwick had been so plagiarized and plundered by other hands – dragged on a European tour by the unspeakable literary villain G.W.M. Reynolds (*Mr. Pickwick Abroad*), forced onto the stage by another, that Dickens may have felt that he too had the right to set Pickwick to work overtime. But all true lovers of Pickwick insist on believing that he did not really visit Master Humphrey. It couldn't be. Dickens must have mistaken someone else for him.

In any case, the "Clock" business broke down. When the reader found that the publication was not a single story, the sales fell with a flop. Dickens at once divined the trouble. He decided to give the readers what they wanted. One of the stories started in the clock was called *The Old Curiosity Shop.* Consequently, at the end of such and such a number, Master Humphrey, with heartless indifference, was kicked out of his own clock and gave place to the serial *The Old Curiosity Shop.* When that story finished, the old man reappeared for a moment to breathe a sigh over it and introduce the next story, called *Barnaby Rudge.* His part, in other words, is only that of the Greek chorus, or the *compère* and the *commère* of a French revue of today.

The Old Curiosity Shop, if not one of Dickens's best works (many of us would think it very far from that), is at least one of his most celebrated. No readers remember the story or the plot as such. But none forget the character and the pathos of Little Nell. It is said that this is preëminently the book which conquered America for Dickens. *Pickwick* and *Oliver*, it is true, had been widely read and greeted with enthusiasm. But it is after *The Old Curiosity Shop*, it seems, and in the name of Little Nell, that Charles Dickens gained with the reading public of America the place that he never lost. The controversies and the angers of later days could never remove the memory of it. All the world recalls how Bret Harte, when Dickens died, centred his poetic tribute round the memory of the imagined child. His word picture of the Western mining camp listening to the story of Little Nell is one of the treasures of literature.

"Above the pines the moon was slowly drifting,
The river sang below;
The dim Sierras, far beyond, uplifting
Their minarets of snow.

"And then, while round them shadows gathered faster
And as the firelight fell,
He read aloud the book wherein the Master
Had wrote of Little Nell.

"The fir-trees gathering closer to the shadows
Listened in every spray,
While the whole camp with Nell on English meadows
Wandered and lost their way."

Master Humphrey had no sooner hatched out *The Old Curiosity Shop* from his clock than he incubated the new story, *Barnaby Rudge*. In its original presentation Master Humphrey introduces it, and reappears to the extent of a few pages at the end to bid it Godspeed and to arrange – with the approval of all concerned – his own approaching demise. But in the usual edition of Dickens's works, *Barnaby Rudge* is printed, like *The Old Curiosity Shop*, as a story by itself.

It is customary to talk of *Barnaby Rudge* as a historical novel and to say that this book and Dickens's other historical novel, *A Tale of Two Cities*, form an exception among his works. But the exception is much more apparent than real. If by a historical novel we mean a book in which appear the actual characters of history – the Queen Elizabeths and the Louis Onzes and such – these books are not so. Apart from a fleeting vision in *Barnaby* of Lord George Gordon, there are no actual characters. All are imaginary. They are perhaps more "real" than the "actual" personages of other writers. But they are not historical in the stricter sense. Neither is the period. We are apt to forget that in Dickens's youth the French Revolution was a vivid memory of yesterday to all people of middle age. When Dickens first visited France, in the pre-railroad days, the routine of life around him was not particularly different from that of the days of Voltaire. With the one exception of the paddle-wheel steamer the journey to France was much like those of Mr. Jarvis Lorry of Telsons Bank. Nor was the London of Lord George Gordon very remote in time or very different in appearance from the London of the Prince Regent. The Maypole Inn was still standing (in hundreds) along the coach roads of England. One would hardly say today that a man is writing a "historical" novel if the plot is laid in the days of Grover Cleveland or Lord Rosebery.

But there is, perhaps, something less of Dickens, personally, in the narration of these two stories. He does not, as much as in the others, invite the reader to step in and out of the book by calling attention in his own person to its applications. Yet consider the opening of chapter IX (*Barnaby*). "Chroniclers are privileged to enter where they list and to come and go through keyholes, to ride upon the wind, to overcome, in their soarings up and down, all obstacles of time and space. Thrice blessed be this last consideration since it enables us to follow the disdainful Miggs even into the sanctity of her chamber," etc. There they go! Dickens and the reader, stepping in and out of the book. If that is the method of a "historical" novel it is a "rum one." Even in *A Tale of Two Cities*, Dickens himself takes a hand in the French Revolution.

In these days, when "detective" fiction and the solution of "insoluble" mysteries cover such a large field, a certain interest attaches to a peculiar incident connected with the story of *Barnaby Rudge* and with its interpretation by Edgar Allan Poe. The narrative has a "mystery" plot with a murder in it. At the very beginning of the novel, sitting in Mr. Willett's immortal Maypole Inn, we are told, with all the proper environment of storm and mystery, the story of the murder of Barnaby Rudge's father, the steward of Mr. Haredale. The mutilated body is found, just as it ought to be, in a pond, and the recollection of it carries through the story a trail of horror, a legacy of crime. But what we are not clever enough to notice is that it is not Charles Dickens who tells us that Rudge was murdered. It is one of his characters, Mr. Solomon Daisy. Seated beside the blazing fire in the Maypole Inn, with the storm of wind and rain outside, to give character to the terror of the tale, he recounts the story of the murder and tells us: "far enough they might have looked for poor Mr. Rudge the steward, whose body, scarcely to be recognised by his clothes and the watch and the ring he wore, – was found months afterwards at the bottom of a piece of water in the grounds." It never occurs to any (ordinary) reader to doubt this statement of apparent fact. In reality Rudge himself is the murderer, a *double* murderer, for he had killed an innocent man to cover up his other crime.

Dickens therefore has contrived to get the living Rudge as dead as he wants, a feat of art that is the despair of the contemporary novelist. He has got him dead, with a license for his resurrection usable at any time. He has only to invite the reader to take another look at Chapter I. He has contrived, by the power and interest of the setting, the old inn, the queer people, the blazing fire, and the storm outside, to lull our critical sense to sleep. In a cheap detective world today, there would be nothing but the story as told by Solomon Daisy, bald, crude, just able to stand on its legs and no more, and inviting criticism of every joint of its unhappy ill-contrivance. But as it is, we never doubt: the sheer truth of the setting lends an air of truth to the story; the phrase "poor Mr. Rudge" clinches the conviction. People are not murdered by "poor Mr. Anybody." Incidentally one notices how fond Dickens was of these "forward references," the insertion of such items of assertion or reflection, only to be understood later. As a literary device the thing is interesting. In its cheapest form it serves as a means of trying to arouse interest and excitement in a dull story by such a remark as, "Had our hero only known it, this simple occurrence was destined," etc., etc. But this form of reference carries its own signpost. Dickens only uses that kind of thing when the signpost itself is a cryptogram. Compare in *Edwin Drood* the famous remark about Edwin's ring: "Among the mighty store of wonderful chains that are ever forging, day and night, in the vast ironworks of time and circumstances, there was one chain forged in the moment of that small conclusion, riveted to the foundations of heaven and earth, and gifted with irresistible force to hold and drag" – an ominous forewarning of which the ultimate meaning passed with Dickens to the grave. But what Dickens loved were forward allusions that could have, at the moment, no possible meaning to a reader not yet acquainted with the book. The reader is supposed to get the benefit of them either by carrying the whole book in his memory, and enjoying the excellence of them at the close, or by reading it over again. The result is that most readers of Dickens are not aware that they are there. The ordinary reader, therefore, we repeat, might easily fail to note the difference between a statement made by one of Dickens's characters and a statement made in the book by the author himself.

But Edgar Allan Poe was not an ordinary reader. He himself dealt in crime and mysteries and had the quick sense of a professional, who doubts every murder in fiction. In his *Essay on Charles Dickens* he tells us that he deduced the fact that Rudge was the real murderer. "The secret was distinctly understood," he writes, "immediately on the perusal of the story of Solomon Daisy which occurs at the seventh page of the volume." In the number of the Philadelphia *Saturday Evening Post* for May 1, 1841 (the tale having then only begun), will be found a prospective notice of some length in which we make use (that is, Poe makes use) of the following words:

"That Barnaby is the son of the murderer may not appear evident to our readers, – but we will explain. It is not the author himself who asserts that the steward was found: he has put the words in the mouth of one of his characters. His design is to make it appear, in the dénouement, that the steward, Rudge, first murdered the gardener, then went to his master's chamber, murdered him, was interrupted by his, Rudge's, wife, whom he seized and held by the wrist, to prevent her giving the alarm, – that he then, after possessing himself of the booty desired, returned to the gardener's room, exchanged clothes with him, put upon the corpse his own watch and ring, and secreted it where it was afterwards discovered at so late a period that the features could not be identified."

Now this is indeed a capital piece of deduction, worthy of Poe's own Mr. Dupin or of Sherlock Holmes plus Watson. The error in it only enhances its interest. Rudge, as told in his final confession, did not seize his wife's wrist. She seized his. But as a way of putting a birthmark of a bloody smear on the wrist of the unborn Barnaby, Poe's method was better than that of Dickens. Dickens didn't make Rudge grasp his wife's wrist: but he should have.

One of the most able of the modern commentators and critics of Dickens's work has derided Poe's whole claim as a characteristic humbug. Even if Poe did write this on May 1, 1841, says the critic, after seeing the mere opening of the story as an American serial, he could easily have read plenty more of it already, since *Barnaby Rudge* began to appear in England in weekly instalments on February 13, 1841, and no doubt had come to America by post. Poe, therefore, it is argued, was merely pretending to be very smart about guessing the outcome of the story from its opening, when in reality he had already seen the English copy. But this argument will not stand. Poe, one admits, was fond of a literary hoax, and loved nothing better than the solemn and dignified make-believe of mock logic or mock scholarship. But because a man is fooling some of the time, it does not follow that he is fooling all of the time. Even if Poe had seen all of the numbers that appeared in England up to May 1, 1841, he would have been no nearer the solution. The story did not end in England till November 27, 1841; and up to the middle of the tale there were no particular clues beyond those given at the start. It is true that Poe may never have written an article on *Barnaby* in the *Post* of May 1st. He may have been lying about that. But what is beyond search now, when the files of the *Post* are no longer in existence, was a simple and easy matter to corroborate or to refute when Poe wrote on Dickens in 1842. What an ass he would have been to stake his reputation on a deceit so easily exposed.

Of course, Poe had seen more than the actual story of Solomon Daisy on page 7. That claim is a mere looseness of expression.

He must have, since there is no mention of Barnaby's existence till Chapter V. Poe had seen five chapters of the book – truly described as a mere beginning of a book of eighty-two chapters. Even Poe could never have claimed that his intelligence was such that having heard of Rudge, and guessed him the murderer, he also guessed that Rudge had a son called Barnaby, born the day after the murder with a birthmark on his wrist. Sherlock Holmes might, but he came forty years later.

In other words, Poe's guess is a brilliant piece of literary deduction, and it is a pity to rob his battered reputation of the benefit of it. Poe did more than that. He showed that Charles Dickens broke the rules of literary honesty, as applied to murders and mysteries, when he speaks in his own voice of Mrs. Rudge as "the widow." He might have called her the "Widow Rudge" in the mouths of the other characters, and then used it as a name of repute, but not on his own authority. He knows and Mrs. Rudge knows that she is not a widow. The thing is grossly unfair: it is not cricket; not even on the hearth.

Nor does Poe's ingenuity stop there. He shows that in spite of Dickens's preface to the book – when *Barnaby* appeared in book form – that the Gordon Riots came into the book only as an afterthought. All readers of the book have noticed that the story comes to a full stop for five years; and this for no particularly obvious reasons. All the characters are held suspended for five years. Dickens announces quite suddenly at the end of chapter XXXII, "and the world went on turning round, as usual, for five years during which this narrative is silent." No one but Charles Dickens could "get away" with that.

The reason was that he had thought of the Gordon Riots and decided to put them into the story. Now the opening at the Maypole Inn was explicitly dated 1775, and the Riots did not happen till 1780. So the story had to stand still, the characters all marking time: John Willett stirring the fire at the inn; Gabriel Varden clicking away at his anvil; Barnaby skipping around in his feathers, and the raven, to whom five years meant nothing, croaking away as usual. To the raven, we repeat, it made no difference.

But for the heroine it was cruel. Emma Haredale, as Poe says, would have been called an old maid in America when the story started again. Even the pert Dolly Varden must have had a lot of the bloom dusted off her. If Dickens had known sooner about the riots coming in, he would have started Dolly at sixteen. But he had no more idea of the riots coming in than he had of Martin Chuzzlewit going to America. And when the riots did come in, there was such a terrific outburst of fire, massacre, crime, and hanging, that this humble little garden murder committed by "poor Mr. Rudge" twenty-seven years before, is hopelessly lost and forgotten in the ensuing horrors. Even John Forster admits that "the story had been laid aside and the form it ultimately took had been compressed only partially within its first design."

It is marvellous that Dickens could do these things. It is high tribute to his genius that such disregard of common sense, fatal to anyone else, made no particular difference and still makes none. It is equally characteristic of Dickens that he could solemnly write in the preface, "No account of the Gordon Riots having been to my knowledge introduced into any work of fiction, I was led to project this tale." What he meant is, "I was led to project them into this tale." Dickens was truth itself. But when it came to talking of his own work he could be as sophistical as anyone.

After finishing *Barnaby Rudge*, Dickens enjoyed something as near to a rest from his labours as he ever allowed himself. It was a period of widening friendships and of rising honours. To the circle of his friends in his Devonshire Terrace home are added such well known names as Macready the actor, Maclise of the Royal Academy, Lord Jeffrey, and Lytton Bulwer. His reputation has long since surpassed the limited fame of an "amusing" or "comic" writer. He has become one of England's great literary men. He did not enjoy, and never enjoyed, the peculiar sanctity of a Tennyson or the majesty of a Carlyle. He dealt with "low and middle life," and he made people laugh. But even these defects could not blind the people whom we now call "high-brow" to the fact that Charles Dickens was a great writer.

It was as this that the nation now began to honour him. When he made, with his wife, in the summer of 1841, a short tour of recreation to Scotland, there was a great public dinner for him at Edinburgh with Christopher North in the chair and all the lamps of Scottish letters and learning illuminating the board. He was given the treasured "freedom of the city" and was made the recipient of a great popular ovation in a leading theatre. Glasgow threatened him with like honours, but he escaped to the wilds of the Highlands, sated and delighted with Lowland hospitality. The Highlanders, it is said, were not to be outdone. We are told they offered him a "free" seat in Parliament. If they did, the offer of a seat only duplicated a proposal already made, for he had already received an offer to represent the borough of Reading.

Dickens wrote to the electors of Reading, "My principles and inclinations would lead me to aspire to the distinction you invite me to seek... but I am bound to add that I cannot afford the expense of a contested election." But he wrote with his tongue in his cheek. He had sat too long *above* the House of Commons to want to sit in it. In any case, he had other and wider fields in mind. His star was rising in the West. Dickens was going to America.

Chapter Four

BOZ VISITS AMERICA

1842

A National Reception – The Roaring 'Forties – Open Arms and Open Ingratitude

THE UNITED STATES, WHEN CHARLES DICKENS first visited it in 1842, was just in the opening of the "roaring 'forties." The earlier agricultural days of the colonies and the gentlemen's republic had given place to the new era of democracy and industrialism. The Jacksonian epoch had initiated the rule of the people. European immigration was beginning to move in a flood. The steamboat was on the ocean, and on land the era of the canals was being forgotten in the wild rush to build railroads. The population was moving west to fill the Mississippi Valley. It had crossed the river to make the new state of Missouri, and Iowa almost ready to become a state. There were settlers out on the plains in Kansas and Nebraska. The frontier line moved onward across the prairie.

Everything was on the move. New towns were being placed on the map every year. The floating of companies and the chartering of banks, the rush to speculate in land, had led to the crash and crisis of Van Buren's time (1837), but it made little difference. The country picked itself up and went on. It was too young to get hurt. The companies and the banks floated on like a drive of logs on a spring flood. The nation was full of power, of noise, of vainglory, of boastfulness, of roaring optimism, of cheerful crookedness and universal hope. It was the land of opportunity, long forgotten now; the land of freedom with its dark curtain of slavery hung as a background.

Here landed the youthful Dickens with eyes trained to different things: expecting something else; an enthusiastic radical soaked in English conservatism; despising forms and ceremonies and good manners till he came to a country that hadn't got them; a spokesman for the common people, but now in a land where they spoke for themselves. The first of Dickens's American notes should have been a note upon himself. It would have saved much disillusionment.

It was, then, on a clear bright Sunday morning of January, 1842, that this young man of thirty, less an odd week or so, conspicuous by his dress but still more by the arresting interest of his eye, stepped off the new steam packet *Britannia* to take possession of North America. The visible sign of his sovereignty was seen in a wild rush of newspaper "editors" on board the ship. As his consort there was with him a good-looking but uninteresting young woman who in our own day would be designated by the adjective "dumb." But the proof of her meaning and utility in the Victorian scheme of life lay in the existence of the four healthy and romping children, left behind in a London nursery.

From the ship "Charles Dickens and lady" (as the papers called them) were borne in triumph through the Boston of those days – a seaport combined with a country town, a place of 100,000 inhabitants. Dickens caught it all with his quick eager eyes and his romantic imagination: the bright red of the brick houses, the still brighter white of the wooden, the gilded signs, the painted railings, all glittering in the morning sun – "all so light and unsubstantial in appearance that every thoroughfare in the city looked exactly like a scene in a pantomime." He kept glancing up at the boards, he tells us, expecting them to "change into something"; he felt certain that "Clown and Pantaloon were hiding in a doorway or behind some pillar," and "the Harlequin and Columbine were lodged over a one-story clock-maker's shop."

Such comparisons were characteristic of Dickens and all his work. He was forever comparing everything with everything else; and, above all, in this way endowing inanimate objects with life and movement: for him windows grin, doors yawn, clocks wink solemnly, and trees talk in the night breeze. The fancies of Barnaby Rudge watching the clothes dance upon the clothes line are those of his creator.

No reception was ever given to any foreigner in the United States quite like that accorded to Boz. The visit of Lafayette a few years before (1826) had been an occasion of greater national honour. The later visits of such people as the patriot Kossuth called forth larger crowds and more public tribute. But the young Dickens was hailed with a warmth of personal affection never manifested before or since. They welcomed in him all the geniality of Mr. Pickwick, all the appeal of little Oliver and Little Nell, all the charm of old English Christmas for the people of a newer England. And Dickens at the first met it with a boyish and buoyant delight that matched his welcome. He was full of life and power and of speech that never nagged: very different from the aged, stricken man whom the Americans – as audiences only – were to see twenty-six years later. "Here we are," he said in his clear and merry voice as he entered the old Tremont House. Later on, after dinner, he was out in the snowbound streets, merry, boisterous, exuberant, delighted with everything. Boz was just what Boz ought to be. No wonder they smothered him with adulation.

The country simply went wild over him. The time of his coming was fortunate. There was at the moment no particular national excitement. The tumult over "nullification" had died down, and secession had not yet come up. It was midway between two presidential elections. There was no cable to bring news of foreign wars, and no foreign wars to bring news of. Under these circumstances the arrival of young Boz became a first-class national event.

The proceedings opened with a rush of reporters to meet the ship, a sort of procession to the Tremont House, where Dickens was to stay, and a crowd of eager faces lined up on the sidewalk to get a look at him. Then followed calls and invitations in a flood. Dickens's table at the hotel was soon piled high with unopened letters. He had to engage a young man, a Mr. Putnam, as a secretary. Years after, as an old man, Mr. Putnam wrote an account of it all. He gives us a picture of Dickens and his wife breakfasting in their sitting room at the hotel, Boz tearing open letters, dictating, eating, and talking all at the same time, and a local sculptor of note (a Mr. Alexander) making a bust of him at the side of the room and occasionally walking around to get a "close-up" look at him. There were dinners and receptions in all directions. Boz was introduced to the leading literary people of Boston and of Harvard. He was taken out to Springfield to see the Massachusetts Legislature, where, we are told by the press, "his appearance in the senate chamber created quite a stir among the members."

Young Boz enjoyed it all to the full. "I can give you no conception of my welcome here," so he wrote home after ten days to an English friend. "There never was a king or emperor upon earth so cheered and followed by crowds and entertained in public at splendid balls and dinners and waited upon by public bodies and deputations of all kinds. If I go out in a carriage the crowds surround it and escort me home: if I go to the theatre the whole house, crowded to the roof rises as one man, and the timbers ring again. You cannot imagine what it is. I have five great public dinners on hand at this moment and invitations from every town and city in the States."

This was a welcome indeed! Here was a proper sort of country. Seen in such a light, all men looked heroic. Dickens wrote home (to Forster) in enthusiasm over the men of Harvard. "The professors at the Cambridge university, Longfellow, Felton, Jared Sparks, are a noble set of fellows. So is Kenyon's friend, Ticknor. Bancroft is a famous man, a straightforward, manly, earnest heart. ... The women are very beautiful ... the general breeding is neither stiff nor formal ... the goodnature universal. ... There is no man in this town, or in this state of New England who has not a blazing fire and a meat dinner every day of his life. A naming sword in the air would not attract so much attention as a beggar in the streets."

This was indeed America! The America of his dreams. For years before his leaving England Dickens had found himself turning with something almost like disgust from the institutions of his native country. What humbug! What pretense and what a tyranny of the classes and what an oppression of the masses. "By Jove, how radical I am getting," he had written to Forster a year back (August 13, 1841). At times he felt like tragically casting off England altogether. "Thank God," he said, "there is a Van Dieman's Land." He wrote and sent to his friend at this time quite a collection of verses to express his radical sentiments. Verses one must call them, not poetry. Dickens's idea of writing poetry never got further than prose with a rhyme in it. Here is the closing verse from the Ballad of the Fine Old English Gentleman – a character already severely handled in his books.

"The bright old day now dawns again; the cry runs through the land,
In England there shall be – dear bread! in Ireland – sword and brand
And poverty, and ignorance, shall swell the rich and grand,
So, rally round the rulers with the gentle iron hand,
Of the fine old English Tory days;
Hail to the coming time!"

What a wonderful relief, then, to find one's self in a country without fine old Tones, where all the women were beautiful, the men noble fellows, where there were meat dinners for the poor and banquets for authors every day.

Such were the first impressions. Later on America was to cure Dickens of his political discontent and make him a loyal subject of monarchy forever; and Dickens was to turn on America and rend it. In any case, it is proper to mention that some of the friendships he now made in Boston were friendships for life. Professor Felton, the admirable Mr. Bevan of *Martin Chuzzlewit*, became a lifelong correspondent. Longfellow and his daughters stayed with Dickens at Gadshill long years afterwards. Boston also had a warm place in Dickens's heart, and New England too, even though he grew to know that it was not a state. The later antipathies and denunciations were against the press, the land grabbers, the uncouth multitudes of the far West, rude and inquisitive, the torrents of tobacco-spitting and the copyright thieves, the denial of honest justice to honest authors, and, above all, the hideous thing behind the black curtain of the South which he would not even go to see. But all that was still to come.

The first great social event of the tour was a huge dinner given to Dickens in Boston on February 1st at Papinte's restaurant by a self-organized body of the "young men of Boston." It was as elaborate, as oratorical, and as liquid as only dinners of the "roaring 'forties" could be. It is interesting to note among Dickens's hosts of the evening a young man called Dr. Oliver Wendell Holmes, then, at thirty years of age, in the early days of his general practice; a young Mr. James Russell Lowell recently out of Harvard. Among the guests were Josiah Quincy, the fine old president of Harvard, Bancroft the historian, and Richard Henry Dana of *Two Years before the Mast.* It was a goodly company, a wonderful honour to the young man of thirty who sat, full of life and spirits and abounding energy, enjoying every moment of it. The company were washed away on a flood tide of rhetoric and good will.

When they had done toasting Boz they toasted his wife – with nine cheers, all standing. Then they toasted the Old World and the New, and then Genius – and Sam Weller – and anything else they could think of. Each round of the toasts called forth speeches of a length proportionate to the cubic content of the drinks. The president, in toasting Dickens, told him that genius had no country – that they claimed his as the property of the English-speaking world.

Dickens's reply was couched in terms of the facile and ever eloquent after-dinner oratory which he grew to command as few have ever done. But in it was struck the first note of that discord which was presently to alienate from him the sympathy of a great part of the American public. At that time there was no international copyright to protect in the American market the interests of British authors. American publishers brought out editions of British books as they liked and paid nothing for the privilege. More than that, they brought them out in any form or fashion they liked, altered, abbreviated, and garbled them as they pleased.

Dickens's own sufferings in this respect had already made him keenly alive to the general injustice to his craft. He took occasion at the banquet to refer to it in very positive terms.

"There must be an international arrangement in this respect. England has done her part: and I am confident that the time is not far distant when America will do hers."

The language was moderate enough, and one cannot doubt that when Dickens expressed these sentiments he expressed them to make a hit. Here was a great wrong, a great shame, and here were generous hearts to hear about it. Who cared which side of the Atlantic was which? "Boz," no doubt, expected an equally noble response.

For the moment, the sentiments passed. There was no challenge. But of the guests many must have been thinking that the moment was ill-timed. After all, was it right to raise the question now Boz had received so much. Was it possible that, like Oliver Twist, he asked for more? There was matter enough in this presently to shipwreck Dickens's American tour.

For the sentiments were presently repeated at Hartford and elsewhere. The grievance grew as Dickens thought about it, grew till it assumed the proportions of an obsession.

It was characteristic of Dickens that his interest as a traveller centred specially round the visiting of public institutions, such as hospitals, prisons, reformatories, and the like. Political institutions he never cared to study: they represented for him from first to last little else than humbug, boredom, and comicality. He took for granted that government must be carried on and only complained that it was not done better, with no sense that it was meritorious and difficult to do it at all. But his mind instinctively turned to anything connected with social betterment, which he was rapidly annexing as a domain of his own; and he was always drawn to anything connected with a sensation – criminals, jails, executions. He had a fine taste in horrors.

In Boston they could show him the asylum for the blind, where he saw Laura Bridgman – deaf, dumb, and blind – for whose mind, thus shut from the world of the senses, so much had been accomplished by intelligent and devoted teaching. Dickens was thrilled and impressed. In the book he presently wrote he devoted pages and pages – still interesting reading – to the marvellous way in which signals of thought and communication had been sent through across the gulf of darkness that lay between Laura and the outside world.

He visited also with intense interest the State Hospital for the Insane; the reformatory where juvenile offenders were specially treated; the House of Correction (the state prison), "in which silence is strictly maintained but where the prisoners have the comfort and mental relief of seeing each other and working together." It all seemed away ahead of England. "In her sweeping reform and bright example to other countries on this head, America has shown great wisdom, great benevolence and exalted policy."

Boz left Boston after a two weeks' stay (Saturday, February 5,

1842) and held a sort of triumphal progress through the New England towns on his way to New York. At Worcester he was the guest of the state governor. At Hartford there was a big dinner at the City Hotel, where again he referred in his speech to international copyright, and a stop-over of two days that allowed him to visit the courts of law, the Institution for the Deaf and Dumb, and the Insane Asylum, where he had much merry conversation with the inmates, duly recorded in his book; and he saw there also the best jail for untried offenders in the world. Hartford was "a lovely place," and New Haven, which came next, "the city of elms, a fine town," in which he found that Yale College with its "rows of grand old elm trees" had "an effect like that of an old cathedral yard in England." The American tour was still seen through the colours of the morning, though already in his letters Dickens was writing of "yearning for home."

So he reached New York. It was time. The metropolitan press was already getting jealous of the favours shown to New England. The *Tribune* expressed the hope that he would spend two or three weeks in its city "if he is not beslavered and lionized into loathing us. We hope," it added, "to get a look at him, but begin to despair of it if he is to be disgusted with such liquorice doses as the Boston *Transcript* is giving him."

But New York got its chance and proceeded to show that in the matter of public entertainment and adulation, in balls, banquets, and receptions, and in prisons, jails, and other places of interest, New England "had nothing on it."

Mr. and Mrs. Dickens reached New York on the 13th of February and remained for three weeks, staying at the Carlton Hotel on Broadway. The welcome was second only, if second at all, to that accorded in New England. The mayor of the city presided at a meeting of leading citizens to frame a vote of welcome. They resolved "That in the opinion of this meeting, it is proper and becoming in the citizens of New York to unite heartily in these demonstrations of respect and esteem which have been, and will be, everywhere in our land called forth by the visit of Mr. Dickens to America; not because of his talents alone, but in consideration of the noble use he has made of those talents, in indicating the rights and claims and feelings of humanity at large, without distinction of rank or circumstances."

If Dickens had been older and had had a less impulsive mind, he would have felt from such words as these a sense of responsibility that would have restrained him from error. Towards his English readers and his English public he was always animated by exactly such a sense. He measured well what they would think, what they would tolerate and what was due to them. But he did not extend this to the States. He expected and received unbounded praise, unstinted hospitality, a national publicity. He was not prepared to pay the price in seemly reticence. The ambassador from England to America had had no training in diplomacy. His own Circumlocution Office could have given him a hint or two.

The New York meeting formed itself into a general committee of entertainment. There was no delay about it. A "Boz Ball" was given the next night at the Park Theatre. There were decorations of garlands and trophies to typify the States of the Union, with designs from the writing of Boz. There was floor space for three thousand dancers. There was a huge programme of grand marches, tableaux vivants of scenes from Dickens's books, quadrilles, and heaven knows what, ending with a gallopade as number twenty-five. The drinks flowed as they could flow only in the roaring 'forties.

A local reporter wrote up the "Boz Ball" with the superlatives of the period. "The agony is over: the 'Boz Ball' the greatest affair in modern times, the fullest libation ever poured upon the altar of the muses, came off last evening in fine style. Everything answered the public expectations."

What a homage to pour out upon one young man! What a scene! What merriment! What colossal fun! If Dickens had had the eyes to see America as he had to see England, what a host of characters, of oddities, of lovable scoundrels he would have found at the Boz Ball. Dickens, who could gather amusement from a reptile like Squeers, fun from a vampire like Mrs. Gamp, and found a holy joy in a hypocrite like Pecksniff, could see in America nothing but crooks and snobs.

What a Dickens book could have been written about these Americans, seen through the same glasses as Mr. Pickwick, if Dickens had been able to do it.

One of the local reports gives a picture of him as he appeared: "The author of the *Pickwick Papers* is a small, bright, and intelligent-looking young fellow, thirty years of age, somewhat of a dandy in his dress, with 'rings and things in fine array,' brisk in his manner and of a lively conversation. If he does not get his head turned by all this, I shall wonder at it. Mrs. Dickens is a little plump English-looking woman, of an agreeable countenance and, I should think, a nice woman."

The New Yorkers were able to satisfy Dickens's curiosity in the matter of institutions, jails, and such, even better than the staid New Englanders. They took him to the Tombs prison, the penitentiary, to the almshouse, to the lunatic asylum. "It is not all parties," he wrote home. "I go into the prisons, the police offices, the watch-houses, the hospitals, the workhouses. I was out half the night in New York with two of their most famous constables: started at midnight and went into every thieves' house, murderous hovel, sailors' dancing place and abode of villainy, both black and white, in the town."

To these delights was added the compliment of a magnificent banquet at the city hotel. All the literati and distinguished men of the town – their names eminent then but mostly forgotten now – were at the board. Washington Irving, with whom Dickens had instituted a real friendship, was of the company; so were William Cullen Bryant, W.B. Astor, Hamilton Fish, and Fitz-Greene Halleck. There were endless toasts. Oratory flowed in a flood. Washington Irving, a silent man, tried to speak and broke down. Dickens spoke with that marvellous and radiant eloquence that was one of the ornaments of his genius.

He spoke – but – one reads in *David Copperfield*, a book at this time still to be written, how poor Mr. Dick, otherwise well balanced, could not keep King Charles's head from coming into things. Dickens had acquired his King Charles head, and its name was International Copyright. It is not true that he came to America on purpose to agitate against the lack of copyright protection for British authors. Later on, when someone said this in England, Dickens wrote a letter to the *Times* and called the man, flat out, a liar.

But the thing had got in his mind. The utter injustice of stealing, without a cent of compensation, the product of a man's creative gift: utter, absolute, robbery – nothing else! So Dickens saw it, and so in a sense it was, except that it had grown up, like so many injustices, through no one's particular contrivance. Dickens felt it as if the American nation – an associated band of crooks – had made a conspiracy to steal the property of British authors, including his own.

In a sense he was right; but, oh! the inconceivable, atrocious bad taste of it! He could at least have waited. He could have gone home and written about it, or agitated about it. He had all the world as his audience at will. But he must needs use the very publicity of his welcome to give publicity to his complaint. The magnificent welcome, outdoing oriental profusion, unparalleled in the world's history of letters, must itself be turned to his account. There he stood like a Tory squire entertained by poachers and talking about the game laws. The odd psychology of it is that Dickens thought himself a noble fellow in doing it and expected a noble response. It was meant as one great-hearted man addressing his generous fellows. When it went all wrong, no one was more surprised than Dickens.

So in the City Hall banquet speech the rushing tide of his oratory rolled in King Charles's head.

"As I came here, and am here, without the least admixture of one hundredth part of one grain of base alloy, without one feeling of unworthy reference to self in any respect, I claim in reference to the past for the last time, my right in reason, in truth and in justice, to approach as I have done on two former occasions, a question of literary interest. I claim

as one who has a right to speak and be heard."

The words were mild enough, and again they passed for the time without hostile comment on the spot. In any case, the guests were authors rather than booksellers, and their interests were identical with those of the speaker. There was a toast drunk to "international copyright, the only turnpike between the readers of two great nations."

But meantime the copyright question and Dickens's attack began to filter through the press to reach the publishers and the booksellers and to call forth recrimination in return. In Dickens's own mind too, as the winter wore on, the subject reached the proportions of an obsession. It coloured all his view of America; it poisoned him.

"Is it not a horrible thing" – so he wrote home later on (but the thoughts were fermenting already) – "that scoundrel booksellers should grow rich here from publishing books, the authors of which do not reap one farthing from their issue by scores of thousands; and that every vile, blackguard, and detestable newspaper, so filthy and bestial that no honest man would admit one into his house for a scullery doormat, should be able to publish those same writings side by side, cheek by jowl, with the coarsest and most obscene companions with which they must become connected, in course of time, in people's minds? Is it tolerable that besides being robbed and rifled an author should be forced to appear in any form, in any vulgar dress, in any atrocious company; that he should have no choice of his audience, no control over his own distorted text, and that he should be compelled to jostle out of the course the best men in this country who only ask to live by writing? I vow before high heaven that my blood so boils at these enormities, that when I speak about them I seem to grow twenty feet high, and to swell out in proportion. 'Robbers that ye are,' I think to myself when I get upon my legs, 'here goes!' "

After New York came Philadelphia, where Dickens spent two

days. But already he was getting "fed up" with public ovations. A notice appeared in the press before his arrival to say that "Mr. Dickens declines all dinners, parties, parades, shows and junketings." But by mistake a newspaper published a notice after his arrival couched in the following style: "Mr. Dickens – this gentleman will, we understand, be gratified to shake hands with his friends between the hours of half past ten and half past eleven o'clock." The result of this was a mob outside of the United States Hotel; the refusal of Dickens to see them; a protest from the landlord that refusal would precipitate a riot; compliance on Dickens's part, and then for more than two hours an overwhelming procession of people shaking his hand. Dickens turned good-natured over it and took it all with smiles. This is the scene introduced in the "levee" in *Martin Chuzzlewit,* calmly announced without asking his leave.

Much more congenial to Boz was a visit to the Eastern Penitentiary, where he spent some time in a minute examination of the awful system of solitary confinement then in operation. It filled him with horror. In his *American Notes* he wrote:

"On the haggard face of every man among these prisoners, the same expression sat. I know not what to liken it to. It had something of that strained attention which we see upon the faces of the blind and deaf, mingled with a kind of horror, as though they had all been secretly terrified. In every little chamber that I entered, and at every gate through which I looked I seemed to see the same appalling countenance. It lives in my memory, with the fascination of a remarkable picture. Parade before my eyes a hundred men, with one among them newly released from this solitary suffering, and I would point him out."

From Philadelphia Dickens and his wife and secretary took the train for Washington. There was a stop for dinner at Baltimore and there, waited upon by slaves, he had his first actual sight of slavery, henceforth more than ever a horror to him. The thought of it aroused in him, as it always did before his tour and to his life's end, a burning indignation. "Though I was with respect to it an innocent man," he writes, "its presence filled me with a sense of shame and self reproach." It seemed to him a "most hideous blot and foul disgrace" upon the face of American civilization. It was not so much the fact of it as the idea of it that burned into his soul. Dickens could chronicle without a quiver of the pen the statement that the girls hired in the new cotton factories of Lowell worked twelve hours a day. But he could not bear the thought of the "slavery" of the coloured waitresses of a Baltimore restaurant. It was the element of coercion, of the utter hopelessness of the individual against the deadweight of compulsion that filled him with a sense of stifled oppression like a man crushed under heavy weights. It was the same sympathetic suffering that he had just felt when he visited the silent corridors of that hideous prison of the Philadelphia of 1842 where "solitary confinement" prevailed and silent prisoners faded to death by slow torture. As against this prison, so against American slavery Dickens cried out with all the intensity of passion. He did not stop to ask, he did not care to know, whether the plantation slave was happier than the factory hand of Lancashire, whether the slave himself felt the degradation of his chain or only the weight of it – Dickens wanted nothing of such talk. He felt, as Longfellow felt, or Channing, that the thing was utterly and hideously wrong in itself, and different from any form of want or suffering that might arise where at least the will is free. Like all the people of his day, he valued individual freedom, if only freedom to die of starvation. Many of us still share his view.

His attitude towards slavery separated Dickens in thought and sympathy from the South. People who lived among slavery took it as they found it – a sort of way of living and working. There were good owners and bad, kind and cruel; but cruelty to any real extent was the exception, not the rule. A slave minded the whip as much and as little as did an Eton schoolboy. He measured it by the sting, not by the moral. People who owned slaves shuddered at the sight of an English factory – its close mephitic air, its clattering machinery, the pale, wan faces working at the looms in the gaslight, the hideous toll of the twelve and fourteen hours of work extracted from little children; the long lines of starving people clamouring for bread in the England of the hungry 'forties and receiving as their answer the cold lead of the Waterloo musket. They contrasted this with the bright picture of the cornfield, bathed in wind and sun, the Negroes singing at their work, and the little pickaninnies clinging to the red gowns of their mothers. On such people of the South in the days of the 'forties descended a fury of anger when a pert Mrs. Trollope, or a prim old maid Harriet Martineau, or a young Mr. Dickens, fresh from the miseries of the English factory and the London slum, should hold up their hands in pious horror over the cheerful darkey of the sunny South. They were no doubt wrong. To many of us, one single family broken up and sold down the river outbalances the whole of Lancashire.

But where Dickens is wrong throughout, in his *American Notes* and in his personal letters and in *Martin Chuzzlewit*, is in his insisting on thinking of slavery as a peculiarly American institution. He should have remembered that slavery was a phenomenon not peculiar to America but belonging then to the whole world. He should have remembered that his own countrymen, from the days of the illustrious Hawkins, had taken a leading share in spreading it about the world. Slavery had died out in England centuries before, because it did not pay, just as it died out in the Northern states and in Canada. But wherever the English founded or conquered colonies they introduced or accepted slavery as the mainstay of colonial prosperity. In this shape British slavery lasted till within eight years of Dickens's visit to America. Nor was it only and solely the tears of Wilberforce and the passion for liberty of the Benthams and the Mills which killed it: there was the added argument of economic value. Charles Dickens shared with all his race that peculiar and almost insulting insular smugness which deplores the sins of other nations, forgetting the recentness of their own conversion. Slavery once abolished, the Victorian contemporaries of Dickens invented a patriotic song (no doubt Charles Dickens often joined in the singing of it) in regard to the moral purity of the British flag:

"That flag may float o'er a shot-torn wreck
But never shall float o'er a slave."

The sentiment is noble. But it should have been sung with the zeal of new converts. The British flag at sea prior to 1808 had flown over more slaves than any other flag in the world.

But in any case, the existence of slavery was one of the causes which alienated the sympathies of Dickens from America and led presently to his denunciation of that country.

Slavery and tobacco-spitting! This later became an even greater offense. He had passed it off lightly enough at first, but now that the first luxury of adulation was waning, he became more and more utterly disgusted at the hideous habit of "spitting all over the place." Those of us who can recall the "tobacco-spitting" customary in the United States and Canada, even of fifty years ago, when it was said to be "declining," may well wonder how it could exist. Men spat great "gobs" of tobacco juice, unrebuked, all over the sidewalk, on the floor of hotel rotundas, barrooms, stations, restaurants – anywhere where fellow men assembled. Students spat tobacco juice as they sat in their examination rooms, informed by a little notice that gentlemen will please spit in the spittoons, but making little false pretense of being gentlemen. In Dickens's time, ninety years ago, the nation swam in tobacco juice. If those are strong words, let us substitute his own. They represent his impressions on arriving at the American capital.

"As Washington may be called the head-quarters of tobacco-tinctured saliva, the time is come when I must confess, without any disguise, that the prevalence of those two odious practices of chewing and expectorating began about this time to be anything but agreeable, and soon became most offensive and sickening. In all the public places of America, this filthy custom is recognised. In the courts of law, the judge has his spittoon, the crier his, the witness his, and the prisoner his; while the jurymen and spectators are provided for, as so many men who in the course of nature must desire to spit incessantly. In the hospitals, the students of medicine are requested, by notices upon the wall, to eject their tobacco juice into the boxes provided for that purpose, and not to discolor the stairs. In public buildings, visitors are implored, through the same agency, to squirt the essence of their quids, or 'plugs' as I have heard them called by gentlemen learned in this kind of sweetmeat, into the national spittoons, and not about the bases of the marble columns. But in some parts, this custom is inseparably mixed up with every meal and morning call, and with all the transactions of social life. The stranger, who follows in the track I took myself, will find it in its full bloom and glory, luxuriant in all its alarming recklessness, at Washington. And let him not persuade himself (as I once did, to my shame) that previous tourists have exaggerated its extent. The thing itself is an exaggeration of nastiness, which cannot be outdone."

From now on it seemed to Dickens as if all America were spitting at him. In Washington the Congress spat at him; at the presidential levee President Tyler spat at him. He met Webster and Calhoun: they spat at him. Such, at least, was the impression now in the youthful Dickens's mind. Henceforth nothing in America could please him. He met the senior senator from Massachusetts and was told that this "is one of the most remarkable men in the country." "Good God," answered Boz, "they are all so. I've hardly met a man since my arrival who wasn't one of the most remarkable men in the country." Later on he took the remark out of his own mouth and put it into Martin Chuzzlewit's.

In such a frame of mind he could see in the city of Washington nothing but a ghastly failure – no trade, no commerce, unhealthy; avenues that begin in nothing and lead nowhere. "To the admirers of cities it is a Barmecide Feast: a pleasant field for the imagination to rove in: a monument raised to a deceased project, with not even a legible inscription to record its departed greatness. Such as it is, it is likely to remain."

One thinks of the magnificent city of today and wonders at the lack of vision. But Dickens had no eyes for the future of America. He was too "fed up" with its present. This was still more so when he went presently to the "far West."

In Washington they showed him the Congress. It seemed to him a pack of crooks. Gone are the "noble fellows" of the Boston days. Dickens in his *American Notes* puts to himself the question what did he think of the lawmakers of America and answers it. His answer, which they presently had the pleasure of reading in their non-copyright, no-royalty edition of the book, must have taken the hide off them.

"In the first place – it may be from some imperfect development of my organ of veneration – I do not remember having ever fainted away, or having even been moved to tears of joyful pride, at sight of any legislative body. I have borne the House of Commons like a man, and have yielded to no weakness, but slumber, in the House of Lords. …

"Did I see in this public body an assemblage of men, bound together in the sacred names of Liberty and Freedom, and so asserting the chaste dignity of those two goddesses, in all their discussions, as to exalt at once the Eternal Principles to which their names are given, and their own character and the character of their countrymen, in the admiring eyes of the whole world? …

"Did I recognize in this assembly, a body of men, who applying themselves in a new world to correct some of the falsehoods, and vices of the old, purified the avenues to Public Life, paved the dirty ways to Place and Power, debated and made laws for the Common Good, and had no party but their Country? …

"I saw in them, the wheels that move the meanest perversion of virtuous Political Machinery that the worst tools ever wrought. Despicable trickery at elections; under-handed tamperings with public officers; cowardly attacks upon opponents, with scurrilous newspapers for shields, and hired pens for daggers; shameful trucklings to mercenary knaves, whose claim to be considered, is, that every day and week they sow new crops of ruin with their venal types, which are the dragon's teeth of yore, in everything but sharpness; aidings and abettings of every bad inclination in the popular mind, and artful suppressions of all its good influences: such things as these, and in a word, Dishonest Faction in its most depraved and most unblushing form, stared out from every corner of the crowded hall."

From Washington Dickens took a steamboat down the Potomac to Potomac Creek, thence to go by train to Richmond. "The train stopped at a lonely cabin in the forest," so wrote afterwards Mr. Putnam, the secretary, in his reminiscences. "We noticed a coloured woman with several small children standing by, who seemed to be waiting for passage. After a little time we heard the woman and children weeping and some one in the car asked the cause. 'It's them damned niggers: somebody bought them and is taking them down to Richmond and they are making a fuss about it.' "

The iron sank deeper into Dickens's soul. He decided that after Richmond he would go no further south. He had seen enough. "The pain of living in the constant contemplation of slavery" was more than he could stand.

Meantime his hosts were unaware of the increasing revulsion in the feelings of their guest. He was received at Richmond, where he arrived on March 16, 1842, with every kindness and every hospitality. He refused to accept any invitation to a public dinner, but his polite Southern hosts begged that they might be allowed to tender to him a "Social Supper" at the Exchange Hotel. The supper was of necessity on a simpler scale than the banquets of Boston and New York. But it let loose an almost equal flood of oratory. Dickens's own speech was brief; he kept King Charles's head out of it, and the report still extant in the *Richmond Enquirer* is thickly punctuated with "Cheers," "Laughter," "Cries of 'Go on,' " and once, when he made a joke about the local railroad from Richmond to Fredericksburg, we are told, "Here the laughter and cheering was overpowering." No doubt the ancient Egyptians roared over jokes on the pyramids.

Dickens made the happiest impression. The company were delighted. The papers called it "a fairy scene," "an Attic supper." "The likenesses of Dickens," wrote a Richmond visitor of the moment, "cannot give the charm of his face, his rich expression of humour and merriment, when he laughs, – his whole face lights up.

All through Dickens's life, people spoke of the light in his face.

Next day Dickens and his wife held a levee – this time of his own making – at their hotel from twelve to two. He left Richmond on March 20 (1842) in a sunshine of good-will. He set his face now for the West. Further south he would not go. His detestation of slavery, shared now by everybody, is all to the credit of his heart and feelings. The chapter on it, appended to the *American Notes,* is one of the most powerful denunciations ever written. But Dickens could have done far more for the cause of freedom if he could have kept his antipathy to slavery from becoming an antipathy to America. His great achievements for social betterment in sinful England were not brought about by antipathy to England. So it might have been in America.

But it was not to be.

By the time Dickens left the South he was utterly and absolutely disillusioned about political freedom in America. To his friend Macready he wrote from Baltimore (March 22, 1842):

"This is not the republic I came to see; this is not the republic of my imagination. I infinitely prefer a liberal monarchy – even with its sickening accompaniments of court circulars – to such a government as this. The more I think of its youth and strength, the poorer and more trifling in a thousand aspects it appears in my eyes. In everything of which it has made a boast – excepting its education of the people and its care for poor children – it sinks immeasurably below the level I had placed it upon; and England, even England, bad and faulty as the old land is, and miserable as millions of her people are, rises in the comparison.

"*You* live here! Macready, as I have sometimes heard you imagining! *You!* Loving you with all my heart and soul, and knowing what your disposition really is, I would not condemn you to a year's residence on this side of the Atlantic for any money. Freedom of opinion! Where is it? I see a press more mean, and paltry, and silly, and disgraceful than any country I ever knew."

To Forster he wrote at about the same time:

"But I don't like the country. I would not live here, on any consideration. It goes against the grain with me. It would with you. I think it impossible, utterly impossible, for any Englishman to live here, and be happy."

Thus Dickens was already "fed up" with America when he left the South. The West was to finish him.

He and his wife left Baltimore on March 23 (1842) and spent a month in travelling to the Mississippi and back. Their route lay by rail to York (in Pennsylvania), then by coach twenty-five miles to Harrisburg, and after that by water to the "far West." Here the railway had not yet reached. Travel was by canal boat and river steamer. To Dickens, the cabins of the canal boats and steamers, crowded, stuffy, and promiscuous, the everlasting tobacco-spitting, and the utter lack of privacy, made the trip almost a nightmare. He could not compare it, as the older Americans could, with the primitive transport of a generation before – the transport of the time of Abraham Lincoln's childhood. In those days the settlers floated down the river in barges and flat boats, "carried" over the forest trails of the portages, and slept in rude cabins of logs and poles, one side open to the weather. To those who remembered all this, the new travel was as palatial as it was rapid – with actual shelter to sleep under, meals on real tables, so that the larger river steamers, to the rude settlers of the Western frontier, seemed glittering with luxury.

Not so to Dickens.

His sufferings began with the coach through the valley of the Susquehanna (beautiful, he admits), with twelve people crammed inside it, and on the box and roof drunken men and dirty boys. Four horses tugged the coach through the rain and mud of early spring.

Then came Harrisburg, the seat of the government, which began at once, like the Washington Congress, to spit tobacco. There "levee" in honour of "Charles Dickens and lady" – "with a great number of the members of both branches of the Legislature. Pretty nearly every man spat upon the carpet." "These local Legislatures," wrote Dickens to Forster, "are too insufferably apish of mighty legislation to be seen without bile."

Next came the canal boat from Harrisburg to Pittsburgh, bridging the gap from the Susquehanna to the Ohio – a marvel of convenience to people who could remember the portage days, to Dickens an awful form of travel in something between a steamer and a floating tavern.

A canal boat, floating in the dity water of the canal – the passengers had to "fish it up with a tin ladle" to wash in – with thirty-three people sitting down to eat breakfast in the foul air of a cabin where eight and twenty men had slept on movable wooden shelves, seven and twenty of them "in foul linen with yellow streams from half-chewed tobacco trickling down their chins"! There was a bar, reeking with gin, with a barber at work shaving, and seventeen men spitting at the stove while waiting. Worse still was the fall of night. "You can never conceive," wrote Dickens, "what the hawking and spitting is, the whole night through. ... As to having a window open, that's not to be thought of."

Here and there on the journey Dickens could see in the forests the newly made clearings and the log huts of the settlers. These his sympathetic imagination endowed with his own sensations. "Their forlorn and miserable appearance," he wrote, "baffles all description. It pains the eye to see the stumps of great trees thickly strewed in every field of wheat; and never to lose the eternal swamp and dull morass, with hundreds of rotten trunks, of elm and pine and sycamore and logwood, steeped in its unwholesome water; where the frogs so croak at night that after dark there is an incessant sound as if millions of phantom teams, with bells, were travelling through the upper air, at an enormous distance off."

This of course is Martin Chuzzlewit in the swamp settlements of the West. Anybody who knows how to compare the lot of a pioneer settler in such a cabin with that of an English factory hand or a London sempstress or a slavery in a London lodging house of the period, can measure, as it should be measured, the value of Dickens's picture of America.

From Pittsburgh the Dickenses went by river steamers to Cincinnati, to Louisville, and thence to Cairo and St. Louis. The steamers in point of accommodation were, some of them, excellent, with better cabins than the Cunard boats on the Atlantic. The hotels, too, were mostly newly built on what seemed a large and commodious scale with a certain touch of "hospitality" about them, carried down from colonial days. Dickens, in his record of discomfort, makes an honorable exception of most of them. But everywhere he complains of the utter lack of privacy, of the rude curiosity of the people pushing to get a look at him.

Everywhere he was received with acclaim, though by this time the copyright question was beginning to boil up in the press of the East, and denunciation of Dickens's "ingratitude" was finding its way into print.

At Cincinnati there was a ball given for the Dickenses by a Judge Walker and attended (according to the guest of the evening) by "a hundred and fifty first class bores." At Louisville, so runs the legend of the local press, reprinted on Dickens's second visit, the "host" of the inn offered to be of service in introducing the distinguished visitor to some of the best families of Kentucky. "When I have need of your services," answered Dickens, "I will ring for you." If it is not true, it is well found. Dickens had travelled a long way from the young radical who dreamed of Van Diemen's Land. What right, anyway, has a hotel keeper to talk to a gentleman?

Thus, pleasantly discoursing, he came to Cairo, where the Ohio meets the Mississippi – "a breeding place of fever, ague, and death, vaunted in England as a mine of Golden Hope, and speculated in, on the faith of monstrous representations, to many people ruin. A dismal swamp, on which the half-built houses rot away; cleared here and there for the space of a few yards, and then teeming with rank unwholesome vegetation, on whose baneful shade the wretched wanderers who are tempted hither, droop and die and lay their bones." "I trust," he wrote, "never to see the Mississippi again except in dreams and nightmares."

On an upper stretch of the river at that time was a little boy of six years old for whom the vast reaches of the Mississippi, moving through the forests to the distant sea, and the lights of the river steamers passing in the night, were the inspiration of a lifetime. Compare the majesty of the picture of life on the Mississippi

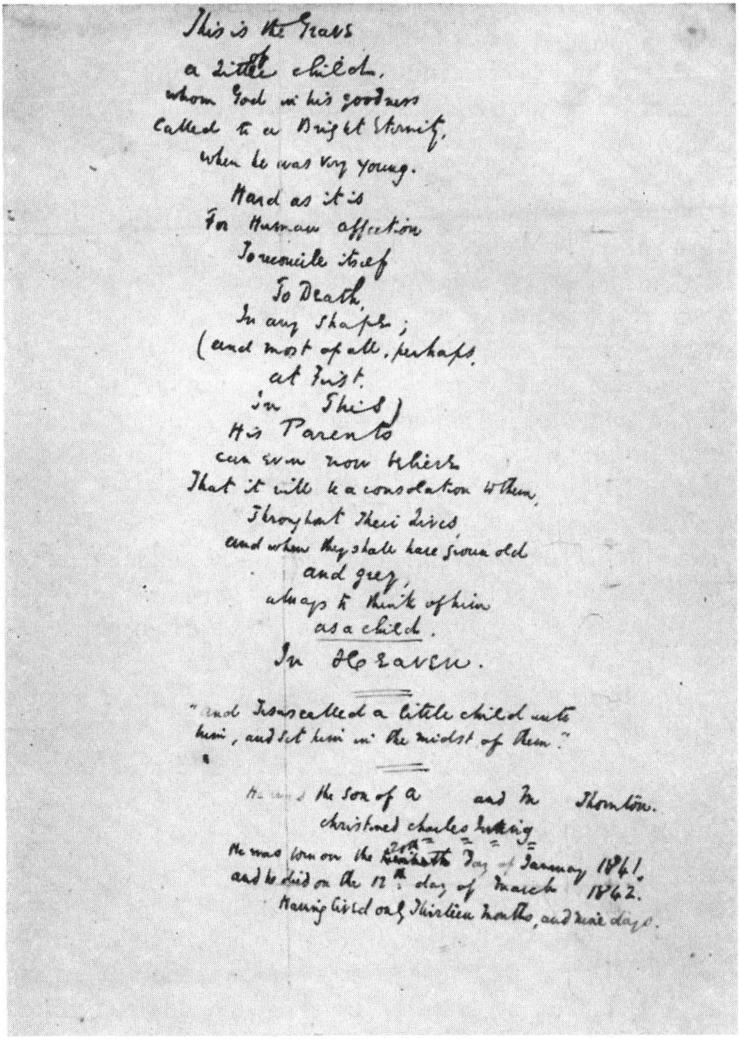

This is the Grave
of a little child,
whom God in his goodness
called to a Bright Heaven,
when he was very young.
Hard as it is
For Human affection
To reconcile itself
To Death,
In any shape;
(and most of all, perhaps,
at first,
in This)
His Parents
can even now think
That it will be a consolation to them,
Throughout their Lives,
and when they shall have grown old
and grey,
always to think of him
as a child.
In Heaven.

"And Jesus called a little child unto him, and set him in the midst of them."

He was the son of   and   Thornton.
christened Charles [illegible]
He was born on the 20th Day of January 1841.
and he died on the 12th day of March 1842.
Having lived only Thirteen Months, and nine days.

An Epitaph

Epitaph on a little child contained in a letter
from Dickens written from Cincinnati, April 4, 1842,
during his first visit to America

drawn in the pages of *Huckleberry Finn* with the cramped and uninspired picture given by Dickens. It is the work of a peevish cockney travelling without his breakfast.

At St. Louis there was, to Dickens's delight, a grand hotel, the Planters' House, "as large as the Middlesex hospital." There was a large public reception spoken of as a "soirée." But for Dickens the charm of being lionized had passed. He set out on his homeward journey, travelling across Ohio by water and stage, through Columbus to Sandusky, and thence by Lake Erie to Buffalo and Niagara. His feelings and impressions as revealed in his *American Notes* are embodied in such recurrent words as tobacco-spit, swamp, bullfrogs, corduroy roads, bugs, politics. For the people he can find little praise. Those of St. Louis as seen at the soirée given for him were declared "pretty rough and intolerably conceited." But they were not as bad as humanity when seen at Sandusky, Ohio – "The demeanor of the people in these country parts is invariably morose, sullen, clownish, and repulsive. I should think there is not on the face of the earth a people so utterly destitute of humour, vivacity or the capacity for enjoyment."

Dickens passed out from the West across the Niagara frontier to Canada (May, 1842). He never saw it again.

The truth was that he did not understand the scenes he witnessed.

What was really going on was a great epic in the history of mankind. It was the advance of civilization down the rivers, and through the forests, and out upon the silent prairies of the West. The woods bowed beneath the age, the forests echoed with voices, the savannahs murmured and rustled to the touch of life. In the mind's eye one could see already the log cabins rising into cathedrals, the villages spreading into great cities, and the swamps and cane-brakes changing to the park and meadowland of a smiling civilization. It was a wonderful epic, this advance of the frontier, moving westward day by day. As beside it the ravaging conquests of early Europe, leaving a track of slaughter, seem things of horror.

But Dickens had no eyes to see it all in its true proportion. Against the crowded canal boats, the jolting stages, and frame

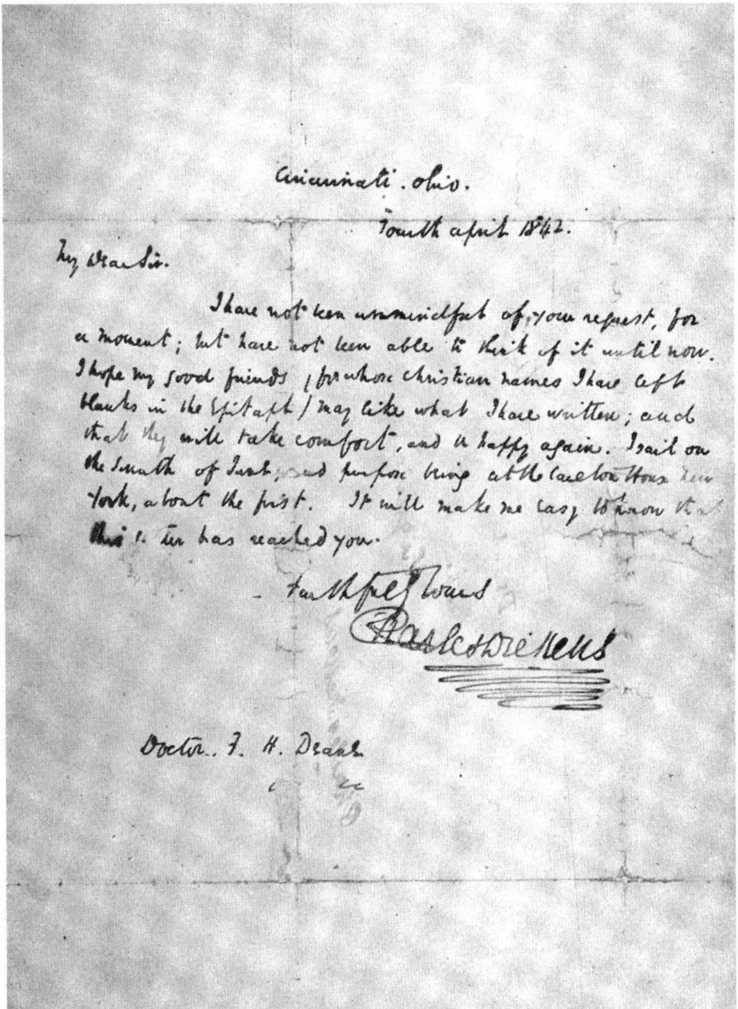

Cincinnati. Ohio.

Fourth April 1842.

My Dear Sir.

I have not been unmindful of your request, for a moment; but have not been able to think of it until now. I hope my good friends (for whose Christian names I have left blanks in the Epitaph) may like what I have written; and that they will take comfort, and be happy again. I sail on the Seventh of June, and purpose being at the Carlton House New York, about the first. It will make me easy to know that this letter has reached you.

Faithfully Yours

Charles Dickens

Doctor F. H. Deane

A Letter

Letter accompanying epitaph on a little child

hotels, the log shanties, and forest villages sunken in the swamps, he set the trim countryside of England, with its neat village commons and parish churches and winding roads lined with thorn hedges – the whole of it a thousand years in the making. Against the cheap frame hotel he set the gabled inns of the John Willetts that had seen two hundred Christmas fires go roaring up the chimney. He suddenly discovered that, after all, the "old Tory gentleman" whom he had denounced didn't spit on the floor, or talk through his nose, or break into the conversations of strangers; that, after all, Mrs. Leo Hunter was a lady, that Mr. Minns and his cousin were gentlemen, and that Mr. Dombey was a dignified and honourable merchant who wouldn't cheat a stranger over a swamp lot in an imaginary settlement.

So it came that Dickens's mind turned back to the England that he knew and cast out the America which he couldn't understand. The fault was his. It has been said – on a foundation difficult to prove conclusively – that Dickens had invested some of his early gains from *Pickwick* in a fraudulent land company of Cairo, Illinois, and went West partly to see the scene of his discomfiture. If so, this gave him an added bitterness against the "Far West."

In any case, there is no doubt that he saw it all with crooked eyes. Could he have seen it right, what a marvellous picture, exaggerated in detail but true in the mass, he could have made of it! Just as at the "Boz Ball" in New York, so here in the New Edens and Thermopylæs a host of "characters" were beckoning to him, like actors waiting to "come on." They were standing there in the wings waiting to catch his attention – as merry and motley a company as those of the pages of *Pickwick* itself. But Dickens, fuming and raving in the foreground over international copyright, tobacco spittle, and slavery, never knew they were there. And when he came back twenty-six years later, he was too old, too broken, too self-absorbed to care whether they were there or not. What a goodly company there was ready to his hand, with their queer clothes, their universal military rank, their magnified eyesight, their generosity, their crookedness! Dickens could *see* them, but saw them only to scoff and denounce. Measured in the same way, the people in *Pickwick* are a pack of dunderheads and fools, Pickwick himself was an amiable idiot on a string, Sam Weller was a crook, and Sam Weller's father smelt of the stable. Dickens was in a land of enchantment and never knew it.

As an epilogue to the American tour came a brief visit to Canada – the two Canadas, Upper and Lower, had been united into one the year before – that lasted from May 4 to May 30, 1842. The visit, if brief, was a pleasant one. After the hustle of the ferocious West the little colony seemed quiet and restful: and Dickens had found a new meaning in the flag that floated over it. More than that, he was now in a rapture of anticipation of getting home again. In Canada he saw and was thrilled by the falls of Niagara and paused a day or two at the pleasant little town (nominally "city") of Toronto, then a place of some twelve thousand people. Here he visited among other places of interest Upper Canada College, founded by Lord Seaton thirteen years before as the Rugby of Canada. The school tradition has it that Dickens spoke in the "prayer hall" to the boys of the school, though no mention of it appears in the chapters of his *American Notes*, where he describes his Canadian tour. From Toronto, Dickens and his wife went by steamer – there was no railway as yet – to Montreal, where he spent eighteen days, the most enjoyable, no doubt, of all his American experience, except perhaps the opening days in Boston. In Montreal was the British garrison, this being still the colonial era, when imperial regiments protected British North America against the rapacity of the United States. The officers of the garrison, the Governor General (then in the city, though Kingston was still the capital) and the citizens at large vied in entertaining Dickens and his wife. But the chief feature of his visit was the organization of the officers of the regiment of amateur theatricals for which Dickens became the leading actor manager and producer. He threw himself into the congenial task with delight. Here was something better worth while than canal boats and swamp villages.

The performance duly came off on the evening of May 25, 1842, at the Queen's Theatre. The pieces presented were *A Roland for an Oliver*, with Dickens and his recent shipmate Lord Mulgrave in the cast; a French scene done by Dickens and Captain Granville (*Past Two o'Clock in the Morning*); and a farce in one act called *Deaf as a Post* in which Mrs. Dickens, for the first and only time, took a stage part.

Dickens wrote home enthusiastically "The play came off last. The audience between five and six hundred strong, were invited as to a party: a regular table with refreshments being spread in the lobby and saloon. We had the band of the Twenty-third (one of the finest in the service) in the orchestra, the theatre lighted with gas, the scenery was excellent, the properties all being brought from private homes. Sir Charles Bagot, Sir Richard Jackson and their staffs were present, and as the military portion in the audience were in uniform it was a splendid scene. We 'went over' splendidly. … But only think of Kate playing, and playing devilish well, I assure you."

In John Forster's account of Dickens's visit to Montreal there occurs one of the few out-and-out errors to be found in that magnificent work. Misled no doubt by Dickens's handwriting in the letters he received, he says that Dickens and his wife stayed at Peasco's Hotel. This is incorrect. Recent researches personally conducted in front of the hotel (still standing, in St. Paul St.) show that the name (still legible) is Rasco's Hotel. All research workers in the history of our literature will find in this correction of a standing error a distinct contribution to our knowledge of the life and character of Dickens and an ample justification of the present volume.

But whether at Peasco's or at Rasco's, Dickens was in no mood to stay there. His mind was set on his departure. He concludes the letter in which he wrote of the theatres with the words, "We shall soon meet, please God, and be happier and merrier than ever we were in all our lives. Oh, home – home – home – home – home – home – HOME."

Dickens and his wife left Montreal Sunday, May 29, 1842,

reaching New York the Wednesday following. While waiting for the ocean steamer he paid a visit to West Point and to the Shaker village at Lebanon. Then, on June 7th, left New York in the *Russia* homeward bound for England.

Chapter Five

YEARS OF SUCCESS

1842–1847
Home Again – "Martin Chuzzlewit" – "A Christmas Carol" – France and Italy

IT MAY WELL BE THAT THE TWO OR THREE YEARS of Dickens's career after his return from America were the happiest in his life. He came back in a tumult of affection for England, for his familiar home, his happy work, and his energetic play, and above all for the nursery of four children waiting to greet him. "How I look forward," he had written, "across that rolling water to home and its small tenantry. How I busy myself in thinking how my books look, and where the tables are, and in what position the chairs stand relatively to the other furniture.... And what our pets will say and how they will look.... We shall soon meet, please God, and be happier and merrier than ever we were in all our lives. Oh, home, – home, – home, – home, – home, – home, – HOME!!!!!'"

And home, when he found it, was happy indeed. It contained a nursery already well filled, and destined to be filled later on to something like repletion. At this time there were, as already said, four children – Charley, aged five, Mary, Kate, and Walter the baby. Two other sons arrived during this happy period between the return from America and the family journey to Italy – Francis (Frank) Jeffrey and Alfred Tennyson. Dickens was an ideal father, never so happy as in romping and laughing with his children, on whom fell family nicknames in an affectionate shower. Frank was "Chickenstalker" and Alfred was "Sampson Brass" or "Skittles." Before the list ended the family had increased to ten.

To this family group one may now add permanently Georgina Hogarth, Mrs. Dickens's sister, at this time a girl of sixteen, who had looked after the children while their parents were in America, and who shared Dickens's home from now till his death. In addition there were Dickens's father and mother snugly ensconced in their villa at Alphington, good for years yet, while Dickens still had about him his brothers and sisters, of whom Frederick and Fanny found an especially warm place in his affections. One notes their names transferred to the pages of *Little Dorrit* later on, with perhaps something of the relationship of the two brothers themselves.

Nor had the shadows that were to come later as yet fallen across the threshold of his home. At this period of his life he had not yet undertaken the burden of overwork which ultimately broke him down. The endless toil of his editorial years had not yet begun. The public readings that eventually did so much to undermine his energy and to hasten his premature death were still far away. What he did now, work or play, was done with equal zest and enjoyment. The writing of his *American Notes* was simplicity itself – a matter mostly of wondering what to leave out, not of searching for things to put in. His writing of *Martin Chuzzlewit*, apart from delays and dilemmas, was on the whole a piece of immense fun. There was nothing in it of that dreary fight against fatigue, that forcing of a jaded and overworn imagination, which is too often seen in his books of twenty years later. As for *A Christmas Carol* – his great achievement of 1843 – he worked on it with a rapt absorption and intense feeling of good to be done and evil to be conquered that was its own reward.

The homecoming to his friends was celebrated by a dinner at Greenwich, the company including such well known names as those of Sergeant Talfourd, Captain Marryat of the sea stories, Tom Hood, and Barham of *The Ingoldsby Legends*. At this time of his life, dinners of this sort were one of the chief delights of Dickens and his circle. They dined to welcome his homecoming from America. They dined presently to celebrate Macready's going away to America. They dined as a way of expressing their regrets at the retirement of Mr. Black from *The Chronicle.* They dined to express their congratulations to Dickens on completing *Martin Chuzzlewit.* In short, they dined for anything and everything.

The dinners were at such comfortable places as the Ship Inn, or the Trafalgar at Greenwich, or the Star and Garter at Richmond. And in those days a dinner was a dinner, a ceremony extending over a multiplicity of courses, a pharmacopœia of bottles, and an endless succession of toasts. One has but to note the generous way in which Dickens lays the table for his characters in his books to know something of the quality and quantity and good fellowship of an early Victorian dinner.

Not that Dickens himself was ever greedy of food, eager for drink or inclined to excess. He was, by disposition and without effort, the most temperate of men. His daughter Mary, in the charming little book on her father (as a father) which she left behind her, has told us that he was "the most abstemious of men, that he rarely ate anything of consequence for luncheon, and that his pleasure was rather in planning and ordering a dinner than in eating it."

It was this moderation, perhaps, which fitted him so well to sing the praises of good wine and a groaning table: he himself knew only the pleasures of good cheer and nothing of the penalties of excess. The last words that he ever wrote were, "and then falls to with an appetite."

Some research scholar – if one may in this place pursue the topic a little further – might well devote a year or two to a scholarly investigation of eating, drinking, and smoking as they appear in the works of Dickens. Even the most casual readers must have noticed the stress that seems laid upon the pleasures of the table. Here, as a sample of the material to be used in such a study, is the bill of fare as ordered – just as a light casual meal – by Mr. Grewgious, the old lawyer, for his young friend Edwin Drood, who has "happened in" at his chambers.

" 'Perhaps you wouldn't mind,' said Mr. Grewgious to his

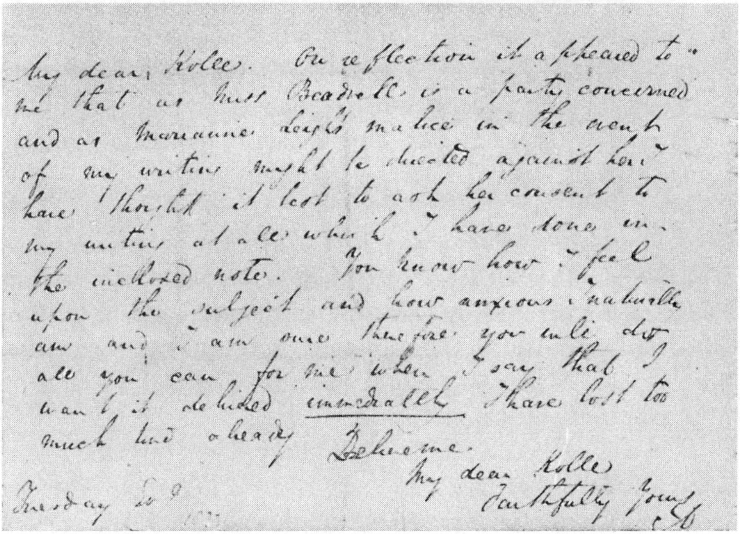

My dear Kolle. On reflection it appeared to me that as Miss Beadnell is a party concerned and as Marianne Leigh's malice in the event of my writing might be directed against her I have thought it best to ask her consent to my writing at all which I have done in the enclosed note. You know how I feel upon the subject and how anxious I naturally am and I am sure therefore you will do all you can for me when I say that I want it delivered immediately. I have lost too much time already.

Believe me
My dear Kolle
Faithfully Yours
C D

Thursday [illegible]

Autographed Letter

A letter signed by Charles Dickens to T. J. Thompson, concerning a sitting for a portrait with Stanfield, and referring to the birth of his fifth child, Francis Jeffrey clerk, 'stepping over to the hotel in Furnival's and ask them to send in materials for laying the cloth. For dinner we'll have a tureen of the hottest and strongest soup available, and we'll have the best made-dish that can be recommended and we'll have a joint such as a haunch of mutton, and we'll have a goose or a turkey or any little stuffed thing of that sort that may happen to be in the bill of fare'..."

A reader not accustomed to the period and to the writer might think that the order is a joke, a burlesque. Not at all. The dinner is brought, as ordered, and they eat it – and eat it all.

Here is another light little collation that is served up in the pages of *Bleak House.* In that story Esther Summerson has been dangerously ill, is now just convalescent and able to sit up a little. To her there comes as a visitor to the sickroom the little old lady Miss Flite – the pathetic victim of the Court of Chancery, so slight, so frail that she looks as if the wind would blow her away. Esther invites her to share what she calls "her early dinner." It consisted of "a dish of fish, a roast fowl, a sweetbread, vegetables, pudding, and Madeira." It would be an ill wind that would blow Miss Flite away after that.

But as to tobacco, the case is just the contrary. If the whole picture were in keeping we would have Mr. Grewgious saying after dinner to the "flying waiter" from the inn, "Now, as to a cigar what would you suggest?" And the waiter answering, "Well, sir, perhaps, a Golden Havana, or a Dry Tortuga!" "Ah," should say Mr. Grewgious, "excellent – half a dozen of each." But no, if Edwin Drood gets a smoke the reader has to supply it to him gratis.

To the private dinner ceremonies spoken of above there began to be added now those public appearances and speeches which from this time on formed an occasional but conspicuous feature of Dickens's life. Few men could excel him in this occasional oratory: as an "after-dinner" speaker he talked with an ease and grace rarely equalled. And in setting forth some great public cause – above all, the cause of the poor – he rose above all others in the matchless appeal of his words and the matchless power of voice and gesture. The fact that he was invited (1843), along with Cobden and Disraeli, to speak at the opening of the Manchester Athenæum shows the place that he was beginning to take in the national life of England. The new institution aimed at promoting the education of the poor, and Dickens pictures to his hearers the lot of the untrained, untaught children of London slums, "condemned to tread the path of jagged flints and stones laid down by brutal ignorance."

At this time public education in England – as apart from the institutions misnamed the public schools – was just struggling into, or rather towards, existence against the inertia of social prejudice. No one could help it more than the man whose *Nicholas Nickleby* had held up to public horror the brutalities committed in dark places under the name of education. Dickens with his voice and pen helped along the cause of the newly founded "Ragged Schools." Through his influence was secured the powerful support of Miss Coutts (later the Baroness Burdett-Coutts), one of the first of the "inspired millionaires" of the industrial era. Now and later she looked to Dickens as a sort of almoner for whose appeal her purse was ever open.

But to return to the private tenor of Dickens's own life as apart from the meals he spread for others. Still more dear to his heart during these early days than even the jovial dinner gatherings were the weeks and months that he spent, at intervals throughout these years, at the seaside. These were passed nearly always at Broadstairs, on the Kentish coast. The various houses and homes which Dickens occupied throughout his life fill a considerable list, as shown in the appendix to this book, and of course at this period of his life his chief place of abode was his commodious home in Devonshire Terrace, London. But there is no place more pleasantly connected with his memory and with his books than the little Kentish fishing village of Broadstairs. For many summers it was his favourite place of rest and recreation. It was at that time (as described by Dickens in a letter to his American friend Professor Felton) "a little fishing place, built on a cliff whereon, in the centre of a tiny semicircular bar, our house stands, the sea rolling and dashing under the windows. Seven miles out are the Goodwin Sands." Dickens first went to the village with his wife in 1837 for a seaside holiday while still busy upon Mr. Pickwick. A house in High Street bears a tablet with the record "Charles Dickens lived here and wrote part of the *Pickwick Papers.*" The "house" as mentioned above was presently incorporated into the Albion Hotel, which therefore bears the legend, "Charles Dickens stayed here 1839, 1840, 1842, 1843, 1845, 1849, 1859 and wrote part of *Nicholas Nickleby.*" As a matter of fact, he also wrote at Broadstairs parts of his *Barnaby Rudge*, of *The Old Curiosity Shop*, the conclusion of *David Copperfield*, and various minor pieces. More than that, it was Broadstairs that inspired more than any other places his pictures of the sea. Dickens loved weather. He loved the wind and the storm, and the waves driving in from the open sea. He himself in his little sketch (of 1851, in *Household Words*), *Our English Watering Place*, has rung the changes of the sun and shadow, the dead flat calm, and the driving storm of the fishing village. The great storm scene of *David Copperfield* is in reality taken from the scenery and impressions of Broadstairs, and the shipwrecks on the Goodwin Sands, though the book places it, literally, off the coast of Norfolk off Yarmouth. "Our house" of Dickens's letter sounds like Bleak House and has often been mistaken for it: but it was not. Bleak House stood inland.

Immediately after his return from America Dickens prepared for the press his *American Notes*, as already described. But before he settled down again he allowed himself a journey to Cornwall with his three friends, John Forster, Clarkson Stanfield, and Maclise – a journey almost Pickwickian in its uproarious merriment. He threw himself with all his characteristic energy into walking, climbing cliffs, peering into dim caves and into churches almost as dim. He wrote to his Boston friend Professor Felton, "I never laughed so much in my life as I did on this journey. I was choking and gasping and bursting the buckle of the back of my stock, all the way.... There never *was* such a trip."

Dickens, Forster, Stanfield and Maclise
Sketched by Thackeray

The fact that the travellers made a part of their journey "by rail" marks the coming of a great change.

The next serious task to be carried out was the writing of *Martin Chuzzlewit*, planned for serial publication in twenty numbers. The terms agreed to by Messrs. Chapman & Hall showed how far Dickens had travelled since the "tempting emolument" of fifteen guineas a month, which was in reality only a few years before. For the new book he was to receive £200 for each number and, over and above it, three quarters of the profit made on each number, after deducting his £200 as one of the expenses. For the twelve months between the making of the agreement and the issue of the first number he was to receive £150 a month as an "advance" against future profits. Princely terms for 1842. Yet today, with picture rights, drama, broadcast rights, world rights, and copyrights, reaching to the grave and beyond it, Dickens would have received not hundreds but millions. "Stars" at Hollywood have made more in a few seasons than Dickens in all his life.

Martin Chuzzlewit duly appeared, beginning its first number in January, 1843. It was produced under the title *The Life and Adventures of Martin Chuzzlewit*, with a long straggling extension intended to be facetious and reading: "his relatives, friends and enemies, comprising all his wills and his ways with a historical record of what he did and what he didn't, showing, moreover, who inherited the family plate, who came in for the silver spoons, and who for the wooden ladles. The whole forming a complete key to the House of Chuzzlewit." This clumsy tailpiece was afterwards dropped in the book editions. The monthly numbers were declared to be "edited by Boz" and the illustrations were again those of Hablôt Browne (Phiz).

For whatever reason it may have been, the new story was not an immediate success. It was published on the *Pickwick* plan, in monthly numbers, and the fact that the stories preceding it had come out and reached a large circulation in *weekly* issues (*Master Humphrey's Clock*) is thought by Forster to have injured the sale. But there seems no reason for this. In any case, the sales amounted to only about 20,000 per number as contrasted with sales of 40,000, 50,000, and even more. Nor did the circulation increase more than two or three thousand when Martin Chuzzlewit was shipped off to America to lend variety to the story.

There seems no valid reason why the sales of the story should have fallen off midway. Many people have liked it best of Dickens's books, and all readers have found it *one* of the books they liked best. Two at least of its characters, Mr. Pecksniff and Mrs. Gamp, have become household names to millions of people, one might almost say common nouns in the English language. The book moreover shares with all Dickens's best work that strange alchemy of transformation whereby even sin and wickedness are softened as things seen far off in retrospect, and horror is replaced by a smile: it is as if one mingled smiles and tears over the half-forgotten pain and sorrows of childhood.

This quality of Dickens, this divine retrospect, this atmosphere in which his characters are made to move, remains the mainstay of his genius.

The book *Martin Chuzzlewit* has on the contrary all the characteristic faults of Dickens: it opens with a perfectly inconsequent piece of burlesque, excellent as a contribution to a comic paper, but of no bearing or use in the story. The plot, as usual, becomes unfathomable, and the motives of old Martin Chuzzlewit in upsetting his whole life to enforce a moral lesson go beyond human comprehension. Most characteristic of all is the sudden transportation of young Martin to America, a pure afterthought of construction. But, after all, what do these faults matter? The real readers of Dickens never notice them. They exult in Martin's journey to America without caring a rush whether it is artistic, or natural, or anything else. As to the plot, no Dickens-lover ever tries to follow it.

When the book reached America it called forth loud outcries at the "ingratitude" of Dickens. The copyright quarrel that had embittered his visit was bad enough: the *American Notes* were worse; but *Martin Chuzzlewit* was an open parody, a vilification, a denunciation of the civilization of the United States. As a matter of fact, it was just exactly that, and it was meant to be that. With the amenities of good-will and the lapse of time, anger fades away and quarrels sink below the horizon. A kind of haze of retrospect colours the enmities of the past. At the present time, stress is laid on the fact that many leading Americans, such as Longfellow, read all of Dickens's criticism of America with tolerant amusement.

But in reality these were the few. Nor does it avail to say that Dickens also satirizes and vilifies countrymen of his own. If Pecksniff is in the book, so is Tom Pinch; the hideous Jonas Chuzzlewit is to be set against the manly John Westlock; and against the damp, oleaginous form of Mrs. Gamp the humble, noble outline of old Chuffey. But the American characters! With the exception of one or two commendable wooden figures such as Mr. Bevan put in to stand for Professor Felton, what a pack they are! Noisy, boastful, mannerless, spitting tobacco juice, defrauding the helpless and the weak, and fawning upon birth and station!

It speaks wonders for the ultimate good temper of life on the American continent that it was all so soon forgiven and forgotten; especially as the picture – even with a dot of truth in the foreground – was hopelessly untrue in its incompleteness, in its background. Dickens in England had no eye to see the dignity and greatness of English government: it was all comic to him; it was all Coodle and Doodle talking platitudes against Foodle and Yoodle; it was all circumlocution, wind, and humbug. In the same way Dickens had no eye to see the nobility of pioneer life in America; no sense of the great epic of the American frontier: to him it was all swamp, ague, and mosquitoes. Others could have looked further and seen in New Eden just what it said, New Eden, the banks and theatres and churches of the maps of Major Pawkins, and they are all there now. But Dickens saw only humbug in England and only ague in America.

While Dickens was still busy on the writing of *Nickleby,* there had come to him a sort of inspiration, the idea of a Christmas story. In the late autumn of 1843 he worked at it – in between the *Nickleby* numbers – with increasing absorption and in something like a frenzy of composition. We are told that as he wrote he wept and laughed at his work, and in the pauses of it walked the London streets at nights, for miles and miles, still absorbed in his idea. It was well worth it: for the idea and the tale were *A Christmas Carol,* one of the famous masterpieces of English literature. In its own form and as converted into plays and dialogues, recitations, and, later, moving pictures, *A Christmas Carol* has quite literally gone around the world. All the world knows at first or second hand of the marvellous transformation of the miser Scrooge, and all the world has rejoiced in the sheer beautiful idealism of it. Literature has no finer picture than the redeemed Scrooge at his window in the frosty Christmas morning, waking to the ringing bells of a new world. It is a new world that is open to each of us at any moment – for that is the point of the story – at the mere cost of opening the windows of the soul. It is of no consequence whether *A Christmas Carol* is true to life. It is better than life.

No story written by Dickens ever met a more sympathetic reception than the *Carol.* The great critics like Jeffrey were not ashamed to shed tears over it.

It is true that now, many readers, most readers, perhaps, would find the mechanism of the story a little melodramatic, the spirits rather too prolix. The reader of today would want it "put over faster." But then the people of today are a generation greatly improved – or is it "badly damaged"? – by the rapid technique of the moving pictures and the hurried emotions of the modern screen. *A Christmas Carol* filled a distinct place in the progress, or the course, of contemporary letters. Dickens did not create the "Christmas Story," but he gave to it an enormous impulse. The *Carol,* and the companion pieces that followed year by year – *The Chimes,* etc. – set the pace for the development of that Christmas fiction which has since become a part of our annual round.

In the financial sense the *Carol* was a disappointment. Dickens had "set his heart" upon receiving a thousand pounds for the sales that season, but his royalties reached only something over seven hundred. *A Christmas Carol,* selling at a shilling, ran (in its initial season) only to a sale of about fifteen thousand copies. Later on, Dickens was able to sell more than a quarter of a million copies of a Christmas number of his *Household Words.*

It was the disappointment over the circulation of *Martin Chuzzlewit* and over the financial returns from the *Carol* which in part induced Dickens to leave England for a prolonged sojourn on the Continent. This was not the sole reason for his doing so. He had begun to feel that new scenes, a new environment, were necessary for the gathering of new material for his work. The idea was more or less fallacious. It turned out that in Genoa Dickens thought and wrote of London. His foreign travel, in the end, only gave him as direct material those "pictures from Italy," which form one of the most ephemeral parts of his work. From it he got also a little of the setting of scenes in *Little Dorrit,* and a part of the background of *A Tale of Two Cities.* But no doubt the timely recreation and the homesickness of exile regilded the inspiration of his own country and his own London.

In any case, he had made up his mind that a foreign residence would aid his declining budget. "My year's bills," he wrote, "unpaid, are so terrific, that all the energy and determination I can exert will be required to clear me before I go abroad: which, if next June come and find me alive, I shall do." As has been said above, Dickens had left poverty or stringency forever behind. But the change of circumstance had brought a change of outlook. He thought now in terms of an expensive and elaborate home, and a wilderness of incidental expense. Even the "economizing" of foreign travels was to mean coaches and couriers and what would have seemed utter luxury but a few years before.

So it came about that Dickens and his family – including his wife, and her sister, and all the family down to the baby – went rolling southward through France in the sunshine of the year of universal peace 1844.

Travelling in France and Italy in those days was a very different thing from travel now. The traveller of today "sees France" by tearing through it in a closed car over a straight cement highway at the rate of sixty miles an hour; by stopping in "international" hotels run in imitation of American methods, where all the waiters talk English; and, as a diversion, playing bridge with other English-speaking tourists, and looking at American moving pictures and English newspapers.

Very different was the world of the early 'forties of last century. Charles Dickens and his family rolled through France in a coach of vast dimensions (it cost Dickens £45) brought over from England, a coach with four horses and a postillion, and with a courier on the box to facilitate the journey. They moved in a leisurely way, stopped at inns, paused at villages, and strolled and picnicked on the roadside. All about them were the burble of a foreign language, the charm and colour of foreign dress, the oddity of foreign customs. Under such circumstances people saw more of France in a day than does the motor tourist in a month.

The case of Dickens was peculiar. It is amazing in one way how much he saw, and in another way how much he didn't. He brought to bear upon the scenes around him the eye and the ear of an artist and the mind of a novelist. He was fascinated with the picturesque costumes, the civility of foreign speech, the light and colour that contrasted everywhere with the drab outlines, the dullness and the mist so frequent in his own country. Dickens was fascinated with the scene, but took but little interest in the meaning. This was the France that still carried everywhere the vestiges of the Napoleonic Empire: Dickens scarcely saw them. Thus in the journey south he talks of seeing by the way, "a silly old meek-faced garlic-eating immeasurably polite chevalier with a dirty scrap of red ribbon hanging at his buttonhole as if he had tied it there to remind himself of something." But other eyes might see in the dirty scrap of red ribbon the Napoleonic Legion of Honour, and looked with something like reverence on the "silly old meek-faced man" who once saw, perhaps, the sunrise at Austerlitz, or the Grand Army struggling in the snow. Later on, when Dickens wrote his *Tale of Two Cities*, his ready reflection and his recollection of remembered scenes enable him to put together a picture of marvellous sympathetic interpretation far better than that of most professional historians. But that was later. His mind was set to another tune.

In his *Pictures from Italy*, he himself indeed disclaims in the little preface of the book (called "The Reader's Passport") any intentions of writing on the history of the country or of the "innumerable associations entwined about it," or "discussing the government or misgovernment of any portion of it." He wrote the book, as he said, as a "series of faint reflections, mere shadows on the water." This was the Europe of the middle 'forties, just passing from the older era to the new industrialism, and stirring already with the mighty forces that were to sweep it from end to end four years later with revolution and war. But if Dickens thought of such things he did not write of them. One cannot have all types of mind at once. Dickens's pen pictures run along in a vein of interested amusement of the surface of things. He gives to everything

French the same half-comic interpretation which he applies to the House of Commons, and the law and government of England.

Take as a typical picture of his foreign travels his account of a "diligence" of the period:

"Then, there is the Diligence, twice or thrice a-day; with the dusty outsides in blue frocks, like butchers; and the insides in white nightcaps; and its cabriolet head on the roof, nodding and shaking, like an idiot's head; and its Young-France passengers staring out of window, with beards down to their waists, and blue spectacles awfully shading their war-like eyes, and very big sticks clenched in their National grasp."

At times his tone is almost as openly comic as that of the famous *Innocents Abroad* of twenty-three years later. Witness, for example, the following description of the arrival of the coach party at a French inn:

"The landlady of the Hôtel de l'Ecu d'Or is here; and the landlord of the Hôtel de l'Ecu d'Or is here; and the femme de chambre of the Hotel de l'Ecu d'Or is here; and a gentleman in a glazed cap, with a red beard like a bosom friend, who is staying at the Hôtel de l'Ecu d'Or, is here; and Monsieur le Curé is walking up and down in a corner of the yard by himself, with a shovel hat upon his head, and a black gown on his back, and a book in one hand, and an umbrella in the other; and everybody, except Monsieur le Curé, is open-mouthed and open-eyed, for the opening of the carriage-door. The landlord of the Hôtel de l'Ecu d'Or, dotes to that extent upon the Courier, that he can hardly wait for his coming down from the box, but embraces his very legs and boot-heels as he descends. 'My Courier! My brave Courier! My friend! My brother!' The landlady loves him, the femme de chambre blesses him, the garçon worships him. The Courier asks if his letter has been received? It has, it has. Are the rooms prepared? They are, they are."

The Dickens family rolled in their coach from Calais to Paris, then southward to Avalon, to Châlons, to Lyons, the Rhone, Avignon, and Marseilles. The opening pages of *Little Dorrit* were to be illuminated thirteen years later with the brilliant sunshine of that Southern coast. Then from France they passed to Italy.

The family settled down in Genoa, which became their headquarters during the year spent in Italy. For the summer months they had a country villa in a suburb of the town, and for the winter quarters they had chambers in the city. Foreign visitors, consuls, officials, and the Governor of Genoa himself vied in doing honour to Dickens. But for a long time, and indeed more or less throughout his Italian residence, Dickens had a feeling of being transplanted. His heart was always in London. He longed for the familiar sights and sounds, and above all for his vigorous walks at night through the London streets. To Forster he wrote these first impressions of his homesickness. "I seem," he said, "as if I had plucked myself out of my proper soil when I left Devonshire Terrace. If the fountains here played nectar they wouldn't please me half as well as the Middlesex waterworks at Devonshire Terrace. Put me down on Waterloo Bridge at eight o'clock in the evening, with leave to roam about as long as I like, and I would come home as you know panting to go on."

But as the summer changed into autumn he found himself hard at work again, and happy in his work. It was not the Italian scenes about him that inspired his pen, but the recollections of his beloved London. The work was planned as a second Christmas story – the setting which most appealed to his nature – and the theme was the vindication of the claims of the poor: the topic that lay nearest to his heart. The story that resulted was *The Chimes*, which owed to Genoa nothing but its title, suggested in a happy moment by the clanging church bells of the Italian city. The work was finished before the end of 1844. Dickens took a brief holiday on his own, leaving his wife and sister behind him, while he visited the great Italian centres of the North. As he travelled, the beauty and the glory of the old cities, especially of Venice, more and more reached his heart. His letters to England in brief description of what he saw have nothing of the tone of easy levity described above. "Nothing in the world," he wrote to Forster, "that you have ever heard of Venice is equal to the magnificent

CHARLES DICKENS READING "THE CHIMES" TO HIS LITERARY FRIENDS
From a sketch by Maclise

FAMOUS LITERARY GROUPS

BIRDS of a feather flock together," may be said to be a proverb specially applicable to literary men and women, whose greatest pleasure has ever been the meeting and comparing notes with kindred spirits, followers of the same strenuous profession as themselves. There have been famous literary gatherings when such giants in the world of letters as Walter Scott, Charles Dickens, and Robert Burns read their works aloud to a favoured company of friends, and fortunately some of these have been immortalised by the painter's brush. Such reunions as these belong unfortunately to a past time, for though writers still meet, and enjoy each other's society as of old, it must be confessed that the enormously increased output of books has brought a certain indifference with it. The publication of a book, even a great book, is no longer an event of almost national importance, as it was when Dickens, for example, was writing his marvellous series of novels, and the whole reading public was strung up to the highest state of excitement and expectancy when the publication of one was imminent. Then it was quite customary for an author to gather his literary friends together and read aloud to them the book about to be given to the world, receiving their criticism and advice before the final step was taken.

Charles Dickens, the most congenial of men, was specially fond of such literary parties. At Lincoln's Inn Fields on December 2, 1844, a memorable gathering of intimate friends surrounded him for the purpose of listening to *The Chimes*. Maclise, the talented young artist, was among those present. Mac, as Dickens affectionately called him, ever full of high spirits, good humour and fun, was considered indispensable at these first readings, and on this occasion, he, as Forster puts it, "anticipating the advice of Captain Cuttle, made a note of it in pencil." Forster assures us of the per-

and stupendous reality.... The gorgeous and wonderful reality of Venice is beyond the fancy of the wildest dreamer. Opium couldn't build such a place and enchantment couldn't shadow it forth in a vision."

He hurried back for a brief visit to London to make arrangements about the publication of the new story, and still more to taste the luxury of reading it aloud to his select circle. He had for weeks looked forward to this pleasure. He had written ahead to get Forster to arrange the time and place, and in due course the reading took place at Forster's house in Lincoln's Inn Fields on December 2, 1844. Forster was there, and among the others Thomas Carlyle, grave and attentive, Douglas Jerrold, and the artist Maclise, who has left a little drawing of this scene, often reproduced.

The reading was such a success that it was repeated, with some new auditors present, among them Thomas Ingoldsby of *The Ingoldsby Legends* (by his true name the Rev. Mr. Barham). Forster afterwards said that the success of these readings and what Barham called their "remarkable effect" on the hearers gave Dickens his first promptings towards those public appearances which added so greatly to his fame and diminished so cruelly his vital strength.

Back in Italy again Dickens left Genoa for a trip to the South, including Rome, which entranced him still more than Venice – not so much perhaps by the appeal of its history, as by the majesty of its appearance and by the loneliness and grandeur of its ruins. Nothing, he said, had ever moved and overcome him as did the sight of the Coliseum.

The journey home was made in June, 1845, the family travelling by carriage through the mountain passes of Switzerland. In Brussels a group of his friends joined him for a holiday week in Flanders; and at the end of the month Dickens set his foot again upon his native land.

The book of travel which he published later under the name of *Pictures from Italy* has long since passed from current interest. He himself was very doubtful whether or not to extend for publication the various notes and letters which he had written on his travels. In the end they were published in part in the *London Daily News* under the head of "Travel Letters Written on the Road," and issued in their final form as a book, *Pictures from Italy*, in 1846.

Apart from the light running commentary on people and things and the little incidents of daily travel – in their nature ephemeral – and apart from the enthusiasm over the masterpieces of Italian painting and the palaces and memorials of Italy, familiar in all books, there are a few passages worthy of note in a study of the art and mind of Dickens. One may cite, for instance, his gruesome account of the torture chamber at Avignon. Here Dickens writes with all the subjective power of his imagination. It was not what he saw, but what was conjured up from the imagined past that formed the fascination and the horror of the picture. Very different is the account of the execution of an Italian murderer under the guillotine, in the open, amid a crowd of curious sightseers. Dickens, with instinctive art, writes the plain circumstance of what he saw, as a De Maupassant or a Zola would have written it.

"He immediately kneeled down, below the knife. His neck fitting into a hole, made for the purpose, in a cross plank, was shut down, by another plank above; exactly like the pillory. Immediately below him was a leathern bag; And into it his head rolled instantly.

"The executioner was holding it by the hair, and walking with it round the scaffold, showing it to the people, before one quite knew that the knife had fallen heavily, and with a rattling sound.

"There was a great deal of blood. When we left the window, and went close up to the scaffold, it was very dirty; one of the two men who were throwing water over it, turning to help the other lift the body into a shell, picked his way as through mire. A strange appearance was the apparent annihilation of the neck. The head was taken off so close, that it seemed as if the knife had narrowly escaped crushing the jaw, or shaving off the ear; and the body looked as if there were nothing left above the shoulder."

Students of the literature of the nineteenth century who contrast the "romanticism" of 1840 with the "realism" of 1890 may mark these passages with interest.

Chapter Six

FLOOD TIDE

1845–1850

The "Daily News" – Switzerland – Paris – "Dombey and Son" – "David Copperfield"

THE YEARS FROM THE TIME WHEN CHARLES DICKENS returned from Italy in 1845 to the publication of *David Copperfield* in 1857 may be taken as marking the highest development of his literary power. They do not mark the height of his fame and reputation, for those increased continually until his death. Moreover, to the celebrity acquired from his written books there has still to be added the celebrity earned by his marvellous public rendering of his written works. But the publication of *David Copperfield* undoubtedly marks the highest reach of his achievement.

These years were for Dickens to a very great extent a migratory period with a repeated change of domicile. For convenience of record one may begin with a recapitulation of his movements from place to place and from occupation to occupation.

He returned from Italy to London in June, 1845; busied himself with the project of the *Daily News*; sat down in his chair as editor of the first number on January 21, 1846, and got up out of it on February 9th. He wrote his travel sketches, the *Pictures from Italy*, then let his house and was off again May 31, 1846, for another year abroad, and settled down at Lucerne to write *Dombey and Son.* He wrote in the autumn, on the Continent, his *Battle of*

Life as his Christmas book for the year; moved to Paris in November of 1846, still writing *Dombey*. Then, after three months, he was called back suddenly to London (early in 1847) by the illness of his son; rented a house at Chester Place, and settled down again in London. That summer (1847) he was at Brighton and Broadstairs working on *Dombey*; back to London in the autumn; busy that winter with various public appearances and a series of amateur theatrical performances for the Shakespeare fund, finishing *Dombey* early in 1848. In the summer of that year he was at Broadstairs writing *The Haunted Man* as a Christmas book, also turned into a play.

The next year, 1849, was Dickens's great year – that of *David Copperfield*. He was busy on the book at Bonchurch in the Isle of Wight in the summer, and the next winter in his own London house at Devonshire Terrace. The book began running in monthly parts in May, 1849. The work went on the next year, in London, and during a summer at Brighton – broken by a brief trip over to France in June. The book drew near its close as the summer ended: it was finished in London in October, 1850.

With its publication Charles Dickens reached what has been called the "pinnacle of his fame."

Such then were the happy and eventful years marking the flood tide of Dickens's success. It would be tedious to pursue in detail each of his varied activities. But some demand a further mention. An outstanding incident of the opening of this period was Dickens's triumphant entry on the field of daily journalism and his rapid and rather inglorious retreat (January-February, 1846). His mind would seem to have been attracted then and always by the idea of moulding public opinion, or rather of dictating it, since moulding is but a slow process. The notion of being an arbiter of merit, a court of resort to award the palm to virtue and to assign to evil its appropriate condemnation, appealed at once to his genius and to his peculiar conceit. Indeed, in the last twenty years of his life he occupied much such a position as the autocratic editor of *Household Words* and *All the Year Round.* Once before, as has already been said, at the very opening of his career, he held a bread-and-butter position as the paid editor of *Bentley's Miscellany.* But the work in that case was purely literary and consisted merely in the consideration and selection of manuscript material, and in the preparation of his own large contribution.

No doubt, in planning and undertaking the adventure of the *Daily News,* Charles Dickens entertained the idea of an editor as a Jove launching thunderbolts, a Nestor warning a nation, a Pallas Athene awarding the palm to virtue. He failed to realize how much of mere routine detail and circumscribed task falls to the lot of the Jupiter and the Athene of the editorial chairs, and how much opinion must be compromised and private wishes subordinated to plain consideration of shillings and pence.

The times were propitious. They always are. England was at a turning point. It always is. At this particular curve in the road the question was of the corn laws, of free trade, of the delivery of England by the cleaving sword of radicalism from the shackles of privilege and aristocracy. In other words, the time was opportune, as it always is, for awakening the nation to a new life.

Various newspapers, and especially the *Morning Chronicle* of his early days, seem to have been anxious at this time to enlist the services of Dickens as a regular contributor, not merely of fiction, but of articles on topics of the hour. From this came the idea that a newspaper might be founded under his editorship, endowed with the prestige of his name, the energy of his temperament, and his recognized championship of the rights of the dispossessed. The project was a noble one, but among Dickens's immediate circle John Forster at any rate was opposed to it. He saw what editorial fetters would mean when clasped on Dickens's hand.

But the proposal went forward. Indeed, in every other respect than that of its original editorship, it was a great and permanent success. Rich men in London put up £100,000 in solid cash. The paper was christened the *Daily News* with a selling price of fivepence (*The Times* then sold at that figure). Charles

Dickens became editor-in-chief with a salary of £2,000 a year. About him were a group of trained and brilliant men, some of whose names – Douglas Jerrold, Mark Lemon – have passed down into literary history. As the sub-editor, the real working editor, was H. G. Wills, afterwards so intimately associated with Dickens in his later magazines. Dickens's quaint old father, otherwise Mr. Micawber, placed at the head of the reportorial staff, supplied a kind of comic relief.

The moral elevation of the new journal was to be on a plane with its literary distinction. The prospectus declared that the *Daily News* would be "kept free from personal influence or party bias" and would be "devoted to the advocacy of all rational and honest means by which wrong may be redressed, just rights maintained, and the happiness and welfare of society promoted."

The editor in a leading article explained further, "We seek, so far as in us lies, to elevate the character of the Public Press in England."

In view of such an auspicious opening and such a fervent avowal of determination, it is almost comic to think that Dickens was thoroughly sick of the whole enterprise in a week, and out of it in less than three. The first number came out on January 21, 1846, and already on January 30th, Dickens, so we are told, was "revolving plans for quitting the paper." On February 9th he resigned, "tired to death and quite worn out." John Forster took over the abandoned task; Wills stayed on as sub-editor, and the *Daily News* rose steadily to national eminence and power.

Fifty years later the paper held a jubilee (1896) in connection with which reminiscences of its early days were in order. Some of them, where they touch on Dickens, are unconsciously amusing. "He was just the man," said one historian, "to become the inspiring force of such an idea. It had a positive fascination for him. He threw his whole soul into it. He was just the man to start such a venture as the *Daily News*." In view of the fact that Dickens threw his whole soul out of it in seven days, this is rather choice. Dickens started the *Daily News* as a man might step on the gas of a motor-car and jump out. Another patriarch, writing a little later, said, "We were, indeed, born fighting, and Dickens began by leading a desperate onslaught on Protection." Thus too did the Duke of Plaza Toro, of Gilbert and Sullivan, cheer on his men.

Of the novelist's own contributions to the enterprise, none are of capital importance. His *Travelling Letters*, later *Pictures from Italy*, as already indicated, appeared in it during and after his incumbency. A letter, over his name while still editor, on the question of Ragged Schools (free schools for the poor), and, later on, three letters on capital punishment, show at least the kind of use he meant to make of the kind of vehicle created. But the whole episode drifted out of the current of his life, forgiven and forgotten. His connection with the political daily press ended for good.

A more abiding feature of the period was Dickens's pursuit of amateur theatricals, henceforth a large element of interest in his life. All professionals and many of the rest of us entertain a sort of phobia against the amateur actor. He is indeed in a class by himself. An amateur cricketer plays as much cricket as a professional; an amateur musician may play music night and day; but an amateur actor means by definition an actor who doesn't act – or whose rare appearances are insufficient for real excellence. As a rule the amateur actor on the stage can neither walk, sit, or stand still, whisper, speak, or shout, without betraying his inefficiency. Amateur acting of grown-up people is at best a thing for sudden inspirations, for occasions ingeniously and quickly contrived, a social effort quickly made and freely forgiven.

But Dickens and his performances, which reached presently even to the feet of royalty, belong perhaps in another class. It has been seen that from his childhood he had a passion for the stage. In the dreary days of the Doctors' Commons he had longed to be an actor. "I went to some theatre every night," so he tells us, "with a very few exceptions for at least three years.... I practised immensely (even such things as walking in and out and sitting down in a chair), often four, five, six hours a day; shut up in my own room or walking about in the fields."

John Forster tells us that a great actor was lost in Dickens. But his very description of Dickens's performances makes us feel that perhaps what was lost was rather an impersonator, an inspired impressionist, than an actor. Dickens, says his friend, "had the powers of projecting himself into shapes and suggestions of his fancy which is one of the marvels of creative imagination, and what he desired to express he became." Forster adds, "His strength was rather in the vividness and variety of his assumptions than in the completeness, finish, or ideality he could give to any part of them." But this is perhaps improvising rather than acting. An actor is a man who can do a thing not once but again and again, who can lose himself in his part and stay lost. It was not, perhaps, as an actor that Dickens came into his own, but when he appeared on the public platform in the dramatic rendering of his written works. Then indeed he carried his audience away with him, took them outside of themselves in a literal "ecstasy" of appreciation.

There seems a certain quality in certain persons, in speech, in gestures, in acting, which performs this miracle. Dickens had it in a high degree. In true acting there is no contact from mind to mind. The orator reaches for the audience; the actor for the theme. In what Dickens did the contact from mind to mind is everything.

But there is no doubt that in any public appearance under any name, Dickens exercised an intense interest and fascination for those who saw and heard him.

Reference has already been made to his early acting at school, to his preparation of little pieces for the St. James's Theatre, and to his triumph at the garrison theatricals at Montreal in 1842. Here Dickens was the life and soul of the performance. He was stage manager, producer, and autocrat at large. He played a part in each of three pieces presented and threw himself into it all with exuberant enthusiasm. But the performance was but for one night. The amateur's little lamp is lighted only to go out. But now in 1846 arose a larger opportunity. As his fortunes enlarged, Dickens often talked with his friends of getting up a play. He spoke of it before his sojourn in Italy, and he was still talking of it when he came back. The recollection of the Montreal success was still warm within him.

The project took shape in the summer of 1846. Dickens and a group of friends rented a little theatre in Dean Street. The play selected was Ben Jonson's *Every Man in His Humour*, with Dickens as Captain Bobadil, Stanfield of the Royal Academy to paint the scenery, and such illustrious names as those of Douglas Jerrold, John Leach, and Mark Lemon billed for the cast. It is cheering for amateurs of lesser note to know that even in such an illustrious company, a number of the actors, including two academicians, got frightened and dropped out. But the performance, to an invited audience, on September 21, 1846, was a tumult of success, and was twice repeated for the benefit of the paying public and of deserving charities.

Later on in the year the "company" presented one of Beaumont and Fletcher's plays with similar success. Indeed, for a moment London seems to have been agog with interest over Charles Dickens's players. In the next year (1847) the enterprise was reorganized on a bigger scale. The "troupe" appeared in aid of certain literary charities before crowded houses in public theatres in Manchester (July 26th) and Liverpool (July 28th). As before, they played *Every Man in His Humour*, following it up each night with a minor piece as a conclusion. The receipts ran to over £900 for the two nights. As is usual with amateur enterprises, the expenses ate up nearly half of the proceeds.

But the moral and artistic glow of the performance was its own reward. The players found themselves carried forward to even greater things. A still larger opportunity occurred next year (1848). A national interest had sprung up in the question of buying Shakespeare's house, and the "Shakespeare fund" afforded a splendid object and an admirable excuse. It is true that in the end the borough council of Stratford on Avon bought the house, but the momentum, once started, could not be checked. The goal was shifted from a house to that of a curator for the house. Dickens and his friends put their plays on with great triumph. After much debate and controversy, they aspired to the presentation of nothing else than Shakespeare himself. Dickens appeared as Justice Shallow in the *Merry Wives*, with Mark Lemon as Falstaff.

For Dickens henceforth the organization and acting of amateur theatricals became a part of his life.

A success and an *éclat* equal to that of his theatrical performances attended Dickens's appearance during this period at one or two great public functions. He presided at a meeting of the Leeds Mechanics Institute, held December, 1847, and acted as chairman at the inauguration of the Glasgow Athenæum a few weeks later (December 28, 1847). This visit to Scotland, in which Dickens was accompanied by his wife, was a tremendous success and was made the occasion of a tumultuous welcome, both public and private. He himself called it "a great demonstration" and wrote home about it in his own exuberant and overflowing terms to his sister-in-law, who had been left behind in charge of the nursery.

"The meeting was the most stupendous thing as to numbers and the most beautiful as to colours and decorations I ever saw. "The inimitable" (this means himself) "did wonders. His grace, eloquence, and elegance enchanted all beholders." He adds at the end of the letter: "Best love from both of us to Charley, Mamey, Katey, Wally, Chickenstalker, Skittles and Hoshen Peck."

All this is characteristic of the Dickens of the time – the success, the energy, the exuberance, the happy home, and the nursery smothered with affectionate nicknames: no enemies, no enmities, no cares. Certainly, if Charles Dickens gave a lot to the world, the world gave much to him. Later the shadows were to fall across it all; but the shadows were of his own making and from his own temperament.

One notes the continuing additions to the family: Chickenstalker is Francis Jeffrey Dickens, born January 15, 1844; after him is Alfred Tennyson (October 28, 1845), and then is Skittles or Sampson Brass; Hoshen Peck means the "Ocean Spectre," a name given to Sydney Smith Dickens (born April 18, 1847) from his far-away wistful eyes. A little later was born the eighth child, Henry Fielding Dickens (January 16, 1849).

The activities described were broken by journeys abroad and brief residences on the Continent. Dickens, as already said, rented his London house for a year in 1846 and went, family and all, to Lausanne. Here he took a villa and settled happily down again to the literary work that was the proper occupation of his life. It was in Switzerland that summer that he wrote the Christmas story called *The Battle of Life* – voted a huge success at the time, though almost forgotten by the Dickens readers of today. A larger occupation was the beginning of *Dombey and Son*, the writing of which filled a great part of the next two years, carried from place to place and never absent from the writer's mind. The story came out as written, being issued after the established fashion in monthly instalments, with illustrations by Phiz. Its success was assured from the start.

His visit to Switzerland brought Dickens for a moment into sharp contact with European politics. He was in Geneva when the Roman Catholic revolution (of the Sonderbund of 1846) broke out. But he had no understanding of such things. His was the complacent assurance of the Englishman, with a generation of peace and security at the back of it. He found foreigners and their revolutions either comic or villainous. He writes home to Forster, chaffing the revolution. "The Sardinian consul," he said, "was gravely whispering the other day that a society called the Homicides had been formed, who were sworn on skull and cross-bones to exterminate all men of property and so forth." The real explanation of the trouble in Switzerland he diagnosed as due to the "dissemination of Catholicity, the most horrible means of political and social degradation left in the world." With this sweeping judgment of an evangelical Protestant, he let the matter go and turned back to *Dombey*.

Indeed, Dickens never really saw the Continent. He carried to it the limitations of his nation – self-assured, impregnable; of his times – unchastened by disaster; and of his temperament, converting it to literary material. Paris, to which he moved that November, was always rather a funny place to Dickens – or partly funny and partly horrible. His house – he rented No. 48 Rue de Courcelles – being French, was funny. "We are lodged," he wrote home to an English friend, "in the most preposterous house in the world. The bedrooms are like the opera-boxes. The dining-rooms, staircases, and passages quite inexplicable. The drawing-room is approached through a series of small chambers like joints in a telescope." The French government, as Dickens saw it, was also an amusing spectacle. "I saw the king the other day coming into Paris," so he writes in the waning days of poor old Louis Philippe. "His carriage was surrounded by guards on horseback and he sat very far back in it, I thought, and drove at a good pace. It was strange to see the prefect of police on horseback some hundreds of yards in advance, looking to the right and to the left as he rode, like a man who suspected every twig in every tree in the long avenue."

Different but equally interesting as a "horror," a thing which always appealed to Dickens, was the Paris morgue, at which he was a frequent visitor.

More natural was his contact with the French stage and his quick eye for its excellences and its peculiarities. The fun which inspires some of his comments, turning on the peculiar inability of the French to use English, is not yet extinct. Here, he tells us, is a so-called English servant in a play who is named "Tom Bob" and who wears a waistcoat that reaches to his ankles. Here, in another play, is the Prime Minister of England – name not given – who refers to "Vishmingster" and "Regeenstreet." In another play, called *English to the Core*, there was a character called "Sir Fakson," and a "Lord Mayor of London" wearing " a stage-coachman's waistcoat, the order of the garter and a low broadbrimmed hat not unlike a dustman."

It is pleasant to think that some sources of amusement are perennial. But of greater interest is the serious side. "There is a melodrama here," he writes, "called the French Revolution, now playing at the Cirque, in the first act of which there is the most tremendous representation of *a people* that can well be imagined. There are wonderful battles and so forth in the piece but there is a power and massiveness in the mob which is positively awful."

Here, surely enough, is *A Tale of Two Cities* – the "echoing feet" and the tumult. It is usual to say that Carlyle's *Revolution* (which Dickens read as a bedside book for years) "inspired" Dickens to write of the Reign of Terror. Yet the germ is here. It is strange that out of such an amalgam of false and true – the comic Paris of 1848, the countryside seen from his rolling barouche, and Carlyle's sound and fury – Dickens could later create his marvellous picture of the horror and heroism of revolutionary France.

Meanwhile Dickens had been busy with *Dombey and Son.* It was commenced in Switzerland. The immortal chapter narrating the death of little Paul Dombey was written in Paris. The work was carried home to England and went steadily on to its completion. The monthly numbers, illustrated by Phiz, had begun to appear in January of 1847.

The story when it appeared was an instant and a conspicuous success. Dickens himself seemed to have the idea that his silence, or relative silence, of two years had, as it were, dammed up in him a reservoir of amusement and interest. In any case, there was no doubt of the public reception of the new story. The monthly numbers from the start outsold *Martin Chuzzlewit* by over twelve thousand, and the praises showered upon the book verged upon adulation. Lord Jeffrey wrote to the author of certain chapters in the book as "the best thing past, present, or to come." "There is no writing against such power as this," groaned Thackeray, "one has no chance."

It may be doubted, however, whether in the estimation of the generations of readers who have lived since, the book retains its relative place. Its abstract theme of the humbling of the pride of Mr. Dombey smacks somewhat of a Victorian copybook. In our days pride can be humbled in less than a whole bookful. But at the time, no doubt, both Dickens and his public thought, or felt, this to be an advance. *Mr. Pickwick* had had no theme or moral at all, and did excellently without one. *Oliver Twist* dealt with the concrete practical theme of neglected childhood. *Nickleby*, at least as an opening motive, carried the practical problem of the Yorkshire schools. These were questions not of abstract qualities but of facts. *Martin Chuzzlewit*, it is true, turns upon the "theme" of the hypocrisy of Pecksniff, but no one ever realizes that it is a theme. *Dombey* is built upon a conscious plan, and carried at the time, no doubt, a certain aspect of grandeur.

But the outstanding and remembered thing in *Dombey and Son* is the sweet and marvellous pictures of little Paul and the infinite pathos of his death. It is doubtful if we would write such things now, even if we could. The literature of every age and time has its peculiar conventions, its peculiar limitations. We do not, in our time, set down extended and harrowing pictures of physical torture; minute and accurate descriptions of the ravages of a loathsome disease. The fact that these things exist is no necessary justification for writing of them. And so it is doubtful at least whether a writer of today, even if he had the requisite literary power, would use it to call forth the agony of suffering involved in the last illness and the death scene of a little child. It is a cup that we would put from our lips.

But in the Victorian age it was different. The expression of sentiment over the common sorrows of life was still a new thing in literature; Shakespeare wrote of kings; Milton, of hell; and Scott, of the Middle Ages. It remained for the nineteenth century to break into a flood of tears over its own suffering. Scholars, who contradict everything, will deny this – their eyes can only peer at exceptions and never open to general truths. No wonder that in the exuberance of this new feeling, the current of this new stream, sentiment was washed into sentimentality. Again and again one feels that Dickens and his readers enjoy their tears. "Come," said someone once in speaking to his disparagement, "let us sit down and have a good cry."

Over a lesser or a trivial object the tears become maudlin or even comic. To what extent are we to go when the occasion as depicted is real, is overwhelming? Take as the supreme example in literature the death of little Paul Dombey. Dickens spares us none of it – the long-drawn-out illness of the little child, fading beside the sea; the waves that sing to the little mind already wandering away; the final illness; the sunlit room; the whispered murmur of farewell, and the unutterable end.

The public of the day read the book – shall we say, enjoyed the book? – in a flood of tears. "I have cried and sobbed over it last night," wrote Lord Jeffrey, "and again and again this morning; and felt my heart purified by those tears and blessed and loved you for making me shed them: and I never can bless and love you enough. Since the divine Nellie was found dead on her humble couch, beneath the snow and the ivy there has been nothing like the actual dying of that sweet Paul in the summer sunshine of that lofty room."

What are we to think of all this? Is this manly, or is it mawkish? Or what?

Dickens himself had written the chapter in a very agony of grief. Indeed, he seems to have carried in his heart ever afterwards a sorrowing memory of little Paul. When he wrote some ten years later a preface for the first cheap edition of *Dombey and Son* he said, "When I am reminded by any chance of what it is that the waves were always saying, I wander in my fancy for a whole night about the streets of Paris, – as I really did, with a heavy heart the night when my little friend and I parted company forever." An author may share the grief of his creations. But to what extent a reader may sit down to enjoy a good flood of tears and then jump up and play bridge – that's another thing. Sorrow as a deliberate luxury is a doubtful pursuit, a dubious form of art.

On the other hand, it may be argued that Dickens knew perfectly well what he was doing. He may have felt that the reader could not sympathize with the main idea of his story unless he could feel to the full the poignant suffering brought by the death of the child and its effect on the character of Dombey and his future life. In *Dombey and Son* the main features of the story, contrary to the method of the earlier books, were firmly constructed in the writer's mind before the work began. The criticism was made at the time that the death of little Paul was needlessly inserted in the story to enhance a sentimental interest, and that the change in the character of Dombey is violent and unnatural. Dickens resented this criticism, which is indeed groundless, and defends himself against it in his preface to the later edition.

Indeed, what he says in the preface is more than substantiated by what he wrote in a letter to John Forster while the story was still in the making. The death of little Paul, far from being incidentally introduced for sensation's sake, is the centre round which the narrative turns. The letter merits quotation. It marks, as it were, a landmark in Dickens's life. It shows the contrast with the unconscious and planless composition of *Pickwick*; it is leading on to the overplanned and uninspired work of much of the later books.

"I will now go to give you an outline," wrote Dickens, "of my immediate intentions in reference to Dombey. I design to show Mr. D. with that one idea of the Son taking firmer and firmer possession of him, and swelling and bloating his pride to a prodigious extent. As the boy begins to grow up, I shall show him quite impatient for his getting on, and urging his masters to set him great tasks and the like. But the natural affection of the boy will turn towards the despised sister; and I purpose showing her learning all sorts of things, of her own application and determination, to assist him in his lessons: and helping him always. When the boy is about ten years old (in the fourth number), he will be taken ill, and will die: and when he is ill, and when he is dying, I mean to make him turn always for refuge to the sister still, and keep the stern affection of the father at a distance. So Mr. Dombey – for all his greatness, and for all his devotion to the child – will find himself at arms' length from him even then; and will see that his love and confidence are all bestowed upon his sister, whom Mr. Dombey had used – and so has the boy himself too, for that matter – as a mere convenience and handle to him. The death of the boy is a death-blow, of course, to all the father's schemes and cherished hopes; and *Dombey and Son*, as Miss Tox will say at the end of the number, 'is a Daughter after all.' ... From that time, I purpose changing his feeling of indifference and uneasiness towards his daughter into a positive hatred. For he will always remember how the boy had his arm round her neck when he was dying, and whispered to her, and would take things only from her hand, and never thought of him. … At the same time I shall change *her* feeling towards *him* for one of a greater desire to love him, and to be loved by him; engendered in her compassion for his loss, and her love for the dead boy whom, in his way, he loved so well too. So I mean to carry the story on, through all the branches and offshoots and meanderings that come up; and through the decay and downfall of the house, and the bankruptcy of Dombey, and all the rest of it; when his only staff and treasure, and his unknown Good Genius always, will be this rejected daughter, who will come out better than any son at last, and whose love for him, when discovered and understood, will be his bitterest reproach. For the struggle with himself, which goes on in all such obstinate natures, will have ended then; and the sense of his injustice, which you may be sure has never quitted him, will have at last a gentler office than that of only making him more harshly unjust."

In the light of this view of the composition of the book, the harrowing description of little Paul's death becomes perhaps a literary necessity.

But of course *Dombey and Son* is not the only book, and Paul is not the only child whose death is set forth with all its painful circumstance for Dickens's readers. There is the equally famous instance of Little Nell, and the "little scholar" in the same book. It was consistent with the mood and taste of the times. We have passed away from it. We demand now a greater restraint, less copious tears – not a greater hardness of heart, but a greater tenderness towards grief itself. It is one thing to portray the bitterness of death and the isolation of bereavement. It is another to exploit it.

Dickens's literary labours did not slacken with the conclusion of *Dombey*. The summer and autumn that followed found him busy on *The Haunted Man*, one of his series of Christmas stories.

It had a great initial success, with an advance sale of twenty thousand, was turned at once into a play by Mark Lemon, and put on at the Adelphi Theatre, with excellent results. A stable feature of the little book was the illustrations, in part, by the young John Tenniel, later on the famous cartoonist of *Punch* whose pictures are still familiar to us in the pages of *Alice in Wonderland.*

Dickens, indeed, was fortunate in the illustrators of his Christmas books. Among those who had a share in the designs for the various Christmas stories were John Leach and Richard Doyle (who also illustrated Thackeray's *The Newcomes*), Sir Edwin Landseer and Frank Stone.

Yet *The Haunted Man* is but little read today. Many lovers of Dickens are probably unaware of its existence. Dickens's shorter tales have not shown the vitality of his longer books. Even *The Christmas Carol* is better known in scenes, in abridgments and adaptations, than at its full length with its full quota of ghosts, spirits, and groans. It would seem as if Dickens's shortcomings in the way of the melodramatic and the fantastic "came shorter" in the lesser stories. There was no space for the sustained attraction of the "characters" to redeem them. Mr. Pickwick would have floated half a dozen "spectres" and "apparitions" without noticing it. But left to themselves they collapsed.

Certainly such a story as *The Haunted Man* in which a lonely and miserable man makes a bargain with *the ghost of himself* for the gift of obliteration of memory, makes a pretty tall demand upon the reader's imagination. Nor are we nowadays impressed with such dialogue as "'Forbear!' exclaimed the Spectre in an awful voice, 'lay a hand on me and die!'" We see too many spectres in our moving pictures, with voices more awful still, to get a thrill out of that. But 1848 was different.

The usual "christening dinner" to celebrate the advent of *The Haunted Man* was hardly over (January 3, 1849) before Dickens was busy again: this time with the greatest achievement of his mature life, *David Copperfield.* The story had grown up out of his plans for an autobiography. He had been turning it over in his mind for months, and groping his way towards an expressive title.

It is strange that Dickens, to whom words and names meant so much, could have proposed for the new story such a ghastly title as *Mags Diversions!* David himself was tried out as Trotfield, Trotbury, and Copperstone before he came into his own as Copperfield.

The book was started early in 1849, and Dickens carried the work about with him, both literally and in his mind, till its completion and publication late in 1850. A lot of it was written down during a delightful summer at Bonchurch in the Isle of Wight. A pathetic memory of the Copperfield period of Dickens's life is the death of his infant daughter Dora. She was born (August 16, 1850) while the book was in the writing and did not live until its close. The little girl was christened Dora Annie, after the characters of the book. She was a fragile creature, marked for early death. When the fatal seizure of convulsions came upon the child, Dickens was not at home. He returned to his house to find her dead. John Forster has told us of the strange and pathetic setting of little Dora's death. Dickens had taken the chair (April 14, 1851) at a dinner given for the Actors' Theatrical Fund. "Half an hour before he rose to speak," says Forster, "I had been called out of the room. It was the servant from Devonshire Terrace to tell me his child Dora was suddenly dead. She had not been strong from her birth; but there was just at this time no cause for special fear, when unexpected convulsions came, and the frail little life passed away. My decision had to be formed at once; and I satisfied myself that it would be best to permit his part of the proceedings to close before the truth was told to him. But as he went on, after the sentences I have quoted, to speak of actors having to come from scenes of sickness, of suffering, aye, even of death itself, to play their parts before us, my part was very difficult. 'Yet how often is it with all of us,' he proceeded to say, and I remember to this hour with what anguish I listened to words that had for myself alone, in all the crowded room, their full significance: 'how often is it with all of us, that in our several spheres we have to do violence to our feelings, and to hide our hearts in carrying on this fight of life, if we would bravely discharge in it our duties and responsibilities.'"

There is a very general agreement that *David Copperfield* is Charles Dickens's greatest book. The only doubt is as between *David Copperfield* and *Pickwick.* But the two are of such a different kind and class that a decision is difficult. They are not the same thing. *Pickwick* among Dickens's books stands by itself. He never did it again and never tried to. It is not a novel; it is not a story; it has no particular plot or plan except what it gathers to it by its own attraction. It is the fortuitous result of setting the exuberant genius of its author to work on a roving commission. Certain unknown forces came together, and *Pickwick* happened. Oddly enough, John Forster, the biographer, whose view of Dickens was one of permanent idolatry, does not rate *Pickwick* as most people do. "I do not think the *Pickwick Papers,*" he says, "comparable to the later books." A strange judgment, not sustained by the verdict of posterity.

But among all the works of Dickens, other than *Pickwick, David Copperfield* on a general vote would stand easily first. Everyone knows, of course, the author's own opinion expressed in his characteristic way. "Like all fathers," he said, "I have a favourite child and his name is *David Copperfield.*"

The book was written at the maturity of its author's powers. He was thirty-seven years old. He was surrounded with all the adjuncts of a happy life – fame, fortune, friends, an affluent home, and a babbling nursery of children. The great domestic tragedy which was later to shadow his life was as yet but a cloud on the horizon. The book was written at Devonshire Terrace, its writing punctuated with the pleasant dinners that were a feature of Dickens's life at this period; and at Broadstairs, where the sight and sound of the sea inspired him with some of its famous passages. It was throughout a labour of love and absorption. "I am in that tremendous paroxysm of *Copperfield,*" so he wrote from Broadstairs (September 17, 1850) to Wills, his sub-editor, as the book drew to its close, "having my most powerful effect in all the story on the anvil, that you might as well ask me to manufacture a cannon seventy-four pounds as to do anything now." The "powerful effect" no doubt is the famous fifty-fifth chapter of the story, with the storm and wreck at sea and the death of Steerforth. Dickens always thought it one of his greatest achievements and read it from the platform as one of his moving selections.

To realize the greatness of the book we have only to remember that not one, but several of its characters have become part of the history of literature, part of the language of the world. Not David himself: there is no such person. But Mr. Micawber, Dora, Uriah Heep, Mr. Dick, and in a lesser degree David's Aunt Betsy Trotwood and Tommy Traddles. What a galaxy is there! What an achievement to have created that. Mr. Dick's difficulty with King Charles's head, the fact that "Barkis is willin'," and the delightful fiction that "Jorkins was inexorable" – these things are a part of Dickens's legacy to human happiness.

One of the strangest things in the book *David Copperfield* is David Copperfield himself. Few people perhaps have noted the fact, but many will admit it when said, that there is, so to speak, no such person. David is merely the looking glass in which we see the other characters, the voice through which they speak. He himself has no more character than a spiritualist medium. He tells us, for example, that he wrote stories for the press, but we don't believe him. He tells us all about his career, his attempts to enter law, his struggle with shorthand reporting, but we take no stock in it. None of it seems real. And none of it is. Our interest is purely in the people who circulate in David's life, Betsy Trotwood, and the Micawbers, Uriah Heep and his mother, and Mr. Spenlow, and, above all, Dora. But in David himself not at all: he is ruined, and we don't feel a pang; goes up in fortune or down or sideways – it doesn't seem to matter. All we want is to hear what happened to the others, not to him.

This instinctive attitude of the reader is entirely justified. It arises out of the origin of the book. Dickens, as everybody knows, planned to write an autobiography, to set down in writing especially all the early recollections of the sufferings of his own life. He began the task. He wrote out various early chapters of his life: then found the revelation too intimate, too poignant, and abandoned it. Later on he changed it into the story of David Copperfield, and in the changing the whole nature of the thing is altered. In the autobiography such as he meant to write the interest is in himself. We can see that in the burning passages which describe the humiliation of little Copperfield degraded to ignoble work, an outcast, on the edge of want and on the fringe of destitution: this is not David Copperfield; this is little Dickens. There are touches of this all through the book, though the intensity washes out of them as it goes on. In the written novel, the autobiography, the revelation of the author's soul, is overwhelmed and absorbed by the characters in the book. If David Copperfield has a soul, we don't care about it. The effect is as if the other characters spoke through the medium of David and sometimes Charles Dickens himself used the medium to do a little talk of his own. The book is therefore neither a real autobiography nor a real novel in first person impersonal. If this is bad art, it doesn't matter. For Dickens there were no more rules of art than there were rules of battle for Napoleon.

It is a supreme excellence of the book that the interest rises continually. For many readers, David's meeting with Dora and his falling in love seem to bring the story to a culmination of interest, when all the points run together, like lights focussed on a single spot. Yet Dora does not come in until the twenty-sixth chapter – halfway through the book. It is a wonderful evidence of the genius of Dickens that could introduce a new character and a new interest at such a stage of the narration. Few writers would even attempt such a thing, and fewer still succeed in it.

Dora herself is one of the great triumphs of the book. The falling in love of David Copperfield, sudden, catastrophic, and idyllic, is one of the masterpieces of English literature. It is so marvellously written that to readers young enough in mind it comes with all the freshness and glory of love itself. The magic words transpose the scene, and the reader shares the exaltation felt by David, carried away on the wings of the morning.

There has been much misunderstanding of this. A false literary tradition has grown up about it. Old maids and jealous women have formulated the idea that Dora was a doll. Men have not dared to contradict. Yet the real masculine judgment is that if these are dolls, let us have more of them. It is expounded by the critics that Dickens meant to contrast the helpless doll Dora with the serene and faithful Agnes of David's later marriage. In a way he did, and in another way he didn't. In depicting Dora – which he did by instinct and not by artifice, recalling from the depths of his own heart the feelings he described – Dickens was showing what love is, what lovers feel, the springtime of life as beautiful as a garden bursting into flower. As compared with this, efficiency, bookkeeping, and buying of butchers' meat is of no account.

It is part of the perversity of genius that, later on, Dickens should have seen fit to blur and smear the beautiful picture. He brought Dora of *Copperfield* back from the dead as the tittering Flora of *Little Dorrit.* But for most readers, luckily, little Dora sleeps on where Dickens left her.

The book has a further merit, in the negative sense, in that it is but very little marred by its author's characteristic defects. There is in it very little of the dense dark complications which take the place of a plot in the later books. The story is in the main straightforward and easy to read. Many readers never quite understand who is who in *Bleak House,* or what is what in *Little Dorrit.* But the narrative of *Copperfield* runs as clear as a stream. Here and there the author's love of the improbable forces its way in. Old Peggotty setting out on a search of the world at large is rather unconvincing. And the writer cannot resist the use of impossible coincidences, such as the drowning of Steerforth at exactly the right time and place. Steerforth, incidentally, be it said, is a blot on the story, not in the moral but in the artistic sense, in that he doesn't come out as Dickens meant him to. He is like a badly taken photograph that develops all wrong. Dickens was trying to portray a dissolute gentleman; what came out was a contemptible cad. Dickens's own impression, no doubt, was that Steerforth was a charming fellow. Most readers find him repulsive. A gentleman was always a difficult thing for Dickens to "put over" deliberately. He could do it only by accident and without trying to, as in the case of Tommy Traddles. But such characters as Steerforth and Eugene Wrayburn of *Our Mutual Friend* are merely "bounders."

It seems to be generally agreed that the famous Mr. Micawber of *David Copperfield*, whose name is now almost a common noun in the English language, was in reality John Dickens, the author's father: as much, that is, as anybody outside of a book is anybody inside a book.

At the time when Charles Dickens began the writing of *David Copperfield* (1849), Dickens senior was not only alive but still "going strong"! His son's generosity had lifted him from his shabby-genteel poverty of twenty years before to a position of ease and comfort. The days of the debtors' prison were long since past. Their squalid pathos, their maudlin tears, their false hopes and bitter disappointments survive only in the pages of the written book. "Mr. Micawber" has passed out of them, as a butterfly kicks out from its entangling web. In the sunshine of prosperity and celebrity reflected from his illustrious son, his latent talents matured, and his character blossomed into geniality. He was to a considerable extent a man of parts. His own exertions had gained him a part in the reporters' gallery in the days before *Pickwick* lifted the family to eminence. Later on, when the *Daily News* was founded, his son was able to award him the position of chief of the reportorial staff. The mimic dignity of this position, its apparent control of the destinies of nations, suited John Dickens to the ground. One of his youthful colleagues on the *Daily News*, writing his reminiscences long afterwards, has given us a charming picture of the father of

Charles Dickens – short, portly, obese, fond of a glass of grog, full of fun, never given to much locomotion, but sitting as chairman, and looking carefully to the regular marking and orderly despatch to the printers of the numerous manuscripts thrown off at lightning speed by the men from the gallery. "It was his habit," we are told, "to come down to the office about eight, at night, and he invariably in all weathers walked down Fleet Street and turned into the passage leading to Whitefriars. Every night as regularly as clock-work he was relieved of his silk pocket handkerchief by the thieves of the great neighbouring thoroughfare, and he would deplore the loss in feeling terms when he tried to wipe the perspiration from his brow: for it was a peculiarity of his nature that he was always hot, whatever the weather might be. He maintained that he knew when his pocket was picked, but that he could not help himself, because the thief was too nimble and he too stout."

John Dickens, like Mr. Micawber, was apparently an orator of sorts, oratory being an acquirement natural to so genial a person in the days when toasts were drunk and speeches were made on any and every possible occasion. "I understand," wrote Dickens to a friend, "that my father went on like the Steam Leg, oratorically speaking, at your dinner." And this too in the last year of the good old gentleman's existence. Nor was the comment meant in criticism. It was affectionate. It was part of the amused and kindly appreciation with which Dickens regarded the oddities of his father. He loved the old man's grandiloquent habit of speech, and used to quote with delight from his letters. "I have a letter from my father," he wrote, "lamenting the fine weather, invoking congenial tempests and informing me that it will not be possible for him to stay more than another year in Devonshire as he must then proceed to Paris to consolidate Augustus's French." When Dickens wrote in his correspondence a high-sounding phrase he would often put in the words, "as my father would say." In short, the elder Dickens was a "character," and "characters" were the preoccupation of Charles Dickens's life. His feeling for his father grew as time went on, and he looked back to the old man's memory with an affection that grew with years. "The longer I live," he said, "the better man I think him."

When he put his father into the pages of his greatest book, it was as a tribute, a mark of his esteem. It conferred upon him immortality. Mr. Micawber, be it admitted, is John Dickens Senior; just as Mrs. Nickleby was Charles Dickens's mother. But one must not overdo this connection between imaginary people and real prototypes in the books of Dickens; and indeed it has been sadly overdone. It seems to slur over the real creative merit of genius and to turn it into mere transcription. A real person put into a book would be sorry reading. The art lies in making them fit to go into a book.

Human beings are made of aspects, not of realities. Each of us is such and such things from certain angles and in certain lights. We are many things to many people and show to the occasion and the hour a different aspect of our being. It is the art of genius to seize the deceiving aspects of real people and turn them into the realities of imaginary ones. The act involved is not transcription but creation. But when we talk of such and such a character in fiction as being taken from such and such a person, we do the author a grave wrong – at least, if the book and the character are worth talking about. When we say that Mr. Micawber is taken from Dickens's father we really mean that Dickens had the eye to see in his father those quaint, elusive appearances which led him to the discovery of Mr. Micawber.

One may well feel sensitive upon the point, inclined as it were to come to the defense of the author as against something like a charge of plagiarism. This is especially so in the case of Dickens. Consider, for instance, the book *Dombey and Son*, discussed earlier in this chapter. Here the commentators give us a list of "characters" which almost fills the book. Little Paul, we are told, is Dickens's nephew Harry Burnett; Carker was a member of a firm of London engineers; Mrs. Skewton was at once "identified" as a Mrs. Campbell; Captain Cuttle's "real name" was David Mainland, a merchant seaman whom Dickens met in the city; the real name of Sol Gills was Mr. Norrie, and John Forster knew Miss Blimber personally.

In other words, all that Dickens had to do was to take a look at these people and then write the book.

Or take the case of Mr. Dombey himself. When Dickens wanted to convey to Hablôt Browne (Phiz) who was to do the illustrations, the "idea" of Mr. Dombey, he suggested that he might "get a glimpse of So-and-so for he is the very Dombey." What this meant was that, having created Dombey in his mind, he saw a man who looked as Dombey ought to look.

One thinks here – to carry the point of art a little further – of the American cartoonist who reduces a national president to a box of teeth, or to a pair of spectacles, or to a jawbone. Dickens did the opposite. He took a jawbone and made a president.

Nor is there in the story except in casual places that overdone and overextended sentiment which so often pushes hard on sentimentality and even hysteria. Mrs. Annie Strong, the young wife of the old doctor, when she makes her general round of confession, autobiography, and psychoanalysis, in speeches straight of the melodrama, is a little hard to bear. But such odd lapses are but as a little mist in the sunshine. Of the works of imagination written in the English language *David Copperfield* to many people stands first.

Chapter Seven

"BLEAK HOUSE" AND SOCIAL REFORM

1850–1854

Amateur Theatricals – "Bleak House" – "A Child's History of England" – "Hard Times"

IT WAS JUST AFTER THE PUBLICATION OF *DAVID Copperfield* that Charles Dickens began, with the first number of his new magazine, *Househood Words* (March 30, 1850), those editorial labours which ended only at his death. Indeed, from this time on, for the remaining twenty years that he lived, the occupations and diversions of Charles Dickens may be said to have swung through a sort of recurrent cycle of activities. There was in the first place the writing of his greater works, the novels so called, of which at least two of the greatest were still to come. There was in addition his work on his magazine, *Household Words*, later to be exchanged for *All the Year Round*, including not only the writing of contributions of his own but the editing of masses of material. There was soon to be added the exhilarating and exacting task of public readings of his works, the first of which took place at the close of 1853. To this – as a diversion, an amusement, but an arduous one – was added his pursuit of amateur theatricals; and the equipment of his new homes in London and in Kent. Migration having become a sort of physical and mental necessity, a very considerable part of the years that here follow was spent in Boulogne and in Paris.

In this middle period of Dickens's life much of his time and thought is turned towards questions of social betterment and social reform. The minor themes of *Oliver Twist* and *Nicholas Nickleby* expand into the broader aspects of the welfare of mankind. All of this appears in his new magazine *Household Words,* his *Bleak House,* his *Child's History,* and above all in his mistaken and unsuccessful *Hard Times.* Later on, the shadows on his own life, the eager craving for activity turned him to other fields.

Written as a chronology of his life, the period runs in outline thus:

The year 1850 found him in London, still living in Devonshire Terrace and embarking on his labours (March 30, 1850) as the editor of *Household Words.*

The next year (1851) saw a bachelor trip to Paris (February); next month, the loss of his beloved father (the good old gentleman died, March 31, 1851, in his own person a few months after he ceased appearing in monthly parts as Mr. Micawber; as such he lives still); a summer at Fort House, Broadstairs (May-November, 1851). In the autumn were the famous theatricals at Devonshire House, London, in the presence of royalty. In this year *A Child's History of England* was running as a serial in *Household Words.* In this year also Dickens moved from Devonshire Terrace, where his lease had expired, to a new home: Tavistock House in Tavistock Square. In the autumn, in his new home, he began *Bleak House* (November, 1851).

In the next year (1852) was born Dickens's youngest son, Edmund Bulwer Lytton Dickens. The summer and the summer following were spent at Boulogne. In the year 1853 *Bleak House* was finished at Boulogne and its completion celebrated by a two-months' trip to Italy, Dickens being accompanied by Wilkie Collins and Mr. Augustus Egg. A notable feature of the close of the year was the rendering of Dickens's first public readings (December, 1853) given at Birmingham on behalf of the new Municipal Institute.

The year following found Dickens busy with *Hard Times,* which came out as a weekly serial in *Household Words* (April–

August, 1854). The children's theatricals in his new home at Tavistock House (after 1851) seemed to John Forster one of the pleasantest things in all his long recollection of his friend.

Of the various activities of these years the amateur theatricals were at first the most conspicuous feature. The first of the presentations of the period – that of *Not so Bad as We Seem*, in London, May 16, 1851 – was unsurpassed in point of distinction and patronage by anything organized by Dickens and his associates – or, for that matter, by any other amateurs. The play was put on in aid of the new Literature and Art Guild. It was specially written by Bulwer Lytton, and the Queen and the Prince Consort promised to grace it with their presence. The royal party commanded seventeen seats with a subscription of £150 towards the fund.

The Duke of Devonshire, with truly ducal munificence, handed over his town residence (Devonshire House) for the performance. He turned into it under professional direction a flock of carpenters to fashion a theatre and to set up the royal box. All of London – royal, scientific, and fashionable – clamoured for seats.

As the time drew near, Dickens himself was quite washed away from his usual anchorage by the affability of the Duke. "The Duke has read the play," he wrote to Lytton. "He asked for it a week ago, and had it. He has been at Brighton since. He called here before eleven on Saturday morning, but I was out on the play business, so I went to him at Devonshire House yesterday. He almost knows the play by heart. He is supremely delighted with it, and critically understands it. In proof of the latter part of this sentence I may mention that he had made two or three memoranda of trivial doubtful points, every one of which had attracted our attention in rehearsal, as I found when he showed them to me. He thoroughly understands and appreciates the comedy of the Duke – threw himself back in his chair and laughed, as I say of Walpole, 'till I thought he'd have choked,' about his first Duchess, who was a Percy. He suggested that he shouldn't say: 'You know how to speak to the heart of a Noble,' because it was not likely that he would call himself a Noble."

We can imagine how delightfully Dickens, in his ordinary personality, would have satirized this scene: the Duke actually reading the play and actually condescending to understand it. But in the august circumstances of the moment the faculties of alert amusement were numb.

The play was "to commence, by Her Majesty's command, at nine o'clock. Therefore the whole of the audience are particularly requested to be seated at least a quarter of an hour before that time."

At the close of the play the Queen rose in her box and commanded the reappearance of the actors to receive the applause of the house. The presence of the aged Duke of Wellington gives an added touch of historic interest.

The same play, accompanied by a short farce, *Mrs. Nightingale's Diary*, written by Dickens and Mark Lemon, was played in various provincial towns, the scenery and appurtenances being carried about in a "portable theatre."

Of less distinction but of a more human interest were the Children's Theatricals which Dickens organized after he moved into his new London home, Tavistock House (1851). Here a large room (the schoolroom) was specially converted into a theatre for such occasions and announced on the printed playbills as the "smallest theatre in the world." The evening of January 6th (Twelfth Night: which happened to be also the birthday of Charles Dickens Junior) was set apart for these revels, which henceforth were an annual fixture for many years. Mark Lemon, of *Punch*, was Dickens's chief collaborator, and his children were fellow actors with the little Dickenses. There were printed play-

DEVONSHIRE HOUSE.

ON FRIDAY EVENING, MAY 16th, 1851,

THE AMATEUR COMPANY

OF THE

GUILD OF LITERATURE AND ART,

WILL HAVE THE HONOR OF PERFORMING, FOR THE FIRST TIME,

IN THE PRESENCE OF

HER MAJESTY THE QUEEN,

AND

HIS ROYAL HIGHNESS THE PRINCE ALBERT,

A NEW COMEDY, IN FIVE ACTS, BY SIR EDWARD BULWER LYTTON, BART.,

CALLED

NOT SO BAD AS WE SEEM:

OR,

MANY SIDES TO A CHARACTER.

THE DUKE OF MIDDLESEX	*Peers attached to the Son of James II., commonly called the First Pretender*	Mr. FRANK STONE.
THE EARL OF LOFTUS		Mr. DUDLEY COSTELLO.
LORD WILMOT	*A Young Man at the head of the Mode more than a Century ago,* Son to LORD LOFTUS,	Mr. CHARLES DICKENS.
Mr. SHADOWLY SOFTHEAD	*A Young Gentleman from the City, Friend and Double to* LORD WILMOT	Mr. DOUGLAS JERROLD.
Mr. HARDMAN	(*A Rising Member of Parliament, and Adherent to Sir Robert Walpole*)	Mr. JOHN FORSTER.
SIR GEOFFREY THORNSIDE	(*A Gentleman of good Family and Estate*)	Mr. MARK LEMON
Mr. GOODENOUGH EASY	(*in Business, Highly Respectable, and a Friend of* SIR GEOFFREY)	Mr. F. W. TOPHAM.
LORD LE TRIMMER		Mr. PETER CUNNINGHAM.
SIR THOMAS TIMID		Mr. WESTLAND MARSTON.
COLONEL FLINT		Mr. R. H. HORNE.
Mr. JACOB TONSON	(*A Bookseller*)	Mr. CHARLES KNIGHT.
SMART	(*Valet to* LORD WILMOT)	Mr. WILKIE COLLINS.
HODGE	(*Servant to* SIR GEOFFREY THORNSIDE)	Mr. JOHN TENNIEL.
PADDY O'SULLIVAN	(Mr. FALLEN's *Landlord*)	Mr. ROBERT BELL.
Mr. DAVID FALLEN	(*Grub Street Author and Pamphleteer*)	Mr. AUGUSTUS EGG.

LORD STRONGBOW, SIR JOHN BRUIN, Coffee-House Loungers, Drawers, Watchmen, Newsman

LUCY	(*Daughter to* SIR GEOFFREY THORNSIDE)	Mrs. HENRY COMPTON.
BARBARA	(*Daughter to* Mr. EASY)	Miss ELLEN CHAPLIN.
THE SILENT LADY OF DEADMAN'S LANE		Mrs. COE.

SCENERY.

Lord Wilmot's Lodgings	Painted by Mr. PITT.
"The Murillo"	" Mr. ABSOLON.
Sir Geoffrey Thornside's Library	" Mr. PITT.
Will's Coffee House	" Mr. PITT.
The Streets, and Deadman's Lane	" Mr. THOMAS GRIEVE.
The distrest Poet's Garret (after Hogarth)	" Mr. PITT.
The Mall in the Park	" Mr. TELBIN.
An open space near the River	" Mr. STANFIELD, R.A.
Tapestry Chamber in Deadman's Lane	" Mr. LOUIS HAGHE.
The Act Drop	" Mr. ROBERTS, R.A.

The Proscenium by Mr. CRACE. The Theatre constructed by Mr. SLOMAN, Machinist of the Royal Lyceum Theatre.
The Costumes (with the exception of the Ladies' Dresses, which are by Messrs. NATHAN, of Titchbourne Street) made by Mr. BARNETT, of the Theatre Royal, Haymarket.

UNDER THE SUPERINTENDENCE OF MR. AUGUSTUS EGG, A.R.A

Perruquier, Mr. WILSON, of the Strand. Prompter, Mr. COE.

THE WHOLE PRODUCED UNDER THE DIRECTION OF MR. CHARLES DICKENS

THE DUKE OF DEVONSHIRE'S PRIVATE BAND WILL PERFORM DURING THE EVENING.

Under the Direction of Mr. COOTE, who has composed an OVERTURE for the occasion.

TO COMMENCE BY HER MAJESTY'S COMMAND, AT NINE O'CLOCK

THEREFORE, THE WHOLE OF THE AUDIENCE ARE PARTICULARLY REQUESTED TO BE SEATED, AT *LEAST* A QUARTER OF AN HOUR BEFORE THAT TIME.

W. S. Johnson, "Nassau Steam Press," 60, St. Martin's Lane

bills, with mock names and announcements in serio-comic style. Stanfield, R.A., was pressed into service to paint scenery, Wilkie Collins to write plays, and among the invited audiences were some of the highest genius and talent of literature and the law. At the famous performance of 1854 Thackeray is said to have "rolled off his seat with laughter." The grown-up people took some of the parts, Dickens appearing on the bills as Mr. Crummles, and Mr. Passé along with Mr. Wilkini Collini and Mr. Mudperiod (Mark Lemon). But the principal feature was the acting of the children. The playbill of 1855 states that the performance is in the Theatre Royal, Tavistock House. It presents the slightly disguised names of seven little Dickenses and three little Lemons, along with their respective fathers and Wilkie Collins and Marcus Stone. The announcement draws attention also to the first appearance on any stage of Mr. Ploorniskmaroontigoonter, who has been kept out of bed at a vast expense. This was the baby of the household, the last of the ten children, Bulwer Lytton Dickens (born March 13, 1852). There were refreshments – "Miss Hogarth will preside at the piano" – and "God Save the Queen." There was everything except the name of Mrs. Dickens.

It was especially at this period of his life – in the conduct of his magazine (as described later), in the planning of his books, and in his public appearances – that Dickens felt himself to be a great social force towards righteousness. It became what the French would call his *métier*.

Such an attitude, no doubt, had led him years before to assume the misguided role of editor of the *Daily News*. It served as the inspiration for the powerful articles which he wrote in the London *Times* against the revolting spectacles of public executions: and it was the denunciation of social wrong – the cruelty of the law's delay – that forms the background and the grandeur of *Bleak House*. In no other book is there such majestic treatment of a theme, such a complete fusion of the story of the book with its theme and purpose. In *Oliver Twist* the workhouse is left behind. In *Nicholas Nickleby*, Dotheboys Hall is forgotten. In *Dombey* the theme at best is abstract.

But in *Bleak House* the theme is real and actual. The issue of a long drawn lawsuit in the Court of Chancery passing from generation to generation and leaving behind the wreck of broken lives, and wasted hopes – there is nothing abstract or imaginary here. It dominates the story from its sombre magnificent opening in the Court of Chancery setting in the London fog, to the climax of the closing scene when the great suit of Jarndyce *vs.* Jarndyce ends – like the fall of an ancient building, eaten into nothingness and collapsing into dust. So ends it with the sardonic laughter of the Court, and Richard Carstone, dazed, unhearing, marked for death. The theme has all the majesty and inevitability of Greek tragedy. Round it is gathered every thread of the narration: the bright loves, the broken lives, and the beauty of renunciation stronger than love itself.

It is no wonder that for many people *Bleak House* is the most impressive of all Dickens's stories. It may fall short in humour – some of its comic effects are somewhat forced, some of its comic people dirty and unlikable, its interior plot (apart from the Chancery) runs to that impenetrable complexity that marked the work of Dickens – but there is no doubt of where it ranks. It is a great book. As a proof of it, consider the array of *Bleak House* characters who stand in the first rank of Dickens's creations. Here is John Jarndyce, as lovable as Mr. Pickwick without the comicality, as kindly as the brothers Cheeryble without their proximity to amiable idiocy. Here is Mrs. Jellaby with her immortal natives of Borioboolagha; Mr. Turveydrop, arm in arm with the Prince Regent; the inscrutable Tulkinghorn, and the doomed Richard and the golden Ada as real as if they stepped out of an old-world canvas. And here inevitably at the last is Dickens's characterless "walking gentleman," Allan Woodcourt, right out of a shop window. Dickens could draw gentlemen like John Jarndyce and Richard Carston because they belonged among gentlemen with oddities, peculiarities, faults, and fates; but when it came to an A I first-class all-round gentleman – that and nothing else – Dickens drew a tailor's dummy.

Many readers of the book think it disfigured by the exaggerated and preposterous lawsuit of Jarndyce *vs.* Jarndyce, described as having been in Chancery for over a generation, as having sent a score of people to jail for contempt and to suicide from misery, and ending at last by the exhaustion of the estate in costs. But Dickens at the time and all his biographers and expositors ever since have shown that there was nothing exaggerated about Jarndyce *vs.* Jarndyce. Dickens didn't need to exaggerate. The facts were good enough.

"Everything set forth in these pages concerning the Court of Chancery," he wrote in the preface, "is substantially true and within the truth. The case of Gridley is in no essential altered from one of actual occurrence made public by a disinterested person who was professionally acquainted with the whole of the monstrous wrong from beginning to end. At the present moment [August, 1853] there is a suit before the court which was commenced nearly twenty years ago: in which from thirty to forty counsel have been known to appear at one time: in which costs have been incurred to the amount of seventy thousand pounds: which is a *friendly suit*; and which is (I am assured) no nearer to its termination now than when it was begun. There is another well-known suit in Chancery, not yet decided which was commenced before the close of the last century, and in which more than double the amount of seventy thousand pounds has been swallowed up in costs. If I wanted other authorities for Jarndyce *vs.* Jarndyce I could rain them on these pages."

Among such accumulated praise of the book, one may without impropriety insert a word of depreciation. How its author loves complexity, and to what impossible devices does he resort to accomplish simple things! Take the case of Krook, who dies of "spontaneous combustion": the foul, dirty creature disintegrated into a shatter of filthy grease of black soot and an acrid smell! Let us grant that Krook had to die. He was in possession of certain "papers" which Dickens and the reader needed. But why not kill

Bleak House

Illustrations from the book

him of indigestion? No, Dickens had heard somewhere of people dying by "spontaneous combustion," and he must needs try it on one of his characters. More than that, he makes an angry refutation of the charge that no one dies of such a thing as that. He tells us that there were quite a lot of deaths of this sort in the Middle Ages and that one of them was described by the Reverend Giuseppe Bianchini only two hundred years ago. There was also a case-called "recent" by Dickens – of a German American saloon-keeper of Columbus, Ohio, who "blew up" in just this way – presumably much like a rum omelette or a Christmas snapdragon. Dickens adds as proof that the story is "very clearly described by a dentist."

Dickens has forgotten his usual lack of faith in medical miracles, and forgot that, very likely, the dentist, as the French say, "*mentait comme un arracheur de dents*." No, no, Dickens wanted Krook to blow up, and blow he must.

Again, how characteristic of Dickens is the dark and complicated plot whereby the "papers" are to be got from Krook. It is thought that some of these "papers" may bear on the question of how and why Esther Summerson was born about twenty-one years before. They may give an opportunity for blackmail. So the prospective blackmailers engage the astute Mr. Chick Smallweed (who has no idea what he is to seek or to find) to change his name and go and hire a room in Krook's house so as to keep his eye on him. Mr. Smallweed has no notion what it is all about – and the reader was lost long ago. But in Dickens a general principle of the solution of mysteries is for people to disguise themselves, change their names, and then "keep an eye" on someone. If enough eyes are kept on enough people, something is bound to "come out."

But all these peculiarities and shortcomings of the book only make it more truly Dickens. They disperse under the effulgence of his genius like the Chancery fog in the sunshine.

The book further illustrates very well Dickens's unconscious disregard of anything in the way of rules or regularity in literary art. If he thought of such things at all, he probably regarded himself as exempt – as did Napoleon in the case of morals. He conducts the

Dombey and Son
Illustration by Phiz
(Hablôt K. Browne)

Bleak House
Title page of
the first edition

story in an in-and-out fashion partly as told impersonally and partly as related supposedly by Esther Summerson. But he doesn't bother to limit Esther Summerson to the kind of ideas and the kind of language that Esther Summerson would, or could, have used. Her personality is maintained by a few little mincing phrases and by a sort of modest decorum or sentiment, but when she needs it she is given all the humour and power of Charles Dickens. The voice is Esther's, but the jokes are Dickens's! Nothing is more false in art than to make a fictitious personage speak out of his character, as if Mr. Pickwick suddenly talked cockney, or Sam Weller dropped into French. But, as usual, Dickens "gets away with it." Few, if any, readers ever bother whether Esther is in character or not; many no doubt think her a mighty humorous girl and that she ought to have written books.

In the case of Esther, also, there is another of Dickens's peculiar licenses. Just as he gave Master Humphrey a clock and took it away again, so he makes Esther go blind – gets the full tragic value of it – and then finding that he needs her eyes, gives back her sight. In all Dickens there is nothing more like Dickens.

Consider how tragically the chapter (No. XXXI) comes to an end. Esther is stricken ill, with fever – dangerously ill – and then, when the crisis comes, she speaks to her little maid at her bedside and says:

"And now come and sit beside me for a little while, and touch me with your hand. For I cannot see you, I am blind."

With what a rush of feeling the reader realizes that the beautiful devoted girl has lost her sight! Blind! What a fate!

But, no, not at all. Dickens leaves her blind while he himself writes three chapters, then she gets her sight back with the simple formula:

"But now, my sight strengthening, and the glorious light coming every day more fully," etc., etc.

Oddly enough, the ordinary reader has no other feeling except joy that Esther can see. If Dickens had been accused of unfair dealing in this he would at once have righteously explained that *temporary* blindness is a frequent accompaniment of fever.

Quite so: but he used it to get all the literary value of permanent blindness. Yet he would have believed himself. He was like that.

An item of literary interest in the book, vivid once but waning now, is the connection of the rather despicable character Mr. Horace Skimpole with Dickens's friend Leigh Hunt. Here in the book is Skimpole – impecunious and crooked, borrowing and never paying, and betraying his friends for a shilling; and here, quite recognizable, scarcely disguised, is Leigh Hunt. Is not such a portrayal, it was asked, as mean as meanness itself? Much ink has been shed on the point. But the name of Leigh Hunt has drifted so far back into obscurity that the controversy loses its interest. The truth probably is that Dickens meant Horace Skimpole to be a charming and lovable character, which he certainly is not. Dickens failed in his aim. Skimpole is a "skunk"; just as Steerforth is a cad and Wrayburn a bounder. Dickens's father could be glad to be Micawber. No doubt Dickens expected anyone to be happy to be Horace Skimpole.

The identification of Bleak House as a "house" is a disputed point with contemporary Dickensian scholars. In the story it is placed in Hertfordshire. The Lord Chancellor is officially informed of that fact by one of the counsel in the case. Indeed, Esther Summerson in her narrative says, "The long night had closed in before we came to St. Albans near which Bleak House was." Arguing like Edgar Poe in the *Barnaby Rudge* matter, we might claim that Esther was mistaken or was lying. But without such subtlety, we have to admit that, in the book, Bleak House was near St. Albans. Indeed, there is a house outside the town known as Bleak House to one school of believers, but another school holds that the windswept house (Fort House) at Broadstairs, where Dickens stayed in 1850, and which was sometimes called by that name, was the original. The best evidence seems to point to Bleak House being situated in Hertfordshire. The controversy about the place has already something of the nicety of Shakespearean criticism and shows that Dickens is coming on. Soon there will be enough of it to get Dickens recognized in the colleges.

Bleak House was published by Messrs. Bradbury & Evans in

twenty monthly numbers from March, 1852, to September, 1853, with illustrations by Hablôt Browne. As a book it appeared September, 1853. It was a colossal success, the monthly instalments reaching sales of over forty thousand. As the story drew to its close, Dickens was able to write of it in triumph (August 27, 1853), "It has retained its immense circulation from the first, beating dear old *Copperfield* by a round ten thousand. I have never had so many readers." But with its writing come the first signs of the breaking of its author's health and energy. The books, the labour of his editing, the claims of society and public service – it was too much. "What with *Bleak House* and *Household Words*," he wrote, "and *Child's History* and Miss Coutts's Home and the invitations to feasts and festivals, I really feel as if my head would split like a fired shell if I stayed here." And with it all was the wear and tear day by day of his distracted home – soon to break up in open disaster.

So Dickens, while *Bleak House* was still in the writing though nearly done, got away to France. There he spent the first of those delightful summers at Boulogne which meant so much, as will be seen later, to his health and happiness.

Along with the composition of *Bleak House* had gone the publication week by week in *Household Words* (January 21, 1851–December 10, 1853) of *A Child's History of England.* It was published by Bradbury & Evans as a three-volume book, just after *Bleak House.* It is now dead, but it deserves resurrection. It is almost forgotten, but it ought not to be. In some senses it is the most notable history of England that was ever written. It never obtained recognition as a manual for either the nursery or the school. Nor was it suited to be such. In the first place, the proportion is all wrong. Dickens wrote at such length about early times that when he at last got to William of Orange and the opening of the eighteenth century, he had to end the book in two pages. He explains this rather lamely by saying that "the events which succeeded the famous revolution of 1688 would neither be easily narrated nor easily understood in such a book as this." It is a little hard to see why children who could tackle the Saxons and the Noblemans, the Middle Ages and the Reformation could not understand the American Revolution and the battles of Waterloo. But there were other objections to such a history in mid-Victorian England. It was far too outspoken; it broke away from the tradition that children must hear only of the glories of history and the majesty of kingship and the pomp of royalty. Witness, for illustration, the characterization of Henry VIII as contrasted with the mass of fulsome flattery and misconception which after four hundred years still cloaks his crimes.

"We now come to King Henry the Eighth whom it has been too much the fashion to call 'Bluff King Hal' and 'Burly King Harry' and other fine names, but whom I shall take the liberty to call plainly one of the most detestable villains that ever drew breath....The plain truth is that he was a most intolerable ruffian, a disgrace to human nature, and a blot of blood and grease upon the history of England."

And here, wholesomely enough, is a plain picture of the "harrying of the north" by William the Conqueror.

"Fire and sword worked their utmost horror and made the land dreadful to behold. The streams and rivers were discoloured with blood: the sky was blackened with smoke: the fields were wastes of ashes: the way-sides were heaped up with the dead. Such are the fatal results of conquest and ambition."

All this is right enough. But Dickens went out of his way to follow the picturesque bypaths of history, the striking stories and the telling incidents, without proper regard to their real importance. More than all, his own strange absorption with the horrors of crime and the cruelties of the criminal law led him to intrude them too brutally on the minds of his readers; at times it goes beyond the necessity of what is wholesome and becomes morbid. Here, for example, are the details of the execution of Lady Jane Grey, which the children might have been spared.

"She came up to the scaffold with a firm step and a quiet face, and addressed the bystanders in a steady voice. They were not numerous; for she was too young, too innocent and fair, to be murdered before the people on Tower Hill, as her husband had just been; so the place of her execution was within the Tower itself. She said that she had done an unlawful act in taking what was Queen Mary's right; but that she had done so with no bad intent, and that she died a humble Christian. She begged the executioner to despatch her quickly, and she asked him, 'Will you take my head off before I lay me down?' He answered, 'No, madam,' and then she was very quiet while they bandaged her eyes. Being blinded, and unable to see the block on which she was to lay her young head, she was seen to feel about for it with her hands, and was heard to say, confused, 'O, what shall I do? Where is it?' Then they guided her to the right place, and the executioner struck off her head."

And here is the execution at full length of Hooper, Protestant Bishop of Gloucester, one of the early victims of "Bloody" Queen Mary.

"At nine o'clock next morning, he was brought forth leaning on a staff; for he had taken cold in prison, and was infirm. The iron stake, and the iron chain which was to bind him to it, were fixed up near a great elm-tree, in a pleasant open place before the cathedral, where, on peaceful Sundays, he had been accustomed to preach and to pray when he was Bishop of Gloucester. This tree, which had no leaves then, it being February; was filled with people; and the priests of Gloucester College were looking complacently on from a window; and there was a great concourse of spectators in every spot from which a glimpse of the dreadful sight could be beheld. When the old man kneeled down on the small platform at the foot of the stake, and prayed aloud, the nearest people were observed to be so attentive to his prayers that they were ordered to stand farther back; for it did not suit the Romish Church to have those Protestant words heard. His prayers concluded he went up to the stake, and was stripped to his shirt, and chained ready for the fire. One of his guards had such compassion on him, that, to shorten his agonies, he tied some packets of gunpowder about him. Then they heaped up wood and straw and reeds, and set them all alight. But unhappily the wood was green and damp, and there was a wind blowing that blew what flame there was away. Thus, through three quarters of an hour, the good old man was scorched and roasted and smoked, as the fire rose and sank; and all that time they saw him, as he burned, moving his lips in prayer, and beating his breast with one hand, even after the other was burnt away and had fallen off."

No purpose can be served in inflicting such stories upon little children. No sensible parent would want to put them into children's hands. The effect is either to brutalize them into a love of cruelty, or to sadden them too soon with a sense of "martyrdom of man."

But for these passages, Dickens's book ought to take its place in any child's library and in any child's heart. No history book ever carried a nobler inspiration.

But meantime Dickens had turned from the England of the Heptarchy and the Tudors to the England of his own day. The opening of the year 1854 found him in London in his residence of the last two years, Tavistock House, where the triumphant revels of the Twelfth Night theatricals had auspiciously opened the New Year. Dickens, filled with the urge for social betterment that occupied so much of his mature thought, set himself to remake Victorian England. The result was the weekly publication in his magazine of the story – half story, half sermon – called *Hard Times: for These Times.* It ran from April till August (1854) and was published as a book immediately upon its completion.

The story *Hard Times* has no other interest in the history of letters than that of its failure. At the time, even enthusiastic lovers of Dickens found it hard to read. At present they do not even try to read it. A large part of the book is mere trash; hardly a chapter of it is worth reading today: not an incident or a character belonging to it survives or deserves to. The names of Mr. Gradgrind and Mr. Bounderly are still quoted, but only because they are felicitous names for hard, limited men, not because the characters in the book are known or remembered. Not a chapter or a passage in the book is part of Dickens's legacy to the world.

This may well seem strange. If the book had been written at the outset of its author's career, its faults could have been laid to immaturity; if at the close, to the waning powers of age; if written ten years later – as was *Our Mutual Friend* – it could have been explained away as the product of a wearied body and an overtaxed mind. But this book was written at the height of Dickens's power, with *David Copperfield* and *Bleak House* just in front of it, and *A Tale of Two Cities* and *Little Dorrit* still to follow.

It may be, of course, that the added exertion involved in assuming the editorship of *Household Words* had already overstrained the abounding energy of Charles Dickens. There are complaints at this time of uncertain health, passed off as "hypochondria." But there was as yet no so such cruel strain of either mind or body as could involve such a literary collapse as this. It may be also that the form of publication week by week in *Household Words* was unfortunate, that it unduly "breaks" the story. But there is really very little to break.

The scene of the book is laid in a factory town (Coketown) intended as typical of the new industry and the new tyranny that went with it. Its leading characters represent the soulless employers of the age, applying the ruthless philosophy of *laissez faire* and the survival of the fittest; and against this, the angelic suffering of the working class. The book is thus an amalgam of Jack the Giant Killer, Ricardo's *Political Economy*, and the Sermon on the Mount; the whole of it intermingled with a comic strain which fails to come off.

The book can be explained only in terms of the old adage that even Homer nods at times. It is the result, perhaps, of oversuccess and overencouragement. You encourage a comic man too much and he gets silly; a pathetic man and he gets maudlin; a long-winded man and he grows interminable. Thus praise and appreciation itself, the very soil in which art best flourishes, may prompt too rank a growth.

In the case of Dickens, failure was likely to be as conspicuous as success. He thought in extreme terms and wrote in capital letters. There are no halfway effects in the death of Little Nell and the fun of Mr. Pickwick. Hence, any of his characteristic methods – comic, pathetic, impressive, or rhetorical-could be strained to the breaking point. This book strains them all: the humour is forced, the rhetoric is rodomontade, and the pathos verges on the maudlin.

But the principal fault of the book is that the *theme* is wrong. Dickens confused the faults of men with the faults of things; hardness of heart with hardness of events. In attacking the new industrial age of factories and machinery that was transforming England, Dickens directed his attack against the wickedness and hardness of his Gradgrinds and his Bounderlys, his brutal employers of labour. Did he really think that they were any wickeder than other people? Mankind at that period had been caught in the wheels of its own machinery and was struggling vainly for salvation; just as it has been caught again and struggles at the present moment. But Dickens insists on regarding the poor and the working class as caught in the cruel grasp of the rich, which was not so, or only in a collective sense, impossible for the individual employer to remedy on the spot. It was the grasp of circumstance and not the hand of tyranny.

At the time the tremendous prestige of Dickens was sufficient to float the book along, and at least to guarantee its sale. But Lord Macaulay, in a well known phrase, damned it as "sullen socialism." Even John Ruskin, whose ideas it is supposed to reflect, sees the weakness of it as art. In a note to his first essay in *Unto This Last* he says, "I wish he could think it right to limit his brilliant exaggeration to works written only for public amusement. The usefulness of the work. *Hard Times*, is with many persons seriously diminished because Mr. Bounderly is a dramatic monster, instead of a characteristic example of a worldly master: and Stephen Blackpool a dramatic perfection, instead of a characteristic example of an honest workman."

These are the judgments of the moment, of contemporaries

among whom Dickens towered as a living reality. With the lapse of time the book has found the place it deserves.

But the inferiority of this book does not in any way detract from a proper estimate of Dickens's genius. In art one must judge a man by his best, never by his worst; by his highest reach, not by his lowest fall.

Chapter Eight

DICKENS AS AN EDITOR

1854–1857

Household Words – France – "Little Dorrit' – Gad's Hill

IN THE HISTORY OF ENGLISH LETTERS *HARD TIMES* ranks as a failure. But in the commercial sense it was far from being that. Its appearance as a serial in *Household Words* was accompanied by a rise of a hundred per cent in the circulation of the magazine.

Dickens had now been seated in the editorial chair – which he never again left – for over three years. His duties in that connection absorbed a large part of his time and thought. They were a constant strain upon his strength and energy. It seems in retrospect a thousand pities that such a transcendent genius as his should have been directed to such a task. What he did for *Household Words* could have been done – more or less successfully – by plenty of other men. Even a genius cannot make a dull contributor interesting. There is no need to set a genius to work with scissors and paste, clipping and arranging, measuring lengths and planning balances. Plenty of people could have done all this. No one else, then or since, could have written Dickens's books. His twenty years of editorial work are in part responsible for his too early death. They gave us in place of the books he might have written and never wrote a mass of contributions which he supervised: ephemeral, mediocre, dead. For posterity, it was a poor exchange.

Not that Dickens took it in that light. The editor of those days fulfilled a function now scarcely known. He was supposed to revise, to suggest, to reconstruct; he was the guide and instructor of his authors: he showed them how. The editor trimmed up a manuscript, as a tailor's cutter might fashion for an apprentice the finer curves in a pair of breeches. Today an editor is a man who has a keen sense of what the public wants to read and buys it from those who can write it. He has, as such, the same connection with literature that a hotel chef has with fish. But he is not a fisherman – unless, as is likely, "on the side."

But Dickens proposed to be vastly more even than the editor of his times. He wanted to be what is colloquially called the whole show. The articles in *Household Words* were not signed. The contributors were lost,amalgamated, absorbed into Dickens. He planned articles for people to write, criticized, in a mass of correspondence, the stories that they had written; put characters in or took them out; suggested titles – there was no end to it.

All this was very clearly indicated in a letter which Dickens wrote to Mrs. Gaskell at the foundation of the magazine: "No writer's name," he says, "will be used neither my own nor any other: every paper will be published without any signature and all will seem to express the general mind and purpose of the journal, which is the raising up of those that are down, and the general improvement of our social condition."

It is significant that among the sixteen other titles which Dickens set down for consideration before he hit upon *Household Words*, one was *Charles Dickens's Own.* Various others indicate a social purpose: *The Forge*, *The Crucible*, *The Anvil of the Time.* Others are domestic, as: *Home*, *Home Music*, and *English Bells.* One, simple and cheerful in its appeal, was *Twopence.* At that humble price the magazine began under the date of March 30, 1850, being dated for Saturday but appearing on the preceding Wednesdays. Journalism was already learning some of its up-to-date tricks.

The magazine was definitely established in offices at No. 16 Wellington Street, North Strand, and the printing and publication carried on by Bradbury & Evans. From this time on, Dickens not only spent a lot of time in the office but still more time in the reading and recasting of the manuscripts offered by his contributions. To assist him he had the services of Mr. H.G. Wills, an able and invaluable man, willing to subordinate himself to Dickens's ideas, but with excellent ideas of his own – when they were asked for. Wills remained with Dickens for twenty years.

But from first to last Dickens was the autocrat of the journal. Not only did his eminence in letters make it dependent on his name, but he controlled it also in the commercial sense. He owned a half share in it, Bradbury & Evans a quarter share, and H. G. Wills and the devoted John Forster an eighth share each. This gave Dickens an actual control of everything, and he used it to the full. He received apart from his share of profits a salary of £500, and payment, at no stated rate, for his literary articles.

But he justified his autocracy by the unremitting labour which he devoted to *Household Words.* A glance at the volume of his correspondence to and from Wills shows how varied was his task and how complete and how minute his supervision.

"Mrs. Crowe's story I have read. It is horribly dismal: but with an alteration in the part about the sister's madness (which must not on any account remain) I should not be afraid of it. I could alter it myself in ten minutes.

"I have cut *Woodruffe* as scientifically as I can, and I don't think Miss Martineau would exactly know where."

"I wish Hanny would not imitate Carlyle. Pray take some of the innumerable dashes out of his article, – and for God's sake don't leave in anything about such a man believing in himself, – which he has no right to do and which would by inference justify almost anything."

"In Horne's 'Ballooning' always insert 'Mr.' before 'Green'. Also insert 'Mr.' before 'Poole', and call him 'the well-known author'. At the end of the third paragraph from the commencement instead of 'the fanatical sentence was carried into execution', read, 'Sentence of the Holy Catholic Church was carried into Christian execution.'"

This is editing with a vengeance. In the days before shorthand secretaries and typewriter machines, this meant a wilderness of writing.

Nor was it, in some aspects, quite fair to the contributors. Nothing being signed, they got no credit for their work. If it was good, the readers thought Dickens must have done it. It was not a method to attract genius. Indeed, some of the contributors, as notably young George Augustus Sala, disliked it strongly from the start.

Yet the contributors included such people as Mrs. Gaskell (whose *Mary Barton* appeared in the magazine); Miss Harriet Martineau; Mrs. Crowe of the *Night Thoughts* that haunted Victorian bedsides; Adelaide Procter, Leigh Hunt, and Wilkie Collins.

But all said and done, the world may well regret that Charles Dickens ever took to editing. It has been often said, and no doubt he himself often thought, that he helped to train up a school of rising young writers; that he educated not only the public but also the aspirants in literature. Yet such a claim is greatly exaggerated. There were a thousand and one traditions and institutions in England, many of them centuries old, for forming the minds of youthful writers: the schools, the universities, the press, a reading public numbered in millions, and a galaxy of great writers of world-wide fame. There was no need for Charles Dickens to play the part of Alfred the Great. In Canada or Natal it would have been a public service; in England it wasn't necessary. Indeed, many of Dickens's authors fell into servile imitation, or attempt at imitation, of his own style – a fault which aggravated him to a high degree. "Her imitation of me is too glaring," he writes of one of his lady coadjutors, "I never saw anything so curious. She takes the very words in which Esther Summerson speaks, without seeming to know it."

And of course, from first to last, the editorial work interrupted, impeded – and later on impaired – his real work in literature. Reference has already been made to *David Copperfield* in this respect. The same was true of *Bleak House*: just at the absorbing moments of its composition, bundles of second-rate manuscripts and hours of trivial correspondence blocked the way. From Boulogne he writes in the summer of 1853, "If I *can* write an article this week, I will. But I am so full of the close of *Bleak House* that I can't for the life of me, get at a good subject for *H. W.* as yet." Again, a few days later, "Can't possibly write autographs until I have written *Bleak House.* My work has been very hard since I have been here. And when I throw down my pen for a day, I throw down myself and can take up neither article."

So it went on from then until Dickens's death: overwork, overcorrespondence, overeffort: and half of it thrown away. Dickens always lived under the conviction that he was indispensable to everything.

Yet *Household Words*, as a popular magazine, was a great success. It took over the idea of the Christmas books in the form of special Christmas numbers. It made plenty of money.

It came to an end, as will be seen, only as a result of Dickens's separation from his wife and the quarrel with Bradbury & Evans which arose out of it. Even when the journal then ended (1859) it merely gave place to the *All the Year Round*, which followed Dickens to the grave, and his memory beyond.

But these editorial labours were but a running accompaniment, or a fixed background to many other activities. During two years of this middle period, as has been seen, Dickens was busy with *Bleak House* and overbusy with the strain of it. From this pressure he had escaped to France for a summer at Boulogne – the first phase of a residence in France which lasted off and on for years. In France he found the rest and the restfulness no longer possible for him in England. It became for these years his second home.

In the first summer at Boulogne (1853) he rented for himself and family a charming suburban retreat – in the country but only ten minutes' walk from the post office – Château des Montineaux (Rue Beaurepaire). Dickens delighted in the place. He called it "the best doll's house of many rooms, in the prettiest French grounds in the most charming situation I have ever seen." He seems to have found in French houses, French towns, and French scenery the same charming and provoking refusal to be English that delighted him in the French people. Especially was he fascinated with his landlord, the owner of the château, an old soldier of Napoleon who had named it all with French magnificence. It was just a little place, but he called it "*la propriété*," and waved his hand at it as if it extended for miles. It had a little grove of trees: he called that "the forest," and in the forest, over a gorge a few feet wide, was a "Bridge of Austerlitz" leading to a chateau of the Old Guard.

Here was a Dickens house without the trouble of creation, and here in the landlord a Dickens character all ready for the pages of a book. Dickens did write him down, but only in a little sketch now forgotten but findable in his complete works and called *Our French Wateringplace.* There is no more attractive character in all his pages than that of the old soldier Monsieur Loyal, drawn in two pages, with the touch of genius.

The old soldier of Napoleon! To us now what an interest would lie in this living contact with the Napoleonic age and the Napoleonic legend. But perhaps it was all too recent. It still needed retrospect. At any rate, it has little hold upon the mind of Dickens.

Consider this: "Three years ago there were three weazened old men, one bearing a frayed red ribbon in his threadbare button hole always to be found walking together among the children on the charming walk arched and shaded by trees on the old walls that form the four sides of the High Town." "They were stooping, blear-eyed dull old men, slipshod and shabby, ... and yet with a ghost of gentility hovering in their company.... They looked as if they might have been politically discontented if they had had vitality enough. Once we overheard the red ribbon complain feebly to the other two that somebody was 'a robber' and they all three set their mouths so that they would have ground their teeth if they had any.... The ensuing winter gathered red ribbon unto the great company of faded ribbons ... another winter came and another old man went and so, this present year the last of the triumvirate left off walking, – it was no good now, – and sat by himself on a solitary bench with the hoops and dolls as lively as ever all about him."

But in France alone, as said, Dickens found rest and, what is harder to find, restfulness. Under the influence of the fresh sea air, of the beauty and repose of his surroundings, he fairly sprang back into health and energy in his first summer at Boulogne. One turns with a sigh today from reading his descriptions of his French watering place: for those of us who live in the cities or even in the country of the present age, it is the vision of a vanished world. No wonder that Dickens spent three summers (1853, 1854, 1856) in such a charming retreat as the Boulogne of last century.

Dickens never understood France. It was always half comic to him. But he had grown to love it and, from now on, his French residences were a part of his life. For French politics he knew and cared nothing. They bored him as much as did the British House of Commons. The Napoleonic legend left him cold: it was just a matter of old men and faded ribbons.

But the place fascinated him in his own way. It seemed like something out of his own books. The French talked and acted as "characters" ought to act: and Dickens loved them for it. He was entranced with the way they mutilated the English language. He wrote home to his actor friend Macready during this first Boulogne summer a joyful description of a French presentation of *A Midsummer Night's Dream*, "In it," he says, "is a poet named Willyim Shay Kes Peer who gets drunk in company with Sir John Foll Stayffe and fights a noble 'night Lor Latimeer, who is in love with a maid of honour you may have read of in history, Mees Oleevia."

Dickens loved France but never understood it. In the same way, the French never understood Dickens's books but loved them. *Pickwick* had hardly run its course in its paper numbers when a French translation appeared. After that Dickens's books were translated into French practically as soon as they came out. The earlier translations were undertaken in a haphazard fashion by different people for different firms without any consent or control or pecuniary profit on the part of the author. They were as literal or as loose as they liked. They improved on Dickens, or parodied him or missed him altogether. *Pickwick* translated (1838) by Mme Niboyet (a French suffragette born out of her time) appears as *Le Club des Pickwistes, Roman Comique par Charles Dickens.* After that comes *Nicolas Nickleby* (1840), and then *Oliver Twist ou L'Orphelin du Dépôt de Mendicité* (1841), and *Le Marchand d'Antiquités*, translated this time by a really competent man, A. J. B. Defauconpret, who is said to have translated several hundred books, including the novels of Walter Scott, Fielding, and Bulwer Lytton.

But the first Dickens books were at best only a qualified success in France. French readers could sit with Walter Scott at mediaeval tournaments or tread the stones of Pompeii with Bulwer Lytton, but they saw no reason to distress themselves with "*la misère et la dégradation de la basse classe Anglaise*." Their feelings at the time were expressed with forcible brutality by a forcible brute – fat, jovial, and emphatic – called Jules Janin, leading critic of Paris before Hippolyte Taine appeared. He undertook to sweep all Dickens's earlier works into the gutter where they belonged.

"Picture to yourself" – so he shouted in the *Journal des Débats*

(1842) in talking of *Nicolas Nickleby* – "a mass of childish inventions in which everything that is horrible alternates with everything that is simple: here pass, in a flood of tears, people so good that they are absolutely silly: further on, rushing round and blaspheming, are all sorts of robbers, crooks, thieves and paupers, so repulsive that one cannot conceive how any society containing them can last for twenty-four hours. It is the most sickening mixture you can imagine of hot milk and sour beer, of fresh eggs and salt beef, rags and embroidered coats, gold sovereigns and penny pieces, roses and dandelions. They fight, they kiss and make it up, they swear at one another, they get drunk, they die of starvation. Do you like stale tobacco, garlic, the taste of fresh pork and the noise of a tin pan beaten against a cracked copper saucepan? Then try to read this last book of Dickens."

With calm insular superiority, a writer in *Fraser's Magazine* demanded in reply by what right an ignoramus like Janin could claim to judge the English and their works: he might, added the writer, about as well undertake to lecture on the literature of the Hottentots. The form of reproof is scarcely happy.

So the translations came to a stop for four or five years. But after 1847 they started up again, including the intervening volumes and the little Christmas books, so that there were no less than eight Dickens books launched in that one year. After that they never stopped. *David Copperfield* appeared in its own place as *Le Neveu de Ma Tante,* or *L'histoire personelle de David Copperfield.*

But the real contact of Dickens with the literary life of France was during his winter spent in Paris just before his third summer at Boulogne. He had already on various occasions made transient visits to the French capital. He had even, as already seen, taken a house there for a time in the winter of 1846, while working on *Dombey and Son.* Now he came back for a more prolonged residence. After a trial of one or two unsuitable lodgments he settled down in the Avenue des Champs Elysées where he lived till the spring of 1850.

During his residence in Paris, Dickens's great delight was in the French theatre, at that time flourishing in the sunlight of an imperial court and the new opulence of the Second Empire. Dickens's knowledge of French was always imperfect for writing and speaking but was ample for the full appreciation of the drama; while his native affinity for the stage, his knowledge of its technique, and his own power as a dramatic writer put him in a class by himself. The long letters which he wrote to England about the plays he saw in Paris evince the intensity of his interest. His letters are full of praise – of the marvellous acting of Lemaître and of the marvellous power of the dramatist Scribe. Only when it comes to French presentations of English scenes does he find occasion for ridicule – for example, of a play in which a character Lord William Falkland is called throughout by all the actors Milor Williams Fack Lorn; and a presentation of *As You Like It* as *Comme Il Vous Plaira* "in which," he said, "nobody has anything to do but to sit down as often as possible on as many stones and trunks of trees as possible."

Meantime the world of art and letters vied in entertaining Dickens. He met all the great actors and playwrights. In particular he was a frequent guest at the house of Scribe – the most prolific dramatist of the day, still going strong, so Dickens tells us, after writing four hundred pieces, great and small!

Dickens indeed saw more of social entertainment – at least, of entertainment in other people's houses – than he was accustomed to accept at home. He was greatly impressed by Lamartine. He met the famous George Sand, who looked to him "the kind of woman whom you might suppose to be the Queen's monthly nurse." He was entertained in the princely style of that lavish period by Emile de Girardin at a banquet of Oriental extravagance: the host said to his guests, "*Ce petit dîner n'est que pour faire la connaissance de Monsieur Dickens: il ne compte pas: ce n'est rien.*"

The moment was of course propitious for the entertainment of an English celebrity in Paris. It was the winter of the Crimean War, the height of the *entente cordiale* that had ripened into military alliance. But the war, as seen through Dickens's eyes in his letters to Forster and others, was not popular. The people were not thrilled by it. As for Dickens himself, the war never reached him one way or the other, either to horrify or to exalt. No war ever did. But he chronicles for us an interesting picture of the Paris of the Crimean War.

"It was cold this afternoon," he writes, "as bright as Italy, and these Elysian Fields crowded with carriages, riders, and foot passengers. All the fountains were playing, all the Heavens shining. Just as I went out at 4 o'clock, several regiments that had passed out at the Barrière in the morning to exercise in the country, came marching back, in the straggling French manner, which is far more picturesque and real than anything you can imagine in that way. Alternately great storms of drums played, and then the most delicious and skilful bands. *Trovatore* music, *Barber of Seville* music, all sorts of music with well-marked melody and time. All bloused Paris (led by the Inimitable, and a poor cripple who works himself up and down all day in a big-wheeled car) went at quick march down the avenue in a sort of hilarious dance. If the colours with the golden eagle on the top had only been unfurled, we should have followed them anywhere, in any cause – much as the children follow Punches in the better cause of Comedy. Napoleon on the top of the Column seemed up to the whole thing, I thought."

But what pleased Dickens most in Paris was that he found himself now quite a well known author for the ordinary people of France – he himself says a "celebrated" author, but French politeness may have had something to do with that. His story *Martin Chuzzlewit* was running in French as a daily serial in the *Moniteur* of 1855. Celebrity in foreign lands has a special appeal, and Dickens wrote to Wills (October 24, 1855) with pardonable pride:

"You cannot think how pleasant it is to me to find myself generally known and liked here. If I go into a shop to buy anything and give my card, the officiating priest or priestess brightens up, and says, '*Ah! C'est l'écrivain célèbre! Monsieur porte un nom très distingué. Mais! Je suis honoré et interessé de voir Monsieur Dick-in. Je lis un des livres de Monsieur tous les jours*.' (In the *Moniteur*) And a man who brought some little vases home last night, said, '*On connaît bien, en France, que Monsieur Dickin prend sa position sur la dignité de la Littérature. Ah! C'est grande chose! Et ses caractères*' (this was to

Georgina while he unpacked) '*sont si spirituellement tournés! Cette Madame Tojair* (Todgers). *Ah! Qu'elle est drôle, et précisément comme une dame que je connais à Calais!*'

"Ever faithfully,
"C.D."

Indeed, during this second residence the translation of Dickens's books took on a new and definite form. The illustrious house of Hachette undertook the publication of all Dickens's works. A special staff of translators was engaged. For the first time the author himself was to get some money out of it, the contract calling for £440 in ten monthly instalments. This, where no legal obligation existed, was generous enough. Dickens himself sat in conference with his translators, fascinated with his new rôle.

In later times, the Hachette translations have been much criticized. The chief people employed on the work were a distinguished lot – distinguished for everything except translation. The bulk of the work was done in a hurry at low prices, and with little realization of the extraordinary nicety of translation. Works on humour, more than any others, depend on the peculiar idioms, the slang, and the conventions of the language concerned. It is not possible to put Sam Weller into French without Mr. Weller being reborn in France. When Mrs. Gamp says "widge" or "dispoge," and calls the steamer to Antwerp the "Ankworks package" – how are we to tell a Frenchman that?

But at least the Hachette edition brought Dickens widely to the knowledge of the French people. The rising generation of the Second Empire heard Dickens's books read aloud at home, just as their English cousins of the day heard and read Victor Hugo. The give-and-take of literature was part of the new entente of Queen Victoria and Louis Napoleon, of Cobden and Bastiat, of Monsieur Guizot and Lord Macaulay. Perhaps, in the long run, Dickens had more to do with politics, French and English, than he ever imagined. The silken skein of thought binds tighter than the chains of diplomacy.

Even at that, it is still doubtful how far Dickens's work was sympathetic to the French mind. The rude denunciation of Jules Janin was presently replaced by the brilliant analysis of Hippolyte Taine, who had the insight to devote to Dickens in his *English Literature* a place and prominence not usually awarded to an author still alive. But Dickens puzzles Taine. He seems a little crazy. His rush of images, his fantastic comparisons, baffle and fatigue. And this touch of commonness – Ruth Pinch (in *Martin Chuzzlewit*) charming in her handling of a beefsteak pudding – but why not a rose?

"And Dickens," says Taine, "like all English novelists, is hopelessly respectable (in the English sense). He and his fellows work under a formula: 'Be moral. All your novels must be such as may be read by young girls. We are practical minds, and we would not have literature corrupt practical life. We believe in family life, and we would not have literature paint the passions which attack family life. We are Protestants and we have preserved something of the severity of our fathers against enjoyment and the passions. Among these love is the worst.'"

This of course is true. These are the limitations under which Dickens and all English and American writers lived and worked, the limitations under which they thought. In his day no one (no one who mattered or counted) wanted to read or write things or use or hear language not fit for a Kensington drawing room or a Boston boarding house. These were the fetters worn by Dickens as he wrote, but he never felt them; he himself was utterly and absolutely respectable. For him the book *David Copperfield* would have been ruined and disgraced by an ecstatic chapter describing the rapturous months of little Emily in Italy with Steerforth before he tired of her and threw her aside. For Mr. Taine that would have been a great improvement – more true to life. That is exactly the difference between Dickens and his French counterpart Alphonse Daudet.

Dickens, one repeats, never felt these fetters. Others did. His junior contemporary in America, Mark Twain, was unhappy all his life that he couldn't put into his books oaths and dirty language such as real people really use: that he couldn't "get after God" if he wanted to and "take a rise" out of hell. All of this –

American profanity and French immorality – was utterly alien to Dickens. He himself was utterly and absolutely respectable and orthodox. He turned his Christianity round to get the bright side out, and he turned sinfulness the other way to make it look black. We English are still all like that. We try hard to be tough in our literature, but we can't – only in our conduct. Thus may Pecksniff have felt towards life in general, and this, since all is pardonable, may be his exculpation.

If a paradox is in place, it may be said that perhaps the best French translation of Charles Dickens is Alphonse Daudet. Not that Daudet copied Dickens. He had begun to write in the Dickens manner before he ever heard of Dickens. Later he read his English senior with delight and took on his influence as naturally as a generation of young Englishmen took on Victor Hugo. The result is that his characters are Dickens's characters turned into French in the real way, in place of the literalism which makes Sam Weller talk the argot of Montmartre for the cockney of the Strand. Monsieur Delabelle of *Froment Jeune et-Risler Aîné* could slip across into *Bleak House* as Mr. Turveydrop.

And Tartarin! He is Daudet's own, absolutely and triumphantly, but he is also a Dickens character fit to sit beside the best of them.

Dickens left Paris in April of 1856. He spent some time in London (till the middle of June) occupied among other things with the purchase of his new house at Gad's Hill; went to Boulogne, as already said, for his final summer there (1856), spent in his original Château des Moulineaux. The winter following was passed in London. On Twelfth Night (January 6, 1857) there were the usual Tavistock House theatricals, the chief piece being *The Frozen Deep*, a romantic drama specially written by Wilkie Collins.

Apart from the editing, which never stopped, the chief literary work was now the writing of *Little Dorrit.* Dickens had begun the story in 1858; much of it was written and some of it had appeared while he was still in Paris. The story came out in the usual monthly numbers, with Phiz (Hablôt Browne) as the illustrator. It ran all through 1856, and for the first six months of 1857. It was published by Bradbury & Evans as a book in June, 1857.

The book is certainly not one of the most readable of Dickens's novels. The plot is intricate and confused. Few readers follow it and none remember it. The separate threads of the story are ill joined. It was the characteristic mode of Dickens – as of Walter Scott and of so many of the writers of the nineteenth-century novel – to start a story from a variety of separate scenes and characters, at first entirely disconnected and presently joining like little rivers to form a single stream. As rivers joining swell in power to a flood, so the convergent streams unite to intensify their common interest. It is doubtful whether such art is ever level with the intensity of a single interest sustained without a break, maintained without digression and without retrospect, moving like life itself. But the method at least allows for greater length, for more characters, for variety and diversity of appeal. A story of the length of a Dickens book told along a single thread would of necessity be without climax or culmination, or would have to keep "culminating" and starting again, like Pickwick. Such a narrative is apt to degenerate into the endless repetition of the picaresque narrative or of the thirty-night Chinese drama. But, on the other hand, the story with a culminating plot arising from separate beginnings can only truly succeed if the parts are really connected and come together as natural components of a common climax. This is done and done with great effect in *Bleak House*, but not so in *Little Dorrit* or the later completed books. The reader keeps wondering what certain people have to do with the story and probably never knows, or finds the connection faint and unwarranted, the motives and actions overstrained and overdrawn.

But the story is at least majestic in the main conception of its pathos. The sombre shadow of the Marshalsea prison lies across its pages. Nor is there any more marvellous depiction of character in all fiction than that of Edward Dorrit. He is drawn not only with all the skill of Dickens but with a different kind of skill from that which Dickens generally cared to use. Even people outside of college classes, who read books only for the pleasure of reading them and never spoil fiction by studying it, have some general notion of the broad distinction of romanticism and realism. The romanticist tries to convey the truth of art by idealizing it, by overstating it, by exaggerating it. The realist seeks to convey truth by describing things, or trying to describe things, just as they are and by reporting language just as said. The danger is that the sheer exaggeration of the romanticism may lead away into unreality, and the attempt of the realist to describe things as they are may lead to an impression of things as they are not.

Thus when Dickens as a romanticist pours out a flood of tears and sentiment from Mrs. Annie Strong, or a moral homily of Kate Nickleby, he fails utterly. But look at Edward Dorrit. Every word that he says is exactly what he would have said, not a syllable, not a sentence, not a pause or an ejaculation, that is not absolutely and literally Edward Dorrit. No Maupassant that ever wrote could have wished the transcription more photographic, the art more literal. There is no need for comment, for direction, for confidential comments with the reader. Dickens and his reader for once have stepped clean out of the book, and there is just Edward Dorrit – living, moving – not even a book at all. It is marvellous. Sustained quotation is not here possible. But let the reader consult again, let us say, chapters XVII and XVIII of part II the concluding scenes of Dorrit's life. The sentence "Amy, my dear," he repeated, "will you go and see if Bob is on the lock" is one of the great things of literature.

Apart from its larger interests, the book contains, unrecognized by those who do not know about it, the record of an interesting episode in Dickens's life, and a unique episode in the history of letters. By this is meant the inside history of Flora and Dora.

It is an episode which Dickens's biographer Forster, who probably knew all about it, prefers to gloss over, without actual names. But what was sacred then is history now.

All readers of Dickens's books recall Dora of *David Copperfield* as one of his chief creations, never forgotten by any reader. The sudden falling in love of David Copperfield, annihilated at sight by the vision of Dora Spenlow, is one of the treasures of literature. Readers of *Little Dorrit* are not so numerous, and many of them could easily forget poor Flora Finching – fair, fat, and forty, and such a contrast to the radiant and juvenile charm of Dora. Yet Flora and Dora are the same person. And Dickens himself was at one time the David Copperfield enslaved by Dora and the Arthur Clenman, from whom fell so easily the shackles he had worn in slavery to Flora.

The story runs thus: In Dickens's youthful days, when he was struggling with shorthand, reading in the British Museum and hoping to become a parliamentary reporter, he made the acquaintance, as already noted, of the Beadnell family. Mr. Beadnell was a banker of Lombard Street and as such was, as already said, a cut above Dickens and his queer half-shabby home. Mr. Beadnell's more genteel establishment was adorned further by the presence of three charming daughters. With one of them, Maria, young Charles fell violently in love: to see how violently we have only to open the pages of *David Copperfield.* We are told that when Dickens undertook to write his autobiography and set down with pen and ink the story of his early and unforgettable love, he tore the pages up as if the story were too sacred for revelation. Later on – and we have his own written word for it – he rewrote it as the love of David Copperfield for Dora Spenlow. Fiction contains no better portrayal of the sudden onslaught of the God of Love.

"'Where is Miss Dora?' said Mr. Spenlow to the servant. 'Dora' I thought, 'What a beautiful name!'

"We turned into a room near at hand, and I heard a voice say, 'Mr. Copperfield my daughter Dora, and my daughter Dora's confidential friend.' It was no doubt Mr. Spenlow's voice, but I didn't know it, and I didn't care whose it was. All was over in a moment. I had fulfilled my destiny. I was a captive and a slave. I loved Dora Spenlow to distraction.

"She was more than human to me. She was a Fairy, a Sylph,

I don't know what she was, – anything that no one ever saw, and everything that everybody ever wanted. There was no pausing on the brink: no looking down or looking back: I was gone headlong, before I had the sense to say a word to her."

For the next year or more (this was in 1830 and 1831) Dickens remained in the same state of agonized love which he has described in the case of David Copperfield. But his passion was scarcely reciprocated. The young Maria – she was nineteen – was what is described in the Victorian days as a coquette, and what has since been called a "vamp." The banker and his family did not regard the lovesick boy as a serious suitor. Maria presently was sent away to a French school. Charles wrote impassioned letters such as he alone could write. Maria sent back the letters but made copies of them to keep – not for love's sake, but as an Iroquois kept scalps. Within a year or so the correspondence died, frozen to death. For twenty years Dickens never saw Maria again. She remained as a "lost love" whose memory carried through his subsequent engagement, his marriage, his home life – unspoken but not forgotten.

Then, twenty years later, she came back into his life. In February, 1855, she wrote to her now famous sweetheart of old days. She too by this time was married, had been married for ten years, to a Mr. Henry Winter, and had a little daughter of her own. Dickens wrote back with wild exuberance. He wrote as David Copperfield would have written Dora. It never occurred to him to wonder what Mrs. Winter looked like now. He wrote to her as she was then; once again he did not pause on the brink but plunged in headlong. He sent her the *Copperfield* book and told her to read in it of his feelings for her and to realize, "How dearly that boy must have loved me, and how vividly this man remembers me." A correspondence followed – love letters one might call them, apart from the outward decorum of the form.

Then came a meeting: and with the meeting all Dickens's passionate love for the sweetheart of his dreams broke instantly and vanished into such stuff as dreams are made of.

The scene may be read in the pages of *Little Dorrit* where the fictitious Arthur Clennam meets after twenty years the imaginary Flora. Change the names, and fiction and imagination are turned into cruel facts.

"In his youth he had ardently loved this woman, and had heaped upon her all the locked-up wealth of his affection and imagination. That wealth had been, in his desert home, like Robinson Crusoe's money; exchangeable with no one, lying idle in the dark to rust, until he poured it out for her. Ever since that memorable time, though he had, until the night of his arrival, as completely dismissed her from any association with his Present or Future as if she had been dead (which she might easily have been for anything he knew), he had kept the old fancy of the Past unchanged, in its old sacred place. And now, after all, the last of the Patriarchs coolly walked into the parlor, saying in effect, 'Be good enough to throw it down and dance upon it. This is Flora.'

"Flora, always tall, had grown to be very broad too, and short of breath; but that was not much. Flora, whom he had left a lily, had become a peony; but that was not much. Flora, who had seemed enchanting in all she said and thought, was diffuse and silly. That was much. Flora, who had been spoiled and artless long ago, was determined to be spoiled and artless now. That was a fatal blow.

"This is Flora?

"'I am sure,' giggled Flora, tossing her head with a caricature of her girlish manner, such as a mummer might have presented at her own funeral, if she had lived and died in classical antiquity, 'I am ashamed to see Mr. Clennam, I am a mere fright, I know he'll find me fearfully changed, I am actually an old woman, it's shocking to be so found out, it's really shocking!'

"He assured her that she was just what he had expected, and that time had not stood still with himself.

"'Oh! but with a gentleman it's so different and really you look so amazingly well that you have no right to say anything of the kind, while, as to me you know – oh!' cried Flora with a little scream, 'I am dreadful!'

"The Patriarch, apparently not yet understanding his own part in the drama under representation, glowed with vacant serenity.

"'But if we talk of not having changed,' said Flora, who, whatever she said, never once came to a full stop, 'look at Papa, is not Papa precisely what he was when you went away, isn't it cruel and unnatural of Papa to be such a reproach to his own child, if we go on in this way much longer people who don't know us will begin to suppose that I am Papa's Mama!'

"That must be a long time hence, Arthur considered.

"'Oh, Mr. Clennam you insincerest of creatures,' said Flora, 'I perceive already you have not lost your old way of paying compliments, your old way when you used to pretend to be so sentimentally struck you know at least I don't mean that, I – oh I don't know what I mean!' Here Flora tittered confusedly, and gave him one of her old glances.

"The Patriarch, as if he now began to perceive that his part in the piece was to get off the stage as soon as might be, rose and went to the door by which Pancks had worked out, hailing that Tug by name. He received an answer from some little Dock beyond, and was towed out of sight directly.

"'You mustn't think of going yet,' said Flora – Arthur had looked at his hat, being in a ludicrous dismay, and not knowing what to do: 'you could never be so unkind as to think of going, Arthur – I mean Mr. Arthur – or I suppose Mr. Clennam would be far more proper – but I am sure I don't know what I'm saying – without a word about the dear old days gone for ever, however when I come to think of it I dare say it would be much better not to speak of them and it's highly probable that you have some much more agreeable engagement and pray let Me be the last person in the world to interfere with it though there *was* a time, but I am running into nonsense again.'

"Was it possible that Flora could have been such a chatterer, in the days she referred to? Could there have been anything like her present disjointed volubility, in the fascinations that had captivated him?"

It is a nice question in the morality of literature, if there is such a thing, whether Dickens was justified in thus putting his old love to the degradation of this appearance as a character in his book. Even as fiction, the fate of Flora is cruel enough, and if Arthur Clennam had really *said* all that is quoted above of a real person in real life, he would have been an utterable cad. We can only excuse it because it is fiction and Clennam enjoys the usual license of fiction in being permitted to think aloud.

But in actual fact. How must Mrs. Winter have thought and felt about it? When *Little Dorrit* appeared in 1857 she must have recognized herself: and her friends, to whom no doubt she had gushed over the story of the great writer's infatuation, must have recognized her: and her friends' friends would soon have heard all about when the whole love affair crumpled flat and Dickens put her in the pillory. For even during her lifetime (she lived till 1886) the story that Flora was Dora was familiar in literary criticism. It is true that Charles Dickens the younger, a kindly man who loved his father's memory, undertook (years after, in an introduction written for an edition of *David Copperfield*) to minimize the connection between Dora and Flora. "There is some reference in Mr. Forster's Life," he writes, "to a 'Dora' who came across Charles Dickens's path very early in his career, – when he was eighteen in fact, – but as she married somebody else and developed afterwards into the 'Flora' of *Little Dorrit*, she could have very little to do with Dora Spenlow." But this won't do. And we must remember too that Charles Dickens Junior tried to deride the idea that Mr. Micawber was in reality his grandfather, old John Dickens – a plea which puts his evidence out of court.

In any case, the question of Mrs. Winter's feelings from and after 1857 was probably not a matter of much moment to Charles Dickens. He was quite definitely done with her. After they had met, their rôles were changed. She gushed. He froze. Presently her husband lost his money: she appealed to Dickens for help. He suggested that her father, or his estate, ought to help. He was writing to her now as "dear madam" and evidently was sick of her. The man was no longer "vivid," and the boy had vanished as completely as the boy on the burning deck. It is a sad story. One turns from it with pleasure to the eternal loves of fiction.

But whatever its merits and its extraneous interest, the book *Little Dorrit* gives other evidence of the wearing down of Dickens and of the breaking strain under which he was now living. There is in it little of the comic element, or little that is successful, and hardly anything of what may be called uproarious fun. The test of this quality is applied when a book is read aloud. Throughout Dickens's life work it appears in a diminishing degree, from the hilarious merriment of *Pickwick* to the sombre *Mystery of Edwin Drood. Pickwick* is, of course, the most laughable of Dickens's books. There is a lot of fun in the books that follow. Mr. Mantalini is gloriously funny. Mrs. Gamp is a treasure: in *Copperfield* the portrayal of Micawber is the embodiment of humour and Big runs close to fun all the time. Even in *Bleak House* Mrs. Jellaby is worthy to sit with Pickwick. But in *Little Dorrit* how little of this is left – insight, pathos of character, yes, but of sheer exuberant fun (to be read aloud), no: not much. Even the circumlocution office is ill satire rather than fun.

In part, one admits this change in Dickens is but the transit of the mind from the laughing years of adolescence to the sobriety, the disillusionment, of age. Dickens, of course, as a young man was filled with high spirits beyond the common lot. He loved laughter, wild pranks, huge jokes, and vast pretenses. At sea he organized the amusement of a ship's company. On land he led in merriment and fun. His life was a game of leapfrog. All of this was reflected in the tumult of his books: the wild images, the crowded metaphors, the rushing thoughts like autumn leaves in the wind. This quality could not be simulated. When it is artificial, the artifice falls into tatters. As Dickens weakened under the strain of his life, this high quality of spontaneous fun slackens and passes away. It is in the pages of *Little Dorrit* that we are first truly conscious of its absence.

The book was written as the shadow – like the shadow of the

Marshalsea wall – began to fall over its writer's later life. Yet even in these later days fate and fortune, which had given him so much, had still one more magic offering. This was the gift of his country home, at Gad's Hill in Kent, and with it the fulfilment of a childish dream. It was like a fairy story come true.

Gad's Hill, where the house stood, is half a mile from Chatham on the road from London to Dover. When Dickens lived at Chatham as a little boy and went out for walks with his father, he used to notice and admire a country house that stood on the summit of the hill. He himself has described in his own unique fashion how the house attracted him as a child. In a paper written in *The Uncommercial Traveller* about a journey on the Dover Road, he draws a picture of meeting his imaginary former self as "a very queer small boy" to whom he gives a ride on the way to school:

"'Do let us stop at the top of the hill and look at the house there, if you please,' said the very queer small boy.

"'You admire that house?' said I.

"'Bless you. Sir,' said the very queer small boy, 'when I was not more than half as old as nine, it used to be a treat for me to be brought to look at it. And now I am nine I come by myself to look at it. And ever since I can recollect, my father, seeing me so fond of it, has often said to me, If you were to be very persevering, and were to work very hard, you might some day come to live in it. Though that's impossible,' said the very queer little boy, drawing a long breath."

It is a pretty fancy and conveys its meaning better than volumes. Not only the Gad's Hill house but all the country was included in Dickens's memory and his affections and connected with his work. On the Dover Road that winds its seventy miles from the south side of the Thames to the Channel, is Greenwich, six miles out, where Dickens and his companions held their uproarious dinners in the early days of success: two and a half miles further is Shooter's Hill, where the coach went tugging upward in the heavy fog of the November night that opens *A Tale of Two Cities*: twenty-three miles from London is Chalk, where Dickens spent his honeymoon: three miles on is Gad's Hill, and beyond that, twenty-nine miles from London, is Rochester, the Cloisterham of *Edwin Drood*, but still more immortal from the fact that "Mr. Pickwick and his three companions had resolved to make Rochester their first halting place." One can almost hear from its cathedral the voice of Mr. Jingle – "glorious pile, – frowning walls, – tottering arches."

The Gad's Hill house fell onto the market in 1855. Dickens chanced that way and saw the notice of sale. "When I was at Gravesend t'other day," he wrote to Wills (February 9, 1855), "I saw at Gad's Hill, a little freehold to be sold. The spot and the house are literally, 'a dream of my childhood.'" By an odd chance the property belonged to one of Dickens's magazine contributors. He opened negotiations at once and finally bought it in March of 1856 for £1,780. He had at the time no intention of making it his permanent or even his principal home. He calculated that by spending a thousand pounds on renovation he could rent it for a good return (£100) on his investment. Meanwhile he could have the joy of possessing it and of occupying it between whiles. He actually moved into it as a summer residence in June, 1857. As it turned out he never rented it except for four months (in 1860). Later on, after his separation from his wife, he sold Tavistock House and Gad's Hill Place became and remained his permanent home. It was there that he died, and the house is more identified with his name than any other of his many residences.

Gad's Hill Place, as the Dickens house is called, stands on the top of Gad's Hill, the rendezvous of Shakespeare's Falstaff. It was a two-story brick house, at that time about eighty years old. It stood in comfortable grounds with gardens, lawns, and orchard. The property included, across the Dover Road, a piece of woodland with two beautiful cedars. This Dickens connected to Gad's Hill Place by a subway. Here he presently set up (1865), as a study, a Swiss chalet sent to him, in ninety-four pieces, as a present from a French friend. Here he sat at work, in the wonderful springtime of Kent, on the last afternoon of his life. But before that, much work, much achievement, and no little suffering were still to come.

Chapter Nine

DICKENS SEPARATES FROM HIS WIFE

1858

TO THE OUTSIDE WORLD, AND TO THOSE WHO KNEW him only as a sort of public character, the life of Charles Dickens in 1857 and 1858 was still a continued round of activity and success. But for those who knew him in his domestic life, the situation in his home was reaching a climax. We are told that there is a tide in the affairs of of men which, taken at the flood, leads on to fortune. So, too, in the written record of a life we may mark the inevitable movement of the ebb tide. For Charles Dickens this ebb tide may be said to date from his separation from his wife in May, 1858.

Up to this time, in the record at least, his adult life looks like one continued and rising success. There had been the phenomenal success of *Pickwick* and its immediate successors from the pen of Boz: the triumphal tour to America; and the series of great novels culminating in *David Copperfield*, which placed him in the foremost rank of the world's men of letters, then and forever. There was as yet nothing, or nothing for the public eye, of the reverse side – the overwork, the overstrain, the inability to rest: and with it the impatient temperament that cannot tolerate criticism or contradiction:

and of the other factors that can sunder lives and break homes, nothing.

But no doubt – and indeed it so appears from what is written below – what followed did not come without a long preparation of circumstance. In most of the books upon Dickens very little is made of the separation of the husband and wife, after twenty-three years of a marriage marked by the birth of ten children. The reason is that at the time when John Forster, and other early biographers, wrote, the death of Dickens was so recent, so many of the family group concerned were still alive, that it seemed indecent to display to the rude eye of public curiosity the sorrows of a broken home. This was no doubt a proper feeling and in a measure still is. Charles Dickens is not yet history, to be mauled about like Charles the Second or Charlemagne. But at the same time it is rather a childish pretense for Forster and such to make out that the separation of Dickens from his wife is of no importance, a mere trivial matter: "an arrangement," as he says, "of a strictly private nature." If Dickens's life is so important that we may chronicle all the sorrows of his childhood, the raptures of his courtships, his every movement from London to the sea and from the sea to London, then it is only natural that some little public curiosity may well surround the most important domestic event of his career.

In one guise or another Dickens "wrote up" almost every important phase of his life: the sufferings of his childhood, the debtors' prison, his father and his mother and his earliest love. But among the assorted and ill-assorted marriages of his books – the Dombeys and the Deadlocks, the Gowans and the Murdstones – one looks in vain for the record of his own marriage. Some instinct withheld his hand.

To the English reading public of 1858 the news that Charles Dickens had separated from his wife came as a sudden shock, with a sense of something like a personal blow. But it had long, long been preparing. Those who knew most said least.

In his intercourse and communications with various friends for some years past Dickens had referred to the increasing unhappiness of his married life. To this was due, in part, the restlessness, which seemed to haunt him, the inability to obtain tranquillity which hurried him from each exertion to the next. The passing years only added to the strain that was reaching the breaking point. That he refrained so long from an open separation was due no doubt largely to his conceit of his own eminence, his acceptance of himself as a sort of trustee of public morality. Of great men we must take the bad with the good. And there is nothing to admire in Dickens's attitude towards his wife and the conduct he saw fit to adopt.

To his friend Forster, to whom he always looked for that vindication of his conduct in the eyes of the world which was so essential to his happiness, he had for years back hinted at the failure of his married life. About a year before the final break, which he evidently anticipated and, one may say, intended even then, he wrote in some detail:

"Poor Catherine and I are not made for each other and there is no help for it. It is not only that she makes me uneasy and unhappy but that I make her so too and much more so. She is exactly what you know in the way of being amiable and complying: but we are strangely ill-assorted for the bond there is between us. God knows she would have been a thousand times happier if she had married another kind of man, and that her avoidance of this destiny would have been at least equally good for us both. I am often cut to the heart by thinking what a pity it is for her own sake that I ever fell in her way; and if I were sick or disabled tomorrow, I know how sorry she would be, and how deeply grieved myself, to think how we had lost each other. But exactly the same incompatibility would arise the moment I was well again: and nothing on earth could make her understand me, or suit us to each other. Her temperament will not go with mine. It mattered not so much when we had only ourselves to consider, but reasons have been growing since which make it all but hopeless that we should even try to struggle on. What is now befalling me I have seen steadily coming ever since the days you remember when Mary was born and I know too well that you cannot and no one can help me. … I claim no immunity from blame. There is plenty of fault on my side, I dare say, in the way of a thousand uncertainties, caprices and difficulties of disposition, but only one thing will alter all that, and that is the end which alters all."

Forster and other friends seemed to have attempted in vain to intercede: to have called Dickens's attention to the singularity of his situation in the eyes of the world: to his responsibility to those whose laughter and whose tears had created out of his matchless books a sort of national heritage. They tried to show him that there was in his lot nothing that honour or conscience need refuse to bear, nothing that had not been borne before by thousands less fortunate than he.

It was in vain. Dickens wanted the separation: and when he wanted anything he wanted it with eager intensity and could find a thousand reasons to justify him in wanting it. Nor is there any reason to maintain the pretense that the separation was really by mutual desire. We have no reason to believe that Catherine Dickens – "amiable and complying" – did anything more than yield to an imperious will and an inevitable fate. But Dickens himself not only wanted the separation: he wanted more than this. He wanted the public, the readers of his books, to accept his separation from his wife as a natural simple matter, like the news of a trip to the Continent or a visit to Scotland. He wanted no trouble made about it, no criticism and no condemnation.

So when the separation came in May of 1858 Dickens announced it in a sort of manifesto, published in the June number of *Household Words*, the magazine of which he was the editor. It runs thus:

"Twenty-and-three years have passed since I entered on my present relations with the Public. They began when I was so young, that I find them to have existed for nearly a quarter of a century.

"Through all that time I have tried to be as faithful to the Public, as they have been to me. It was my duty never to trifle with them, or deceive them or presume upon their favour, or do anything with it but work hard to justify it. I have always endeavoured to discharge that duty.

"My conspicuous position has often made me the subject of fabulous stories and unaccountable statements. Occasionally, such things have chafed me, or even wounded me; but, I have always accepted them as the shadows inseparable from the light of my notoriety and success. I have never obtruded any such personal uneasiness of mine, upon the generous aggregate of my audience.

"For the first time in my life, and I believe for the last, I now deviate from the principle I have so long observed, by presenting myself in my own Journal in my own private character, and entreating all my brethren (as they deem that they have reason to think well of me, and to know that I am a man who has ever been unaffectedly true to our common calling), to lend their aid to the dissemination of my present words.

"Some domestic trouble of mine, of long-standing, on which I will make no further remark than that it claims to be respected as being of a sacredly private nature, has lately been brought to an arrangement, which involves no anger or ill-will, of any kind, and the whole origin, progress, and surrounding circumstances of which have been throughout, within the knowledge of my children. It is amicably composed, and its details have now but to be forgotten by those concerned in it.

"By some means, arising out of wickedness, or out of folly, or out of inconceivable wild chance, or out of all three, this trouble has been made the occasion of misrepresentations, most grossly false, most monstrous, and most cruel – involving, not only me, but innocent persons dear to my heart, and innocent persons of whom I have no knowledge, if, indeed, they have any existence – and so widely spread, that I doubt if one reader in a thousand will peruse these lines, by whom some touch of the breath of these slanders will not have passed, like an unwholesome air.

"Those who know me and my nature, need no assurance under my hand that such calumnies are as irreconcilable with me, as they are, in their frantic incoherence, with one another. But, there is a great multitude who know me through my writings, and who do not know me otherwise; and I cannot bear that one of them should be left in doubt, or hazard of doubt, through my poorly shrinking from taking the unusual means to which I now resort, of circulating the Truth.

"I most solemnly declare, then – and this I do, both in my own name, and in my wife's name – that all the lately whispered rumours touching the trouble at which I have glanced, are abominably false. And that whosoever repeats one of them after this denial, will lie as wilfully and as foully as it is possible for any false witness to lie, before Heaven and earth.

"CHARLES DICKENS."

It seems deplorable that Dickens should have stooped to an act of such atrocious bad taste. In still worse taste was what happened after. He insisted that the publishers of *Household Words*, Messrs. Bradbury & Evans, should also publish the manifesto in another of their publications with which Dickens himself had no connection, namely, the gay and youthful *Punch*. Their common sense compelled a refusal. Dickens in a frenzy of anger broke off all dealings with them. He raged and fumed at the comments, the condemnations, and the innuendoes that appeared in the press. He prepared and gave to an American newspaper correspondent an intimate account of his domestic troubles, excusing himself from blame. Then he raged and fumed again when the correspondent printed it all in the New York *Tribune*. Dickens claimed that it was only a private letter, a plea which shows how unbalanced was his mind.

The letter read:

"Mrs. Dickens and I lived unhappily together for many years. Hardly any one who has known us intimately can fail to have known that we are in all respects of character and temperament wonderfully unsuited to each other. I suppose that no two people, not vicious in themselves, ever were joined together who had a greater difficulty in understanding one another, or who had less in common. An attached woman servant (more friend to both of us than a servant), who lived with us sixteen years, and is now married, and who was and still is in Mrs. Dickens's confidence and in mine, who had the closest familiar experiences of this unhappiness, in London, in the country, in France, in Italy, wherever we have been, year after year, month after month, week after week, day after day, will bear testimony to this.

"Nothing has, on many occasions, stood between us and a separation but Mrs. Dickens's sister, Georgina Hogarth. From the age of fifteen she has devoted herself to our house and our children. She has been their playmate, nurse, instructress, friend, protectress, adviser, and companion. In the manly consideration towards Mrs. Dickens which I owe to my wife, I will merely remark of her that the peculiarity of her character has thrown all the children on some one else. I do not know – I cannot by any stretch of fancy imagine – what would have become of them but for this aunt, who has grown up with them, to whom they are devoted, and who has sacrificed the best part of her youth and life to them. She has remonstrated, reasoned, suffered, and toiled, again and again to prevent a separation between Mrs. Dickens and me. Mrs. Dickens has often expressed to her her sense of her affectionate care and devotion in the house – never more strongly than within the last twelve months.

For some years past, Mrs. Dickens has been in the habit of representing to me that it would be better for her to go away and live apart; that her always increasing estrangement aggravated a mental disorder under which she sometimes labours – more, that she felt herself unfit for the life she had to lead as my wife, and that she would be better far away. I have uniformly replied that we must bear our misfortune, and fight the fight out to the end; that the children were the first consideration, and that I feared they must bind us together 'in appearance.'

"At length, within these three weeks, it was suggested to me by Forster that, even for their sakes, it would surely be better to reconstruct and rearrange their unhappy home. I empowered him to treat with Mrs. Dickens as the friend of both of us for one-and-twenty years. Mrs. Dickens wished to add, on her part, Mark Lemon, and did so. On Saturday last, Lemon wrote to Forster that Mrs. Dickens 'gratefully and thankfully accepted' the terms I proposed to her. Of the pecuniary part of them I will only say that I believe they are as generous as if Mrs. Dickens were a lady of distinction and I a man of fortune. The remaining parts of them are easily described – my eldest boy to live with Mrs. Dickens and take care of her; my eldest girl to keep my house; both my girls, and all my children but the eldest son, to live with me, in the continued companionship of their aunt Georgina, for whom they all have the tenderest affection that I have ever seen among young people, and who has a higher claim (as I have often declared for many years) upon my affection, respect, and gratitude than anybody in the world."

But he got what he wanted. Out of his house went Mrs. Dickens, and he never looked upon her again.

After the first rancorous splutterings in various newspapers about Dickens's separation from his wife, there seems to have settled down over the whole matter a sort of decent conspiracy of silence. It still lies under a veil. The relation of Charles Dickens to those who read his works was of a unique character: it was a sort of personal bond in which admiration was fused into affection. He seemed not a writer but a friend, a comforter whose wide human sympathy brought consolation to the afflicted and laughter to the disconsolate. To such readers it seemed painful to think that the writer who had depicted a hundred happy marriages of people who lived happily ever afterwards had put aside his wife; that he could not exercise the tolerance he extolled nor the quiet devotion which he loved to exalt. On his own statement there was no question of those grave faults which even then could break asunder the marriage bond. It seemed, and it still seems, amazing that one who enjoyed fame and fortune and adulation could not find the manhood to endure such minor misfortune as came to his lot.

So there arose the conspiracy of silence. Take as typical the almost ridiculous explanation given by a biographer of his "life," published just after the great novelist's death, at a time when there were still thousands of people who must have had some knowledge of the inner aspects of his family life.

"The simple explanation was," he writes, "that a misunderstanding had arisen between Mr. and Mrs. Dickens of a purely domestic character, – so domestic, – almost trivial indeed, – that neither law nor friendly arbitration could define or fix the difficulty sufficiently clear [*sic*] to adjudicate upon it. All we can say is that it was a very great pity that a purely family dispute should have been brought before the public, and saying this much, we trust the reader will think we add wisely in dropping any further mention of it."

"A misunderstanding of a trivial character"! So trivial that Dickens put aside his wife for it; put her out of his beautiful home and went on living there himself; that on account of it the children were divided up; that the eldest son left his father's house; that Dickens, on account of it, never saw his wife again; that when he was stricken and dying no one sent for her and in the wording of his will his antipathy to her spoke from beyond the grave.

It is not possible to gloss over so utter a catastrophe, such a complete collapse of what should by rights have been the happiest home in England.

What then was the trouble? It is amazing how little information in regard to Dickens's wife is given in the voluminous mass of biographies, criticisms, articles, and letters which record the incidents of his life. She was younger than he was by some years: it was no case of crabbed old age assorted with glowing youth. She was little over forty years old when he put her aside. The portrait painted by Maclise of the Royal Academy about 1846 shows her as a beautiful woman. In point of intellect one looks in vain in the record for any sign of a brilliant mind or a cultivated intelligence. It would seem probable that Mrs. Dickens had not a mind of a high order, that she was even what is called in the slang of today "dumb." Her husband in one of the few letters from America in which he gives her more than a casual mention as "Mrs. Dickens," writes of her acting in garrison amateur theatricals at Montreal (1842): "But only think of Kate playing! And playing devilish well, I assure you!" And on the playbill which he enclosed, where her name appears as taking the part of *Amy Templeton* in a farce called *Deaf as a Post,* he puts no less than eight notes of exclamation after it !!!!!!!! As who should say, what do you know about this! Such comments as applied to a good-looking young woman of twenty-six seem to mean only one thing.

But after all a woman who brings ten successive children into the world in sixteen successive years, and carries the burden of a noisy nursery, may well shine with a different illumination than that of the footlights of the stage and the chandelier of the drawing room.

Mr. A.W. Ward, who wrote in 1882 a critical account of Dickens's career, implies that Dickens had never loved his wife. The causes of the separation he says "were an open secret to his friends and acquaintances. If he had ever loved his wife with that affection before which incompatibilities of temper and disposition fade into nothingness, there is no indication of it in any of his numerous letters addressed to her."

And on the other hand, what a difficult person, what an almost impossible person, must Charles Dickens have been to live with and to live up to. It was not alone the sheer exuberance of his energy, the intensity of his mental life, his thought, his conversation. It was, as he grew older, his impatient temperament, his inability to brook criticism or contradiction, his inordinate desire to be always right. The very meekness which bowed before it became in itself an added offense.

In the vast mass of literature which has grown up about Charles Dickens, it is strange what a silence envelops the personality and the memory of his wife. He himself lived in a blaze of notoriety and in his later life in the limelight of publicity. Public attention was naturally focussed upon him. She passed unnoticed. In the American tour of 1842 she got no further than to be chronicled in the press as part of "Charles Dickens Esq. and lady," and the polite generalities already quoted. Hardly a word is said about her in all the contemporary pictures of Charles Dickens and his entourage at home. There is extant a letter in regard to her written by a Mrs. Christian which carries a description of what she looked like:

"I thought her a pretty little woman, with the heavy-lidded large blue eyes so much admired by men. The nose was a little *retroussé*, the forehead good, mouth small, round, and red-lipped, with a pleasant smiling expression, notwithstanding the sleepy look of the slow-moving eyes. The weakest part of her face was the chin, which melted too suddenly into the throat. She took kindly notice of me, and I went down with a fluttering heart to be introduced to 'Boz.' "

There is also a description written by the dreamy little Dane, Hans Andersen of the Fairy Tales, who had formed a pen-and-ink friendship with Dickens and visited the family just before the crash. Mrs. Dickens, he says, "had a certain soft and womanly repose about her: but whenever she spoke there came such a light into her large eyes and such a smile upon her lips and there was such a charm in the tones of her voice that henceforth I shall always connect her and Agnes together." Hans Andersen, in short, saw, or thought he saw, the vision of a happy home graced by the noblest heroine of Dickens's works. But little Hans Andersen had eyes only for Snow Men and enchanted mermaids and not for the realities of life.

What was Mrs. Dickens like, anyway, as a person? If the accusation of Dickens's letter to Arthur Smith is true, she must have been a creature to shudder at. Notice the force of the words used: *that he cannot by any stretch of fancy imagine what would have become of his children if left to the care of their own mother.* These are terrible words to cast at a woman. Was it right that child after child should be brought into the world to face such awful risk as this? Dickens ought to have talked to their father about it.

What did Mrs. Dickens think? Again silence. When she abandoned her children – or when they were taken from her (which is the proper phrase?) – the youngest was a little boy of six years old. There were two grown girls of eighteen and twenty, and in between a group of five little brothers: in all, a bevy of bright sweet children halfway between the nursery and the world. Is it nothing to be taken from all that? When they laughed and romped with their clever father at the beautiful Gad's Hill home, and Mrs. Dickens sat in her lodging alone – what a tragedy Dickens could have made with a pen and ink of a scene like that!

But all is wrapped in silence.

The most brilliant living interpreter of the books of Charles Dickens has sought to explain it for us by saying "His selfishness was wholly a selfishness of the nerves." But this explains nothing or too much. There are a lot of nervous fellows in the penitentiary.

It is to Mrs. Dickens's honour that she took the separation without complaint, without protest. She did not write to Bradbury & Evans; she did not communicate her side of the story to the correspondent of the New York *Tribune*; she did not take all England into her confidence; she did not wish to have her sorrows chronicled in the pages of *Punch*; nor had she an affectionate brother-in-law to whose home she could retire.

Here Dickens was fortunate: he had – or at least a sister-in-law.

Ever since his return from America his wife's younger sister, Georgina Hogarth, had lived in their house. After the separation she continued to live with Dickens and to look after his children to the end of his life. She was with him when he died.

Mamie Dickens, in her little book to which reference has been made, has spoken in affectionate terms of the part played by her aunt. "She has been to me," she says, "ever since I can remember anything, and to all of us, the truest, best, and dearest friend, companion, and counsellor. To quote my father's own words, 'The best and truest friend man ever had.'"

In his will Dickens left to his sister-in-law the sum of £8,000 free of legacy duty. To his wife he left an annuity of £300 a year. In his will he says, "I also give to the said Georgina Hogarth all my private papers whatsoever and wheresoever and I leave her my grateful blessing as the best and truest friend man ever had." And when he had finished in his will (it was dated May 12, 1869) the "form of words necessary to the plain objects" of it, he went out of his way to add, "I desire here simply to record the fact that my wife since our separation by consent, has been in the receipt from me of an annual income of £600, while all the great charges of a numerous and expensive family have devolved wholly upon myself." That is to say that even after his death he wanted the world to understand what a generous fellow he had been. The extent of the generosity might have been measured better if he had added that in the last year completed before the will was written the £600 came out of an income of over £30,000. In the same part of the will he wrote, "I solemnly enjoin my dear children how much they owe to the said Georgina Hogarth and never to be wanting in a grateful and affectionate attachment to her, for they know well that she has been, through all the stages of their growth and progress their ever useful self-denying and devoted friend."

Thus the story of Dickens's broken marriage makes rather sad reading. It leaves a great and unforgettable imperfection in a life otherwise filled with devotion. Nor does it correspond with what one might have expected from the general character of Charles Dickens. In him was nothing of the philanderer, the Lothario, the Don Juan. He drew Mr. Mantalini out of his head, not out of his life. He was a man who loved his home and his home life. But outside of it, he seems to have preferred the society of men to that of women. Female friendships formed no particular part of his life. One might think perhaps of his long connection with Miss Coutts (the Baroness Burdett-Coutts) to whom he is said to have written over six hundred letters. But then Miss Coutts was a multi-millionaire giving away money. Any of us would have written six hundred letters to her. And the connection implied was not with Miss Coutts but with the causes she so nobly served. In the volume of such letters recently published the warmth is regulated to the temperature of charity. Dickens enjoyed also to a certain degree the friendship of the somewhat dubious Lady Blessington of Gore House, patroness at large of art and literature. But she was, after all, twenty-three years older than he was and died when he was thirty-seven. In all the records of his comings and goings there are no surreptitious pages.

Indeed, in regard to women Charles Dickens from first to last took what one might call an entirely Victorian point of view. He lived well before the days of women's rights, women's votes, women in college, and women in the business world. Like all his generation, he rated women, intellectually, away down. While nominally placed upon a pedestal as angels, fairies, and ministering spirits, in reality they were the inferior sex. Their function was to adorn life, to soften it, to beautify it, and so on; under these flattering terms was concealed the fact that it was the men who ruled and thought and acted and created. One may realize the position of women as Dickens saw them and depicted them by turning to the pages of the poets.

> *"0 woman!* [thus sings one of them] *in our hours of ease*
> *Uncertain, coy, and hard to please,*
>
> • • • •
>
> *When pain and anguish wring the brow,*
> *A ministering angel thou!"*

In accordance with this a generation of women set themselves to be as uncertain and as coy as possible – no doubt with success. Yet in our day an uncertain stenographer and a coy female police magistrate do not sound quite so convincing; and the pain and anguish business is handed over to the professional care of a trained nurse with a chart and a thermometer. The women of course cannot have it both ways, coming and going. And in Dickens's day they still took it in only one.

It was out of such gossamer as thus indicated that was created the convention of the Victorian heroine: and Charles Dickens took his "heroines" from the accepted Victorian convention.

What he really thought of the intelligence, the intellect, of women can be seen not through his heroines, but through his female "characters." Mrs. Nickleby is and remains for Dickens the real embodiment of female intellect: not an exception or a departure from it, but the type itself.

To Dickens the female mind – not Mrs. Nickleby's alone but the female mind in general – is incapable of logic, incapable of a plain sequence of thought, incapable of common sense. It replaces the current of thought by a flow of words. Take, for example, almost at random, any of the Nickleby "tirades" or orations which passed for conversation with that amiable lady:

" 'I am sure,' said the worthy lady, with a prefatory cough, 'that it's a great relief, under such trying circumstances as these, to have anybody else mistaken for me – a very great relief; and it's a circumstance that never occurred before, although I have several times been mistaken for my daughter Kate. I have no doubt the people were very foolish, and perhaps ought to have known better, but still they did take me for her, and of course that was no fault of mine, and it would be very hard indeed if I was to be made responsible for it. However, in this instance, of course, I must feel that I should do exceedingly wrong if I suffered anybody – especially anybody that I am under great obligations to – to be made uncomfortable on my account. And therefore I think it my duty to tell that gentleman that he is mistaken, that I am not the lady who he was told by some impertinent person was niece to the Countess of Pavingstones, and that I do beg and entreat of him to go quietly away, if it's only for,' here Mrs. Nickleby simpered and hesitated, 'for *my* sake.' "

To Dickens, as to many others, the joy of this is that it is not only the way Mrs. Nickleby talked, it is the way women talk. It is, as it was for Dickens, every man's mother, wife, sister, and aunt. One could, if need be, compile a whole repository of feminine thought from the conversations of Mrs. Nickleby, Mrs. Gamp,

Mrs. Micawber – a hundred Dickens women. Never, or hardly ever, does there appear in Dickens's books a woman of what one might call a clear intelligence. One thinks of David Copperfield and Betsy Trotwood only to remember that the whole point about her was that she was just like a man. When she breaks away into idiosyncrasies and absurdities, that reveals the fact that after all she was a woman. Hence all the really successful female characters of Dickens – the Mrs. Micawbers and the Mrs. Nicklebys and so forth – are really oddities, freaks, queerities, but truly female because illuminated always with the kaleidoscope of the feminine intelligence. If Dickens's women readers only realized it, his books are one vast panorama of women as the inferior sex, the lesser sex – not through injustice or lack of privilege, but as turned out by the hand of nature. In other words, Dickens really thought very little of women.

One asks: What about the "heroines": the Agneses and the Madeleines and the rest? But the answer is that the "heroines" were not women at all, but were abstractions, conventions, idealizations of what women were wanted to be. The freaks were facts; the heroines were fiction. Thus one may compare with interest the speeches of Mrs. Nickleby with those of her heroine daughter Kate. Dickens meant Mrs. Nickleby's speeches to be funny: so they are. But so are Kate's funny, and he didn't know it. Kate is the type of heroine who requests the presumptuous villain to "unhand her" – a form of manipulation since lost. Mark the way in which she gives her wicked uncle a "telling off" for introducing her to bad men.

"'In the meantime,' interrupted Kate, with becoming pride and indignation, 'I am to be the scorn of my own sex, and the toy of the other; justly condemned by all women of right feeling, and despised by all honest and honourable men; sunken in my own esteem, and degraded in every eye that looks upon me. No, not if I work my fingers to the bone, not if I am driven to the roughest and hardest labour. Do not mistake me. I will not disgrace your recommendation. I will remain in the house in which it placed me, until I am entitled to leave it by the terms of my engagement;

though, mind, I see these men no more! When I quit it, I will hide myself from them and you, and, striving to support my mother by hard service, I will live, at least, in peace, and trust in God to help me.'"

Any girl who could *really* say all this would find that the men, good and bad, had all left her before she finished. One admits, of course, the combination, as in the charming and unique Dora of *David Copperfield*, unsurpassed in fiction. But Dora could only belong in a world where women were the satellites of men. The same is true of the devoted Ada, who married Richard Carstone in *Bleak House*.

To sum it up in a word, Dickens's women heroines were built on the Victorian convention of the gossamer angel, and his women "characters" were the real women which he saw about him. But the "angel" as a standing chivalrous compliment to women has counter-balanced the standing insult of the freak.

At the time when Dickens's home was broken up his eldest son, Charles, was twenty-one years old and was employed in the firm of the Barings in London and was presently sent to Hong Kong by his father to enter the tea trade on his own account. Of his two daughters, Mary, the elder, remained permanently with her father and her aunt. The second, Kate, was soon after (1860) married to Charles Collins, a brother of the famous novelist. The second boy, Walter, went out to India as an ensign and presently became a lieutenant in the 42nd Highlanders. Frank was sent away to school in France and Germany to qualify to join his brother in business, and came home again in 1860. Little Sydney, "the Ocean Spectre," was training for the navy. The other two boys were away at school, only the youngest, "Plorn," stayed on at home, studying with a tutor. Except for gatherings at holiday time, the family circle was gone.

Chapter Ten

DICKENS TAKES THE PLATFORM

1858–1865

Public Readings – "All the Year Round" – "A Tale of Two Cities" – "Our Mutual Friend"

IT WAS JUST AT THE TIME OF HIS SEPARATION FROM his wife that Dickens began his public and professional readings from his books which henceforth filled a large part of his life. His genius was unique in this lesser sphere, as it was in the larger field of letters. It is doubtful whether anyone before or since has ever given the same kind of "performance" as Dickens in his public readings. They were not "readings" in the strict sense; still less were they recitations; nor were they "monologues" such flourish in the world today; nor was Dickens "acting," because he was not appearing in character, and was portraying not one personage but half a dozen. Moreover, he was talking to his audience: a thing done only by by actors who cannot act. What Dickens did was "interpretation," a sort of mesmeric art which combined acting with reciting, direct appeal with histrionic detachment, and above all contained a sort of hypnotic power of suggestion. Dickens's audiences were quite truly carried away. They were outside of themselves. They laughed, they sobbed, they were in an "ecstasy." And Dickens controlled them with hand and voice and eye – like a magician.

The idea of giving this sort of public entertainment had long been in his mind. As far back as December, 1853, he had given public readings of his *Christmas Carol* and his *Cricket on the Hearth* at Birmingham to aid the funds of the town institute. They were followed by other random appearances for various charities. Everywhere the readings were vastly successful. At Birmingham the Institute gained £500 from them. It occurred to Dickens at the time that a new form of art and a new source of income was here opening for him. John Forster dissuaded him, thinking, quite wrongly, that it would hurt the sale of his books. Dickens laid the idea aside. But in 1857 it came up again. The sudden death (June 8, 1857) of his friend Douglas Jerrold, who left behind him an impoverished family, led Dickens and various others to raise a fund in aid. Among other things Dickens and Wilkie Collins put on their *Frozen Deep* at the Gallery of Illustration, the Queen and the Prince Consort graciously attending. The Queen, still more graciously, commanded Mr. Dickens's presence after the performance to receive congratulations. Dickens, being in "farce dress" and being more royal than royalty itself, refused to come. The lesser of the two sovereigns gave way. The Queen after that saw Dickens only once – thirteen years later.

For the same fund Dickens gave three public readings of his *Christmas Carol* in St. Martin's Hall, London (1857). Their success revealed to him more clearly still his uncanny power before an audience. "The two thousand and odd people were like one," he wrote, "and their enthusiasm was something awful." This decided him. The breaking strain of his home life, now grown intolerable, made him doubly eager for outside diversion. He took on the role of a professional public entertainer – an occupation which terminated only with his life.

The public readings which Dickens gave fall into four great series, or tours, in England, Ireland, and Scotland, with a trip to the United States in 1867-68. The first of these tours was organized by his friend Arthur Smith and consisted of eighty-seven readings, beginning at Clifton on August 2nd and ending at Brighton on November 13, 1858. There was a second series in 1861-63, managed by a Mr. Headland. Later on, under the celebrated and genial

George Dolby, Dickens toured England, 1866-67, and visited America, 1867-68. His last series of readings of 1869-70 was curtailed by the illness which ended in his death.

To describe any one of Dickens's public lecture tours is to describe them all. They were from first to last a wild success, a pilgrimage of triumph. He had come into his own. He writes home from his first tour to his sister-in-law, henceforth the sole guardian of his hearth, in terms of constant elation, "We had a most wonderful night at Exeter" (this is August 5, 1858). "It was a prodigious crowd and we turned away no end of people. ... I think they were the finest audience I ever read to. ... I don't think I ever read so well." "A wonderful audience last night at Wolverhampton" (August 12, 1858). "If such a thing can be, they are even quicker and more intelligent than the audience I had in Edinburgh. ... I never saw such people." "We had a tremendous night": (this time it is Liverpool Aug. 20, 1858) "the largest house I ever had since I first began: two thousand and three hundred people." Nor was there any change except in intensity of sentiment when Dickens crossed the Irish Sea and exchanged his English for an Irish audience. His first Dublin lecture (August 24, 1858) proved to him that the Irish could laugh. The next question was, could they cry?

"I very much doubt," Dickens wrote home, "the Irish capacity of receiving the pathetic: but of their quickness as to the humorous there can be no doubt. I shall see how they go along with little Paul in his death presently." He did see, in a second reading given that same day, and he appended a postscript to his letter: "Their crying was universal and they were extraordinarily affected. There is no doubt we could stay here a week with that one reading."

It presently appeared that the protestants of Ulster could laugh and cry like the catholics of Dublin. "We turned away half the town," he wrote from Belfast.

From Ireland he went to the north of England, where his two daughters joined him, and thence to Scotland. The reception was everywhere the same. "At Aberdeen we were crammed to the street twice in one day. At Perth … the whole town came and filled an immense hall."

And so on, throughout the tour. There is no doubt that Dickens found in the work not only the fascination of artistic success, but a sort of fierce distraction that helped him to forget his broken home.

But the work was a great strain. From the very beginning it overtaxed his strength.

At first he writes – still in his first fortnight of it – "I have not felt the fatigue to any extent worth mentioning: though I get every night into the most violent heats." But only a little later: "My cold has been oppressive and is not yet gone. I have been very hard [*sic*] to sleep, too, and last night I was all but sleepless." But he had enough reserve power still to stand the fatigue. "The work is hard, sometimes overpowering," he wrote at the end of the Irish tour, "but I am none the worse for it."

In a sense, the novelty and the effort restored him, momentarily, to something like his earlier self. James Payn, who met him for the first time at Edinburgh – he was then editor of *Chambers' Journal* – speaks of him as "full of fun and brightness" and says, "in five minutes I felt as much at ease with him as though I had known him as long as I had known his books." And Dickens wrote home: "Payn went with us" (with himself and his two daughters) "to Hawthornden and we laughed all day." This is again the Dickens of *Martin Chuzzlewit* days and the Cornwall trip.

Dickens's audience gave vent to their feelings in roars of laughter, in floods of tears, in fits of hysteria unknown today outside of a revivalist meeting. In part, of course, this was a matter of the social habit of the day. The expression of sentiment both in words and acts, we must remember, was much more free and unrestrained then than now. It was "the thing" to burst into a generous flood of tears. We have seen how Lord Jeffrey sat and sobbed over the death of little Paul, and Thackeray rolled off his seat at the amateur theatricals. But even with all allowance made, the effect of Dickens's presentations was extraordinary. Could anything today – even the Irish annuities – occasion "universal crying" in a Dublin audience? Or this (it is from Scarborough, on the first tour, as told in a letter to Miss Hogarth): "There was one gentleman at the 'Little Dombey' yesterday morning ... after crying a good deal without hiding it, covered his face with both hands and laid it down on the back of the seat before him and really shook with emotion."

"Last night," he writes this on the second tour January 8, 1862, "I read *Copperfield* (the storm at sea) and positively enthralled the people. It was a most overpowering effect." The culminating effect was on Macready, at Cheltenham (this was Dickens's friend the famous actor):

"When I got home after *Copperfield,* I found him quite unable to speak, and able to do nothing but square his dear old jaw all on one side, and roll his eyes (half closed), like Jackson's picture of him. And when I said something light about it, he returned: 'No – er – Dickens! I swear to Heaven that, as a piece of passion and playfulness – er – indescribably mixed up together, it does – er – no, really, Dickens! – amaze me as profoundly as it moves me. But as a piece of art – and you know– er – that I – no, Dickens! By –! have seen the best art in a great time – it is incomprehensible to me. How is it got at – er – how is it done – er – how one man can – well? It lays me on my – er – back, and it is of no use talking about it!'"

The public readings given by Dickens were all taken from his written works. But they were specially edited, altered, and selected so as to suit them for presentation. In at least one case he even had the selections reprinted in the form as used on the platform. On his first tour the material used was *A Christmas Carol* (his favourite rendering), *The Chimes,* the trial scene from *Pickwick,* Little Dombey, "Boots at the Holly Tree Inn" (a *Household Words* story), "The Three Poor Travellers" (ditto), and Mrs. Gamp.

The profits, though small compared with the receipts of the later American tour, were very handsome. Meantime the editorial labours went on. During Dickens's lecture tour, Wills remained in charge at the office of *Household Words,* but his chief still sent directions by correspondence. There was the usual "Christmas

Charles Dickens as he appeared when reading

Number" with a Dickens article as a special feature, a practice which had gone on without a break since 1851. The number always carried a special title (*What Christmas Is*, 1851, *Stories for Xmas*, 1852, etc., etc.), and Dickens always contributed a leading portion of it. This year (1858) the number was called *A House to Let* and Dickens wrote for it a chapter on "Going into Society."

But the magazine was doomed. After his quarrel with the publishers Bradbury & Evans about inserting in *Punch* a notice of his separation from his wife, Dickens wanted nothing more to do with them. He bought out all and whatever rights they had in the property for £3,500 and replaced the magazine with a new one, *All the Year Round*; the offices changed from No. 16 to No. 11 Wellington Street. For publishers Dickens now returned to Chapman & Hall, with whom his works remained till his death.

The new magazine was just the old one under a new name. Nothing was changed. In point of proprietorship, the name and the good-will belonged to Dickens alone: the profits and losses were to be shared as three quarters and one quarter between Dickens and Wills. Dickens was editor with a salary of £504 a year; Wills, subeditor, with £420. To make sure that there would be no interregnum between the two magazines, *All the Year Round*, began appearing (May 28, 1859) while *Household Words* had still five weeks to run.

From this time on, the conduct of *All the Year Round* was an essential part of Dickens's life. It was a continued success. Not only did Dickens's own writings guarantee for it a wide popularity, but he was fortunate in obtaining the aid of various contributors of the first rank. Wilkie Collins's *No Name* ran as a serial in 1862, Charles Reade's *Very Hard Cash* in 1863. Among other contributors of this period were Edmund Yates, Anthony Trollope, and Charles Lever.

But Dickens himself had given to the new periodical its greatest impetus by beginning in its opening number his own novel, since so celebrated in fiction and in drama, *A Tale of Two Cities*.

According to his notes and correspondence, he had been revolving in his mind the basis of this new tale for a year or so. It originated in the idea of having "a story in two parts with a lapse of time between like a French Drama." This led him to the idea of the French Revolution. His suggested titles, *Long Ago*, *Buried Alive*, *The Doctor of Beauvais*, indicate the movement of his thought. At last (in March, 1859) he found the exact title that he wanted: *A Tale of Two Cities*. After that the writing went on at breakneck speed – only one month ahead of its running publication as a serial. *A Tale of Two Cities* appeared as a weekly serial in *All the Year Round* (April to November, 1859), beginning thus with the opening number of the new magazine. It came out also in monthly numbers with illustrations (June to December) and was published in book form at the end of the year. It was the last of Dickens's work to be illustrated by Hablôt Browne (Phiz). Dickens, after twenty years of work together, broke off the connection without a word. After this Marcus Stone and, at the end, S.L. Fildes were his illustrators.

Whatever may be its shortcomings, *A Tale of Two Cities* is a great book. It conveys, imperfect or not, a marvellous picture of the French Revolution. The self-sacrifice of Sydney Carton giving his wasted life upon the guillotine, has become a legend of the ages. Many of its passages, such as the opening picture of the coach on Shooters Hill on a November night, are full of power; others even of majesty. Of its characters, Mr. Lorry of Telson's bank belongs with John Jarndyce and such – the elderly men worth more than the youngsters about them, whom Dickens loved to draw; and the figures of Ernest Defarge, the republican patriot, and his wife, the woman of the Terror, remain in the reader's mind.

It is wonderful that Dickens could have depicted the Revolution so well. It is done by sympathy, not by scholarship. The time, as said in an earlier chapter, was still fairly recent. It had not yet drifted into history. Nor had the industrial life of France when Dickens first knew it, in the days of diligences and mail coaches, changed much from that of half a century before. All the old people still remembered the Revolution, and everyone of middle age looked upon Napoleon and Waterloo as things of yesterday.

Dickens, of course, never having been to college or trafficked with learning, has no notion of the prolonged and assiduous labours of the historical scholar. Because he had looked over Mercier's *Tableau de Paris* and such ABC as that, he imagined that he had profoundly studied the French Revolution. Thus did his American counterpart Mark Twain, because he read books about Joan of Arc in the intervals of writing a shelf of books, giving lectures, telling stories, playing billiards, and smoking cigars, truly believe himself to have spent twelve years of research into the Middle Ages. For such scholarship, the true college historian, buried in book dust to the neck, has but a feeble smile and an unconfessed envy.

It was said of Alexander Hamilton that without having seen Europe he had "divined" it. So with Dickens and the Revolution. From his own knowledge of France, and a fragment here, a fact there, he built it up. Those who know the history intimately will admit the value of the picture which he draws. But it has its limitations. It is *coloured*, just as Thomas Carlyle's picture (Dickens's bedside book for years) is all smoke and fury, like a huge genie emerging from a bottle; so with the work of Dickens. His Revolution has not exactly the comic touch of his France and his Boulogne, as discussed above, but it has, all through it, a sort of stage effect. The French scenes all have a touch of play-acting about them, as if the mob were pretending to be a mob, the seigneur acting as a seigneur, and revolutionists "doing" the Revolution. Yet withal it reaches the mind as few histories do.

Even Dickens's own admirers, like Forster, admitted that the new book lacked the usual humour. This aspect of Dickens's work, at least the humour of uproarious fun, the humour that is read aloud to make people laugh, was fading out of Dickens's work. In *A Tale of Two Cities*, Jerry Cruncher, the body-snatcher, is meant to be funny but is not. Dickens is so crafty and mysterious about Jerry's gruesome trade that the reader never suspects he has any.

"'Jerry,' says Mr. Lorry in the opening pages of the book, 'say that my answer was "Recalled to Life."'

"Jerry started in his saddle. 'That's a blazing strange answer too.' said he, at his hoarsest."

The reader can have no notion of the meaning, nor will have for hundreds of pages. This is Dickens's "forward reference." The reader is supposed to carry a hatful of them as he goes along.

Nor are there many "characters" in the book in the Dickens sense. Sydney Carton is rather a character by his fate than by his individualities. Charles Darney is the best of Dickens's "walking gentlemen," but little more. Apart from Carton the names are not quoted.

But the book is after all a beautiful book with a wonderful

quality of interest. It is just as well that Dickens left "fun" out of it. He was no longer capable of producing it. It was not that his genius had worn out. But his mind had shifted and saddened. The "fun" of his books after this is jaded and mechanical.

It would be without point to chronicle in detail the minor events of Dickens's life from his taking up his abode at Gad's Hill until his second tour in America. There was after this no novelty in his life. After the first tumultuous success of the first lecture tour, even that had lost all attraction other than as excitement and as a refuge from restlessness. At the period when Dickens's life might have been settling down to a long evening of domestic tranquillity he found himself, by the misfortune of his fate, thrust back into the world. He had no home. His boys were growing up and passing out into the world. He moved restlessly from place to place: rented temporary houses in London, spent odd months in Paris, meditated huge tours in the antipodes, presided at great meetings, plunged headlong in and out of lecture tours, wrote with a hurried pen that could not wait for inspiration – and rested never. The world has seen fit to shroud the tragedy of Dickens's later years.

The chronicle of these intervening years shows of itself the hurried and ceaseless activity that could find no peace.

Dickens was at Tavistock House in London in the winter of 1858-59. He went on his first lecture tour, as already said, in the autumn of 1858: continued it by Christmas readings in London. In 1859 he started his new magazine and wrote for it *A Tale of Two Cities*. In the summer he wrote at high speed a special story, *Hunted Down*, for an American paper, the New York *Ledger* – a unique form of proceeding induced by an offer of $1,000 down. He went to Broadstairs for a fortnight (September, 1859) and was off lecturing in the autumn. The next winter, 1859-60, was his last in Tavistock House. In the next year he was chiefly busy with *Great Expectations.* The marriage of his second daughter, Kate, in this year – she married Charles Collins – left him with only one girl at home.

In 1861 he took a house in London from February till the spring and in March began a second series of readings, which went on, with breaks, till 1862. His old friend and manager Arthur Smith, being dead, the tour was very much muddled in its arrangement by a cheerful but incompetent Mr. Headland. A further disruption of the tour was the temporary break occasioned by the death of the Prince Consort (December, 1861). *Great Expectations*, as a book, appeared that summer.

In February, 1862, Dickens swapped Gad's Hill for a London house for three months and gave readings in London that went on intermittently till June. In the autumn he went over to Paris for three months. There too he gave readings – at the British Embassy – again with terrific *éclat.*

To his restless mind and flagging intellect there were added at this period the successive shocks of various bereavements. The sudden death of Thackeray (December, 1863) affected Dickens deeply. They had quarrelled, over a nothing, years before; had been estranged; had just come happily together; then on Christmas Eve Thackeray was taken.

Nearer to him still was the death of his soldier son Walter of the 42nd Highlanders in India, just as the old year went out (December 31, 1863). His brother Frank was on his way out to join him. The year 1864 found Dickens working as best he might – a very poor best – on *Our Mutual Friend.* This winter again (February-June, 1864) he took a house in London. All through this time he seems like a haunted man, living in strange homes.

Meantime his book was finished – the last he was destined to finish – and appeared in 1865.

One turns a moment to the chief literary work of this closing period – apart from minor sketches and stories – the two novels, *Great Expectations* and *Our Mutual Friend.*

Lovers of Dickens are unwilling to accept any idea of a decline or waning of his powers in later life, of an inferiority of his later books. For affection's sake and for contradiction's sake, many judgments have been given, warm in praise of the work of his closing years. One notable novelist of the present century has even called *Our Mutual Friend* Dickens's best novel. Longfellow tried to think of *Edwin Drood* as Dickens's most beautiful book; John Forster persuaded himself that the few additional scraps of it discovered later in his papers were among his friend's best work. But speaking according to the opinion of the many, the books of the decade of the 'sixties – *Great Expectations, Our Mutual Friend,* and *Edwin Drood* – cannot rank among the great works of Dickens. A canvass of opinion anywhere shows that Dickens is widely read – but the books read are *Pickwick* and *Martin Chuzzlewit, David Copperfield,* and *A Tale of Two Cities,* and not the books of the closing years. *Edwin Drood* is somewhat an exception. It was only half finished. We cannot truly judge it; and, in any case, its author shifted entirely the emphasis of his work from character to plot. Conceivably he might have opened a new vein with it.

But there are plenty of reasons why the books should be inferior. It is obvious that authors write themselves out; that some songs can be sung once only, whether early in life or late; that the wear and tear of overwork and overworry can impair any literary output; that commercial reasons will force publication when art would demand delay.

All of these reasons combined in the case of Dickens in *Our Mutual Friend* to make it an unhappy child of adversity, the weakling of a robust family. But even *Great Expectations,* we may expect, could hardly have survived except for its cousinship to still greater.

The opening of the book – the hunted convict among the gravestones – the churchyard on the marshes by the sea – a picture taken from the view from Gad's Hill – is as wonderful an opening as only Dickens could make. But the story is throughout on a lower level than the greater books, the characters less convincing, the nullities more null, the plot more involved, the fun, what there is of it, apt to sound forced and mechanical. One looks in vain in its pages for world-famous characters. The ending, unexpectedly altered from tragedy to relief, at the suggestion of Bulwer Lytton, is as unconvincing as any end must be when fitted onto the beginning of something else.

It is fitting to chronicle here – for chronicling's sake – Dickens's interest at this period in the Guild for Literature and Art. This was a foundation intended to aid necessitous genius with which he had been associated since his early dramatic days. It was an inauspicious enterprise. It meant well, but genius is proverbially difficult to manage. The attempt to build and equip a sort of camouflaged workhouse at Stevenage in Hertfordshire for authors put out to grass, proved unsuccessful, a subject even for comic merriment. But from first to last Dickens devoted much time and work to the starred guild. It led a twilight existence till buried by an act of Parliament at the close of the century.

Like the earlier book, *Hard Times*, the novel *Our Mutual Friend* is interesting only as illustrating the failures of genius. It seems amazing that even the prestige of Charles Dickens in 1865 could have sustained so poor a book. It is amazing that the prestige of his memory can to some extent still sustain it. It is in reality of little interest or value except for the interest of asking why it has so little value.

For its own sake, the book never is, and never was, very readable. Not even the sentimental Victorians could have tolerated its maudlin tears; not even the long-winded reader of the "sixties could have stood for its prolixity; nor the most inquisitive of minds attempt to understand the outline of its plot – except for the commanding prestige of its author.

Even the kindliest critics have damned it with faint praise. The biographer Forster, whose life was dedicated to his admiration of Charles Dickens, admits that "the book will never rank with his higher efforts," and confesses that it "wants freshness and natural development."

The very title of the book is dubious as an English phrase and is without any bearing on the book itself. It so mystified the readers of the opening monthly parts that Dickens had to insert in the next instalment a printed slip that announced: "The reader will understand the use of the popular phrase 'Our Mutual Friend' as the title of this book on arriving at the ninth chapter." When the reader reaches this exciting spot he finds that two of the characters refer to a third one as "our mutual friend," and reiterate the phrase twice more. In other words, Dickens has stepped out of the book to talk rather severely to his readers. But any other two characters could equally well have used the designation about any other third one. Dickens apparently had thought of the title long before and had decided to call a book after it. For any point it has, he might just as well have called the book the *Declaration of Independence* or *Jessica's First Prayer.*

But with or without a title, the plot is what is called by the vulgar "fierce." Dickens's plots – as in *Little Dorrit* par excellence – grew more and more involved and intricate as time went on. It is not so much that they were "impossible." There's no great fault in that. Most of the best books in the world are impossible. The trouble is that they got so abstruse and involved that no one could follow them. Hence, the true Dickens reader learned, and still learns, to leave out the plot. But in *Our Mutual Friend* the plot is not *impossible,* and it is not difficult to grasp. It is just idiotic.

The book originated, as did many of his books, with a sort of "root idea." Sometime before he started, Dickens wrote to Forster: "A man feigning to be dead, and *being* dead to all intents and purposes external to himself, and for years retaining the singular view of life and character so imparted, would be a good leading incident for a story." So it might: the only trouble would be how to get him dead. Dickens's solution of the difficulty is as dull and wooden as a tired brain could make it. John Harmon, returning to England as heir to a great fortune, decided to be dead in order to "get a line" on the unknown girl whom his deceased father wanted him to marry. Dickens then proceeds to drown and half drown various people in the Thames with lots of melodrama, midnight fog, and riverside stuff. Again he had to take his readers sharply to task in case they would think themselves too smart in fishing out their real John Harmon from the river. So Dickens added a postscript to the book with a reproof to such readers. "I foresaw," he said, " the likelihood that a certain class of readers would suppose that I was at great pains to conceal exactly what I was at great pains to suggest: namely that Mr. John Harmon was not slain and Mr. John Rokesmith was he." Dickens adds that "an artist may perhaps be trusted to know what he is about in his vocation, if his readers will concede him a little patience." This is certainly a comfortable doctrine for those who write books, as it dispenses with the reader's opinion altogether.

More than that. In the construction of most of Dickens's books the current of the narrative springs not from one source but from several. It begins with a particular scene and a particular group of people. Then it starts over again, more than once, perhaps, with other scenes and other people – at first totally without connection. Gradually the streams come together, the currents at last unite in one swift flood moving with the power of all. This form of narration has its merits and defects, as already said. It lacks the simple, breathless interest of the unified narrative. But it lasts longer and allows for a greater width and diversity.

But in *Our Mutual Friend* the streams have no connection and never come together in any really convincing way. Dickens's construction of the story is like the work of a tailor making a coat of odd pieces which he had in the shop. Apart from the wet and dripping John Harmon, he had thought of the idea of two people marrying one another each for the other's money and neither really having any; and he had thought of the idea of new people in society (what we now call, especially in English, *nouveaux riches*). These two ideas fuse together to make the Veneerings and the Mr. and Mrs. Lammle of the story. But with John Harmon, his fortune, and his bride, they never connect at all. The effect (speaking with a little exaggeration) is much as if one told the story of Conan Doyle's Brigadier Gerard and the story of Stevenson's Dr. Jekyll and Mr. Hyde in alternate chapters, and then in the last chapter explained that the Brigadier Gerard was a cousin to Dr. Jekyll.

Even that wouldn't have been fatal if the rest were there. One could mix up Mr. Pickwick and David Copperfield half and half and make an agreeable mixture (with a final chapter perhaps to explain that David was Mr. Pickwick's son). But in *Our Mutual Friend* – alone among Dickens's sustained stories – the people as a lot are not agreeable, not likable. They are on the whole a mean, disagreeable lot. Now Dickens's people, crooks, freaks, and villains included, live upon their charm. That was, as said elsewhere, the very magic of his genius. Alfred Jingle was a crook and a cheat: and we like him. We also are drawn to the major Pawkins (of New Eden in *Martin Chuzzlewit*) who "had a most distinguished genius for swindling, who could start a bank or negotiate a loan or form a land jobbing company with any gifted creature in the union." We feel we'd like to meet him. Even Wackford Squeers, endowed apparently with every brutal instinct of the bully and the child beater, somehow weaves around his evil character an atmosphere of amusement. One good hiding for the sake of poetic justice squares his account. Only here and there across the pages of Dickens squirms – designedly on the writer's part – the evil figure of a Bill Sikes, or a Jonas Chuzzlewit, unredeemed and hideous. All the rest are caught up into the atmosphere that rarefies evil into human kindliness.

But this only genius can achieve; and in *Our Mutual Friend* genius was, for the time, at any rate, wanting. Hence the characters are nearly all disagreeable and offensive. The Veneerings and all their group are either idiots or horrors. The "Barnacles" of *Little Dorrit* who plunder and mystify the British people are amusing and appealing. The similar people in the Veneering group are just a pack of rascals. Or take the case of Silas Wegg with the wooden leg, who read to Mr. Boffin "the decline and fall of the Rooshan empire." Here, indeed, should have been – he began as being – a true Dickens character. But the tired brain and the faltering hand of his creator cannot hold him up. Wegg becomes a loathsome creature, the fun all out of him. Even Dickens turns against him, intensifies his evil side, and, quite undesignedly, spoils him. Or take the incidental Mr. Venus with his little shop of skeletons, articulated joints, and pickled specimens. He arose thus. While Dickens was writing the story, Marcus Stone, the illustrator, told him about finding such a shop and such a trade in some odd corner of London. So Dickens must needs drop him into the story. Or take the Jew, the venerable Mr. Riah. Someone had complained to Dickens about his having vilified the Jewish race in the person of old Fagin in *Oliver Twist.* So, as a compensation, in goes the venerable Mr. Riah, beard, gabardine, speech, and all, right out of the Old Testament. What more could the Jews ask than that?

One might say that this is the method of the *Pickwick Papers.* It is. But it can be used only under inspiration. It is like Edward Longshanks' sword. You need Edward Longshanks to use it.

What then was wrong? Is it that Dickens was getting old? And what light does it throw upon the perennial "old man" question? Is it true that men succeed when they are young by the force of their mind and the power of their body, and later on in their old age encumber the offices of honour and emolument, monopolize through the prestige of what once was theirs the pages of the press and the drama, the dead ashes of extinct genius choking the living fires below? Is the world being ruined by "venerable" statesmen, wars lost by "veteran" generals, and spiritual life numbed by "venerable" prelates? *Si jeunesse savait, si vieillesse pouvait!* – or should it be, *Si jeunesse pouvait, si vieillesse savait?* If youth only had a chance or old age any brains.

It would seem that, in Charles Dickens's case, all the reasons indicated combined to lower the character of his work, whether in a temporary eclipse or in a permanent darkness: we cannot now tell. His incessant overwork and overstrain, the editing, the readings, his broken home, his restless life all told against him.

Added to all this, his writing of his last finished book was rudely affected by the special and terrible shock received by him as one of the passengers in the appalling railroad accident at Staplehurst (June 9, 1865).

He himself escaped with only a severe shaking up, but the harrowing scenes of which he was an eyewitness made a terrible and lasting shock upon his system. The haunting recollection that would not leave him added one more item to the distress of mind and weariness of body under which he sought to carry on his work.

Chapter Eleven

THE SECOND VISIT TO AMERICA

A Quarter Century Later – Dickens and Dollars – Mark Twain Listens to Charles Dickens

AT THE CLOSE OF HIS LABOURS ON *OUR MUTUAL FRIEND* Dickens found himself greatly exhausted in mind and body. He seems, moreover, to have been haunted during his remaining years with the idea that his literary powers were waning. No fading beauty questioning the looking-glass suffers more keenly than the author drowsing toward old age. With Dickens it was mainly the fatigue of overstrain. But the sense of apprehension was no less.

Nor could his labour stop. He had to busy himself at once with the Christmas number of his magazine. To his delight it turned out a great success. As usual it bore a special title – *Doctor Marigold's Prescriptions* – and Dickens himself contributed a considerable part of it. At the time *Doctor Marigold*, though forgotten now, was a decided success. Dickens used it from now on as one of his reading pieces for the platform. In the commercial sense this Christmas number and the one that followed, *Mugby Junction*, 1866, were among Dickens's greatest successes. *Mugby Junction* sold a quarter of a million copies, – an interesting comparison with the fifteen thousand of *A Christmas Carol*. Cheap literature (it sold for twopence) was coming into its own.

Meantime, with the New Year (1866) Dickens plunged again into his public readings. This time he cut himself loose entirely from the business management and the hazard of profit and loss. He accepted an out-and-out fee of £50 per lecture for the thirty that made the series. The tour began early in the year, ended in June, and included a visit to Ireland and Scotland. It was a vast success, much helped by the able management of George Dolby, henceforth a tower of strength for Dickens in his public work. In the book which Dolby afterwards wrote, about his association with Dickens, he tells us that the gross receipts of this tour were nearly £5,000, leaving a handsome profit for the firm (Messrs. Chappell of London) who financed it.

The readings met everywhere with the same enthusiasm, the same tumultuous success. Any failing there may have been in Dickens's literary power had no effect upon his histrionic art. But it was the same old story of exhaustion and fatigue. From Liverpool he wrote "the enthusiasm has been unbounded. On Friday night I quite astonished myself: but I was taken so faint afterwards that they laid me on a sofa in the hall for half an hour. I attribute it to my distressing inability to sleep at night."

Partly to be near his work and partly from sheer restlessness Dickens made his usual spring migration to a London house (No. 6 Southwick Place). With the departure of his children into the world, Gad's Hill was not the family centre it had been at first. Only when at intervals the boys came back from school and from the sea it turned again into a home like that of earlier years in London. At such intervals the boys published a family newspaper, the *Gad's Hill Gazette*, purporting to be sold for twopence.

With the public readings went a few public appearances such as the dinners to the Dramatic Equestrian and Musical Fund (February 14, 1866) and the Royal General Theatrical Fund (March 28, 1866). Assistance to the cause of arts and letters and the drama always appealed strongly to Dickens. He was ever ready to take the chair at such gatherings, and his wonderful eloquence in appeal was a valuable asset to them. But society at large he avoided. He was of too self-centred, too dominant a temperament for the ordinary give-and-take of social life.

Dolby arranged and conducted certain further readings. But there was now larger game to be seen on the horizon. For some time past suggestions had been made for visiting America in a professional way. Dickens's circle of leaders had grown enormously in that country. His experiment of publishing a story direct in New York (*The Haunted Man*) was followed by similar publication of two others.

Then, as now, America valued genius more – in terms of dollars and cents – than did the Old World. The great upheaval of the Civil War had sunk into oblivion all the animosities that had grown out of Dickens's tour of 1842. Everything was forgiven and forgotten, and slavery itself was no longer there.

The time was ripe for a great artistic and financial success. Dickens's intimates – Wills, Forster, and the rest – sought to dissuade him. They knew too well the risks – one might almost say the certainties – involved for Dickens's broken constitution. It was in vain. The bait was too tempting, and Dickens, in any case, measured consequences. There was a farewell dinner at the Freemasons Tavern (November 2) and he sailed (November 9, 1867) on the *Cuba*, outward bound from Liverpool to Boston.

Charles Dickens's second American pilgrimage began with his landing in Boston in November of 1867 and ended with his departure from New York on April 22, 1868. The whole of the intervening time, with one brief and unintentional cessation, was filled with his work on the platform. The state of his health compelled him to forego all social engagements and all external activities. The tour as originally planned was to have extended into the Southern states and westward to the Mississippi. But in the sequel this proved impossible, and, in a financial sense, unnecessary.

The circumstances of Dickens's second visit to America differed greatly from those of the first. In 1842 he came with all the exuberance of youthful energy and early success, at a time when celebrity was still new enough to be a constant joy. Moreover, he was, or was prepared to be, intensely interested in America. Like all the people of his generation, he marvelled at the rise of this wonderful new republic where civilization was spreading in a flood over a vast new continent. Like many of his generation, he had idealized the republic from a distance. There is a certain type of human who is a radical when among conservatives, and a republican when living under a monarchy; who despises the forms and ceremonies of the Old World until he finds himself where they don't exist and becomes a loyal and ardent royalist when outside of the domain of kingship. There is no reference here to the revolutionist who conspires to destroy the government under which he lives: but only to the peaceful citizen who prefers the luxury of discontent to the subservience of approval.

Charles Dickens and His Former American Acquaintances

Dickens himself has often portrayed this type of mind. Mr. Jerry Cruncher, the body-snatcher of *A Tale of Two Cities*, is a fine atheist till he gets to France, where they all are.

So was Dickens a first-class radical till he got to America, where they all were. He despised all hereditary and clan privileges, all powers and distinctions, precedence and formalities. But when he got to a country where these things did not exist and where human nature and human impulses ran riot without the restraint of ancient custom, it seemed to him that he was lost in a sea of vulgarity. As a consequence, Dickens, on his first visit, as already seen, felt bitterly disillusioned with America.

But that does not alter the fact that in 1842 he came to it with intense interest, intense eagerness, intense enjoyment. The mingled admirations and angers of his first visit were at least an acknowledgment of the importance and interest of America. His attitude of 1842 might be thought insulting, but it was at least complimentary in its intensity.

Far more deprecating in reality was his attitude towards his second visit. When he came in 1867 he took not the faintest interest in the place. He didn't care whether he saw much of it, any of it, or none of it; whether he went to many cities or a few; whether he visited Canada or cut it out. His wearied energies and his excited mind left him without any interest in the country in which he moved. At this period the great epic struggle of the Civil War had just drawn to a close. Dickens had had time to realize that after all the Jefferson Bricks and the Major Pawkinses and all the other oddities and crooks of *Martin Chuzzlewit* were a terrible people when in arms: that the South might have nourished the evil institution on which he had poured the burning contempt of his indignation, but that it had paid for its sins with a nobility of sacrifice on the field never excelled in history.

But Dickens thought nothing of these things. He had come to America to make money, and his thoughts never wandered far from the box office: this and the personal and artistic interest in his own performances filled all his mind. He chafed to begin, and counted the days and nights till he could end. The weariness of mind and brain, the breaking energy and the ill-health which pursued him in these closing years, no doubt explain it all. The Fates were whispering already and holding the open shears close to the thread of life. It is no cause for blame that Dickens took so little interest in America and had no vision to see it. But of the facts there is no doubt. We have only to open the pages of the letters that he sent home to his daughter and to Miss Hogarth to realize his frame of mind.

"Parker House, Boston

"Nov., 21st, 1867.

"I arrived here on Monday night after a very slow passage from Halifax against head winds. All the tickets for the first four readings were sold immediately on their being issued."

"Nov. 25, 1867.

"I am constantly chafing at not having begun tonight instead of this night week. The tickets being all sold for next week and no other announcement being yet made there is nothing new in that way to tell of. Dolby" (Dickens's manager, as already seen) "is over in New York, where we are at our wits' end to keep the tickets out of the hands of speculators.... My anxiety to get to work is greater than I can express because time seems to be making no movement towards home until I can be reading hard. Then I shall begin to count and count the upwards steps to May."

This wearied frame of mind is revealed in practically all of the letters that follow. On November 5th he writes to his eldest son from Boston:

"The tickets for the first four readings here were all sold immediately and many are selling at a large premium. The tickets for the first four readings in New York were on sale yesterday and were all sold in a few hours. The receipts were very large indeed, but engagements of any kind and every kind I steadily refuse, being resolved to take what is to be taken myself."

This same strain of weariness and of eagerness to be at home follows through all of Dickens's correspondence from America in the ensuing months. It is broken only with remarks on the tremendous success of his lectures, the public enthusiasm, and the personal kindness which he met everywhere, and the incessant fatigue and illness which pursued him. Of the country itself, even at this moment of its history when emerging from the titanic and heroic struggle of the war – nothing, or practically nothing.

Dolby himself, the manager, seems to have played a hero's part. He took all Dickens's troubles and difficulties on his broad shoulders and carried them gaily along. He fought against the speculators that haunted the box office, the press agents, the bores, and the nuisances who would have persecuted his suffering celebrity. Dickens's one prayer was for rest and peace, and as far as could be, Dolby, aided by the kindliness of sympathetic friends, contrived it for him.

"The Bostonians," writes Dickens, "having been duly informed that I wish to be quiet, really leave me as much so as I should be in Manchester or Liverpool."

"I have been in bed all day" (New York, December 20) "till two o'clock and here I am now at three o'clock, a little better. But I am not fit to read and I must read tonight." ...

"We arrived here" (Philadelphia) "last night" (January 13, 1868). "... This is one of the immense American hotels (it is called the Continental) but I find myself just as quiet here as elsewhere.... My cold is no better.... If I could only get to the point of being able to hold up my head and dispense with my pocket handkerchief for five minutes, I should be all right."

"The people" (this is New York, January 15th) "are exceedingly kind and considerate and desire to be most hospitable beside. But I cannot accept hospitality and never go out, except at Boston, or I should not be fit for the labour." …

"My cold sticks to me" (January 21st) "and I can scarcely exaggerate what I sometimes undergo from sleeplessness."

Only now and then does this melancholy cloud of exhaustion and illness and overwork lift for a little while: and then more by the stimulus of anything that seems like the routine of his life at home than the interest in anything that he saw abroad. As has already been seen, the exercise of active walking was throughout Dickens's life his favourite pastime and restorative. Even in his present condition he turned to it whenever possible.

"Dolby and Osgood," he writes to Miss Hogarth from Baltimore at the end of January, "who do the most ridiculous things to keep me in spirits (I am often very heavy and rarely sleep much) have decided to have a walking match at Boston on Saturday Feb. 29th. Beginning this design in joke they have become tremendously in earnest, and Dolby has actually sent home (much to his opponent's terror) for a pair of seamless socks to walk in. Our men are hugely excited on the subject and continually make bets on 'the men.' Fields and I are to walk out six miles and the men are to turn and walk round us. Neither of them has the least idea what twelve miles at a pace is. Being requested by both to give them a 'breather' yesterday I gave them a stiff one of five miles in the snow, half the distance up hill. I took them at the pace of four miles and a half an hour, and you never saw such objects when they got back. …"

The walking match, moreover, actually came off as planned when Dickens returned to Boston at the end of February. "The walking match," he writes, "came off on Saturday, over tremendously difficult ground, against a biting wind and through deep snow-wreaths. It was so cold, too, that our hair, beards, eyelashes, eyebrows, were frozen hard and hung with icicles. … In the evening I gave a very splendid dinner, eighteen covers, most magnificent flowers, such table decoration as was never seen in these parts. The whole thing was a great success, and everybody was delighted. I am holiday-making until Friday."

The reason for this break in the clouds of depression was that Dickens had had to stop lecturing. American politics had got in his way. The impeachment of President Johnson in connection with the reconstruction policy had set the country in a turmoil of excitement. Not even Charles Dickens's overwhelming popularity could keep an audience quiet in their seats.

Dickens himself, needless to say, did not share in the excitement. "Nothing in this country lasts long," he wrote to his sister-in-law, "and I think the public may be heartily tired at the president's name by March 9th when I read at a considerable distance from here. So behold me with a whole week's holiday in view."

The tour was originally planned to include an extended journey westward to the Mississippi and the South, to visit Canada and Nova Scotia. But the condition of his health, and the fact that audiences were obtainable anywhere in shoals, without hunting for them, somewhat contracted the original plan. As it was, he lectured in Boston and in New York many times in each of these cities and in various New England centres, in Philadelphia, Baltimore, and Washington: then westward to Syracuse, Rochester, and Buffalo; from Buffalo he allowed himself a two days' visit to Niagara, his only glimpse of the newly formed Dominion of Canada (a formation which he had probably not remarked), and then his farewell appearances in Boston and New York.

The lectures were everywhere an overwhelming, a colossal success. "Success last night beyond description and exaggeration," he wrote to his son Charles after the first reading in Boston. "The whole city is quite frantic about it today and it is impossible that prospects could be more brilliant." As Dickens had himself anticipated, the audiences who were prepared to be enthusiastic over the mere notion of hearing Dickens actually read from his own works, passed from enthusiasm to delight when they found that "reading" was but a feeble name for what he actually did. "They were accustomed," he said, "to mere readings out of a book and I am inclined to think that the excitement will increase when I shall have begun." The "lectures," of course, like those already given in England, were utterly different from men "reading out of a book." Dickens gave a dramatic rendering of the scenes described, in which every tone and gesture, every movement of the features and every expression of the eye was calculated with the highest art to call forth a vision of the thing portrayed. The "pieces" that he selected were chiefly the Trial Scene from *Pickwick*, Doctor Marigold, the storm scene from *Copperfield*, and, more than anything else perhaps, *A Christmas Carol*, and whether known already by the auditors or not, the effect was everywhere the same magnetic appeal. The excitement, as he had foreseen, did increase. The success was everywhere the same. In New York the people clamoured in thousands for seats. Dolby, said Dickens, had become the most unpopular man in the United States because he could not put four thousand people into a hall meant for two thousand. Before his appearance in Brooklyn the ticket speculators, such was their literary enthusiasm, lay out all night on mattresses sucking bottles of whisky to keep them warm for the opening sale. The receipts were enormous: £500 sterling in a single night in New York: £1,300 per week clear profit to Dickens in Boston. These were the days of greenbacks and small denominations, and Dolby went about with what looked like great bundles of paper. The final gross receipts reached $228,000. Dickens's own profits on the tour, after deducting all commissions, all expenses, and all money which he previously spent in America, and converting the balance from greenbacks to sterling – as Dickens with no faith in anything American hastened to do even at a discount of 40 per cent – amounted to £19,000.

In Washington President Andrew Johnson – impeachment or not – took a whole row of seats every night of Dickens's appearance.

At Washington Dickens relaxed on one or two occasions his self-imposed avoidance of hospitality. He writes on February 4, 1868, to his sister-in-law, "I dined (against my rules) with Charles Sumner on Sunday, he having been an old friend of mine. Mr. Secretary Staunton" (War Minister) "was there. He is a man of very remarkable memory and famous for his acquaintance with the minutest details of my books. Give him a passage anywhere and he will instantly cap it and go on with the context. He was commander-in-chief of all the Northern forces concentrated here, and never went to sleep at night without first reading something from my books which were always with him."

Dolby himself in his book on Charles Dickens has left us a glowing account of the tour. Even judged by the statements of the harassed and overwrought lecturer, Dolby was a marvel of good-nature and a tower of strength. The papers reviled him: he passed it off with a laugh; in Buffalo a sheriff's officer of the Inland Revenue department undertook to forbid the lecture for the want of a license. Dolby, not understanding that all the man wanted was "his share," annihilated him by nourishing a special authorization from the head of the department at Washington. "Jerusalem!" said the discomfited sheriff, "I'm beat." On which Dolby took him into the bar and put a pint of champagne into him. Dolby understood America if Dickens didn't. On another occasion (it was at one of the Boston lectures) Dolby had to deal with a man who left the hall in a fit of anger, because he said that Dickens's presentation "was no more like Sam Weller than a cow." And once, later on, he had to assist in taking out of the hall a young girl reduced to a passion of hysterical tears by the rendering of Tiny Tim.

Only now and then did Dickens's health and energy allow him to carry on any of the visits and investigations which had occupied so much of his time in his earlier American tour. But his abiding interest in the treatment of crime and criminals led him while at Baltimore to accept the invitation of the Governor of Maryland to visit the penitentiary. Dolby, who went with Dickens, gives a long and interesting account of their visit, which seems to have restored Dickens for a moment to his old inquiring self. Some of the details given are perhaps of greater interest in our own day than in his.

"In one large carpenter's workshop there were as many as fifty men (and amongst them half a dozen men convicted of murder) busily engaged making door-frames, panels for doors, window-frames, etc., having the free use of the usual carpenters' tools and with no guard over them other than one warder (in plain clothes and smoking cigars all the time) perched up at a high desk with no other means of defense, in the event of an *émeute* than one six-barrelled revolver.... On enquiry, we ascertained that the warden was not placed there so much for the purpose of preserving order as to prevent the prisoners from making an improper use of the materials supplied to them for their trade ... for as a result of experience, it had been discovered that these worthies applied such materials on the sly to the manufacturing of skeleton keys, with which they supplied their friends in the burglary trade 'outside' on visiting days."

The long-term prisoners and the murderers we are told "had a capital bill of fare – cocoa coffee or tea with a choice of fish and bread and butter for breakfast: soup and meat for dinner: and cocoa coffee or tea with bread and butter for supper." The murderers, it appeared, were never executed, public feeling being against it; and practically all the other prisoners were "pardoned" – if only ten minutes before their sentence ended – so as not to lose their votes to their political party.

This Utopian establishment was declared by Dickens to be less of a prison than "a huge hydropathic establishment without the privilege of going out for a walk." The governor was delighted with the compliment.

One other of these inquiries into crime in all its aspects which always fascinated Dickens occurred while at Boston.

Since his first visit to the city there had occurred (1840) at Harvard University the appalling crime of Professor Webster, who had murdered his colleague Professor Parkman and burnt his remains in the laboratory furnace. The crime is remembered to this day with a shudder. When a theologian burns a theologian, that is history. But when a professor burns a professor, that is "*wieder was anders*." Yet few of us would for that reason want to go to see the actual furnace where he did it. Yet such was Dickens. He went to see the furnace, just as in Italy he went to see the man have his head cut off by the guillotine. It was a queer taste. If it is said that it was necessary in order to write books, some of us would feel that we would rather write on gardening. But Dickens went, and he writes (January 12, 1868) to his fellow crime expert Wilkie Collins:

"Being at Boston last Sunday, I took it into my head to go over the medical school, and survey the holes and corners in which that extraordinary murder was done by Webster. There was the furnace – stinking horribly, as if the dismembered pieces were still inside it – and there are all the grim spouts, and sinks, and chemical appliances, and what not. At dinner, afterwards, Longfellow told me a terrific story. He dined with Webster within a year of the murder, one of the party of ten or twelve. As they sat at their wine, Webster suddenly ordered the lights to be turned out, and a bowl of some burning mineral to be placed on the table, that the guests might see how ghostly it made them look. As each man stared at all the rest in the weird light, all were horrified to see Webster *with a rope round his neck*, holding it up, over the bowl, with his head jerked on one side, and his tongue lolled out, representing a man being hanged!"

One minor incident of Dickens's lecture tour may be cited as not without interest in the history of letters. Among the audience at one of his New York lectures at Christmas time (December 23, 1867) sat a robust, vigorous young man of thirty-two, with a shock of reddish hair and a blue eye with something of the arresting power of Dickens's own glance. This was Mr. Samuel L. Clemens who had just had a sudden rise to literary success as "Mark

Twain" almost as phenomenal as that of Boz. Mark Twain had just returned from his immortal European tour as an "Innocent Abroad." The travel papers which he had written for the press (the book was not yet out) had carried him deservedly to the crest of the wave of popularity. Mark Twain also was a lecturer, though as yet his appearances had been confined to one wild tumult of success in San Francisco, a tour of the California mining camps, and one evening – before the *Quaker City* sailed – at the Cooper Union in New York, where an audience of "deadheads" had paid their way in uproarious laughter. Within the years immediately following, Mark Twain was to prove the only rival of Charles Dickens on the platform, in point of popularity and success. Their methods and their conception of lecturing were very different. Dickens on the platform acted – he threw himself into the characters he portrayed. He was Mr. Weller, he was Bill Sikes, he was Tiny Tim. Mark Twain was always Mark Twain: it was not his characters that convulsed the audience, it was "Mark."

There seems to be no record of Dickens's having heard of Mark Twain, or having even later read his books. In point of date, he could easily have done so, for before he died in 1870 the *Innocents Abroad* (published in July, 1869) was selling round the world. But it is more than likely that he knew nothing of the young man from the West who was to rival him.

We may well imagine with what absorption Mark Twain listened to Dickens. But if we did we should be wrong. For though Mark Twain was absorbed that night it was not with Charles Dickens. Beside him sat a sweet-faced girl whose gentle fragility contrasted with his own rude health and energy. The beautiful love story which adorned Mark Twain's life till it ended at the grave began that night. The girl was Olivia Langdon, with whose picture in a miniature young Clemens while in the Quaker City had fallen irretrievably in love. Now at last he had met her, and this evening was their first night out together.

So, like ships that pass in the night, the life orbits of these two men, who did more than any others of their century to bring to saddened hearts and dull lives the priceless gift of laughter – met and parted. A few years later, when Mark Twain lectured in London (1873) with a success second only to that of his senior in New York, Dickens was gone.

The strain of the evening appearances, the two hours easy of intense concentrated effort on the platform was terrible and increasing. But Dickens would not give in. Dolby tells us how Senator Sumner, coming to see Dickens one afternoon in Washington, was shocked by his condition. "Surely, Mr. Dolby," protested the senator, "you are not going to allow Mr. Dickens to read tonight?" Dolby assured him that if Dickens had determined to read, nothing but death would stop him. And as usual, when the hour for the platform came, by some singular exercise of internal will power his voice and strength came back to him.

"Mr. Dickens's health," writes Dolby, after their return to New England from the Western tour, "was becoming a graver source of anxiety every day." From Portland, Maine, he himself wrote at the end of March (1868) to Miss Hogarth, "I have coughed from two or three in the morning until five or six, and have been absolutely sleepless. I have no appetite beside and no taste."

The rest of the tour (the farewell appearances in Boston and New York) was a struggle against time, a fight against collapse. At Boston, where Dickens felt more at home than anywhere else in America, he rallied somewhat to take occasional walks by the sea and to gather strength for the strain of the final lectures. Each fresh effort left him prostrate again, without sleep or appetite. But he found the strength for it all.

One great occasion still remained for which fortunately he was able to find the strength and energy. This was the press dinner arranged in his honour at Delmonico's in New York on April 18, 1868. It was, as said, a great occasion, in the sheer point of speech-making, a terrific occasion. It was intended as an expression of farewell on behalf of America, and with over two hundred press-men trained in the art of expression to say it, the farewell was said at full length. Horace Greeley of the *Tribune* took the chair with the guest of the evening on his right. Among those present whose names are still with us today were George William

Curtis, Charles Eliot Norton, Charles Nordhoff, Thomas Nast, J.A. Lippincott, and S.S. McClure. There were representatives of all the great journals of New England and the Eastern states, and letters of regrets and congratulations from Oliver Wendell Holmes, Thurlow Weed, and a list of other celebrities. And speeches, speeches, speeches! Thirty pages of close print as chronicled in the records – and when the speeches were done, then came the "remarks" of Professor Youmans. It was like a professor to reserve that for them! But what did they care? They were out for a night of fun! And the speeches in the record are liberally punctuated with "Hear, hear!", "Applause," "Bravo, bravo," "Tremendous applause!", "Laughter," "Tumultuous applause, the company rising to its feet and greeting the sentiment with enthusiasm." These were the days before the eighteenth amendment to the Constitution turned an American banquet into the gloomy ordeal that we have known since.

Dickens spoke with his accustomed power and charm. He laid stress on the friendship of England and America. "It would be better for the globe," he said, "to be ruined by an earthquake, fired by a comet, overrun by an iceberg and abandoned to the arctic fox and bear than that it should present the spectacle of those two great nations, each of whom has, in its own way and hour, striven so hard for freedom, ever again being arrayed the one against the other." This, in fact, was the sentiment that brought the united audience to "its" feet.

But Dickens said more on the occasion than this noble sentiment. He realized, now that he about to say good-bye, how warm had been his welcome; with what honour he had been acclaimed; with what enthusiasm he had been heard; with what hospitality he had been received; and with what considerate good feeling he had been spared. He realized this and decided to make the *amende honorable* for the past, to blot out with a generous repudiation the record of the *American Notes* and *Martin Chuzzlewit.* In reality there was no need. Americans had long since forgotten and forgiven. There was nothing left in the pages but laughter. But Dickens wanted to set it all right forever. So he said:

"But what I have intended, what I have resolved upon is, on my return to England, in my own person, in my own Journal, to bear, for the behoof of my countrymen, such testimony to the gigantic changes in this country as I have hinted at to-night. Also, to record that wherever I have been, in the smallest places equally with the largest, I have been received with unsurpassable politeness, delicacy, sweet temper, hospitality, consideration, and with unsurpassable respect for the privacy daily enforced upon me by the nature of my avocation here, and the state of my health. This testimony, so long as I live, and so long as my descendants have any legal right in my books, I shall cause to be republished, as an appendix to every copy of those two books of mine in which I have referred to America. And this I will do and cause to be done, not in mere love and thankfulness, but because I regard it as an act of plain justice and honor."

The testimony when given consisted in the publication of all the parts of his speech which dealt with the question as an appendix to every copy – as far as he could control it – of all future editions of the two American books.

In return Horace Greeley of the *Tribune* followed suit with a tribute to Dickens and a warm acknowledgment of his "apology." "As for those old darts of offence which have rankled so long in the wounds of a few of us, he drew them out with a deft and tender hand, and salved the injury with the unction of a little national flattery. We do not know that he was under any obligation to do this but we are glad that he has done it, for we would have him leave none but warm friends here, and we trust that when the ship bears him away, the American people will wish him with entire unanimity God-speed and long life and happiness."

Dickens lectures with great difficulty and pain, one last time (April 20, 1868), and then the tour was over. In April he sailed from New York.

On the voyage home there was nothing, for Dickens at least, of the jollity and the organized fun of the voyage of June, 1842, with the "United Vagabonds' Club" to keep the ship in a roar. This time Dickens kept to his cabin, while the ship drove in a "record" passage before an Atlantic storm. In eight days the anchor was dropped in Queenstown Harbour.

Even more than the farewell American oration, Dickens may well have valued the warmth of the local greeting of his return. The villagers of Higham (his railway station) planned to meet him and to draw his carriage to Gad's Hill. Circumvented in this by Dickens going by another station, they turned out, as he came along, in carts and in gigs and on foot, and he reached home surrounded by a tumultuous escort in a little forest of flags. Next day the parish church rang a peal of bells after service in honour of his return home.

Chapter Twelve

CLOSING IN – THE CLOSE

1870

Last Readings – "Edwin Drood" – Death

DICKENS REACHED HOME AFTER HIS AMERICAN tour in May of 1868. The voyage had greatly relieved and restored him. After a few days' rest at Gad's Hill he was back in his editorial chair in London busy with *All the Year Round.* There were to be no more Christmas numbers, as he had decided that the novelty of them had worn off, but there was much to do in the conduct of the magazine itself. Wills the sub-editor was laid off by an accident and presently had to resign and Charles Dickens Junior became the sub-editor of the journal for the last two years of his father's life. He himself has left his tribute to the constant assiduity of Dickens in his work as editor. "I hardly remember a week," he says, "in which, after making up the number in London, he did not devote the two or three succeeding hours to going with utmost care over the proof of each article selected. Even when, on his absence from town on reading tours, he had to be content to leave some of the proofs to me, his instructions as to the manner in which they were to be dealt with were so precise and definite that any work done upon them might still almost be said to be his own."

As if he feared that even with the work of editing on his hands this summer (1868) would be too full of rest, Dickens undertook the ridiculous task of sorting out for publication a litter of manuscripts called the "Religious Opinions of the Rev. Chauncey Hare Townsend." The writer was a deceased friend who had imposed this task in his will. Dickens wrote a preface for the "Religious Opinions." The Estate paid him £1,000. It seems doubtful if the opinions were worth it.

In this summer of rest appeared at Gad's Hill as visitors the American Longfellow and his daughters; the Eliot Nortons from Boston, and other random visitors. A further distraction was a short trip to Paris in the summer.

Already Dickens was planning a new book and making notes of varying titles dealing with disappearance and mystery, and murder that presently fashioned themselves into the words *The Mystery of Edwin Drood.* There were to be a boy and a girl in it "pledged to be married and then going apart." What else was to happen, he had not yet quite settled.

But the work on the new book was delayed in order that Dickens might undertake what he promised himself should be the last of his series of readings – a trip designed to embrace the principal cities of England and Scotland and to consist of one hundred appearances.

The arrangement had been made before he left England for America. When he came back, his shattered health should have warned him against new efforts. He was, and he must have known it, a broken man, but he could not resist the temptation of the profits of the proposed tour.

The offer was magnificent – over and above all expenses, £8,000 for a hundred readings, with no share of the risk and no trouble of management.

Dickens could not resist. The figures were too tempting. It was like entering a treasure cave. The receipts at one of the early lectures totalled more than four hundred pounds. "If all goes well," wrote Dickens, "I shall have made of these readings £28,000 in a year and a half." His biographers unite in telling us that his eagerness for money arose from his anxieties for the future of his children. It may be so; but even then the anxiety was itself inordinate and overstrained – a mark of his condition. His children were all capable young people either already out in the world for themselves or close to it. Dickens himself was already rich. Reckoned on an ordinary commercial basis, as apart from the appraisal of an inheritance tax, he was "worth" more than a hundred thousand pounds. Without any readings at all, and with only a leisurely use of his pen, he had an income from book writing at his hand, over and above his investments, of easily £10,000 a year. The *Edwin Drood* sales – even as far as it had gone – represented about £16,000. Over and above this was his salary of £500 on *All the Year Round* and his share – three quarters of the profits from it. All this at a time and at a range of prices when people lived in England comfortably on £500 a year, and lived like princes on £2,000.

It was characteristic also of Dickens's condition that he was anxious to touch up, to intensify the tenor of his readings. There must be no falling off in his success, no danger of monotony. Not even the success of the past could reassure his foreboding mind. He must have something new – more dramatic, more melodramatic than before. He must have crime – murder. So he worked up the murder scene of the book *Oliver Twist*, the killing of Nancy by Bill Sikes and the murderer haunted by his crime, an unparalleled presentation of horror. He himself was absorbed and fascinated with the sheer terror of it. "I have no doubt," he wrote, "that I could perfectly petrify an audience by carrying out the notion I have of the way of rendering it. But whether the impression would not be so horrible as to keep them away another time is what I cannot satisfy myself upon."

He wanted murder. But he didn't want to kill the box office.

So the tour began – with the long railway journeys; the crowded halls; the roars of laughter and the thrills of terror; the crowning tumults of applause with which Dickens's public was ushering him off the stage of the world.

REDUCED FACSIMILES OF DRAWINGS BY DICKENS

There was no doubt of its success – and above all of the fascinating horror of Dickens's murder scene. We cannot tell now how Dickens acted it. There is no record to call to our eyes what those people saw. But some terrible and uncanny power must have gone from Dickens, as Sikes the murderer, to clutch his audience by the throat. At one place – it was at Clifton – though the room was not hot, for it was winter – twenty of the women of the audience fainted and were carried out rigid and unconscious. Dickens himself tells in a letter of a man who as he finished the murder scene, sat on the platform, motionless, with every vestige of colour gone from his face, his eyes staring in front of him in the wildest way.

But the price that Dickens was paying for this artistic success was his own life. He was exhausted. He was sleepless. He lay for hours upon sofas waiting for strength. His sight failed. At times on the street he could see only the half of the letters on the shops – the top, not the bottom. Words slipped from him. Gaps opened in his memory. His hands groped wrongly in the air for things elsewhere. If he wished to lay his left hand on the table he must look first where it was to go. At times he could not raise his hand up to his head. His left foot was a dead weight. This was paralysis – cerebral haemorrhage – approaching – imminent. As Dickens stood upon the lecture platform there was a shrouded figure standing behind him waiting to strike.... And the blow was coming....

For the moment it was deferred. An authoritative medical man of the real sort – it was Sir Thomas Watson – dragged him off the platform with a signed certificate that for the time saved Dickens's life. This was in April of 1869.

The tour as planned was never completed. But with medical permission Dickens gave twelve more readings, in London, without the fatigue of travel, in the opening months of 1870. A doctor sat at his side. A great crowd filled St. James's Hall for every occasion. Then at last, on a March evening in 1870, Dickens reached his final reading. This time he left aside the murder. He read from *A Christmas Carol* and then from *Pickwick.* Where he had begun he ended.

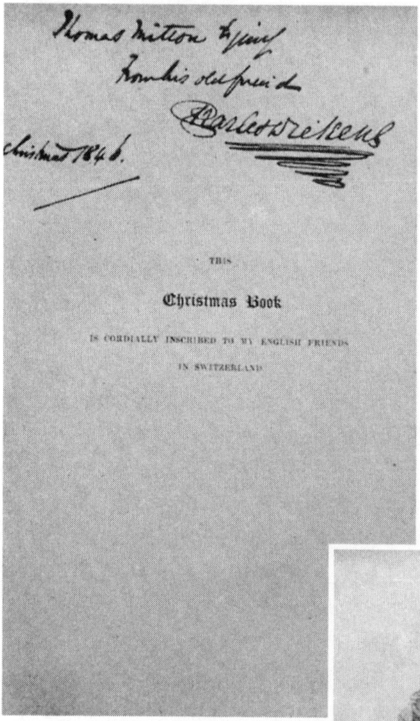

Inscription
Presentation inscription
to Thomas Milton, Esq.,
in Dickens's
The Battle of Life

Martin Chuzzlewit
Illustration by
Phiz
(Hablôt K. Browne)

As he finished he closed the volume of *Pickwick* and spoke a moment, as himself, a farewell to his last audience. "From these garish lights," he said in conclusion, "I vanish now forevermore, with a heartfelt, grateful, respectful, affectionate farewell."

"When he ceased to speak," so writes his son Harry (Sir Henry Fielding Dickens, looking back over sixty years to his recollection of the scene), "a kind of sigh seemed to come from the audience, followed almost at once by such a storm of cheering as I have never seen equalled in my life. He was deeply touched that night, but infinitely sad and broken."

So Dickens took himself back to Gad's Hill to resume the proper work of his life, the writing of books. It was a relatively empty place compared to its first days. Dickens's sister-in-law, Georgina Hogarth, was there, and the eldest daughter Mamie. But of the other children the soldier son Walter was dead. The eldest son and Kate the second daughter were married. The little wistful midshipman Sydney, affectionately called the Little Admiral and the Ocean Spectre, was at sea. Harry was at Cambridge with a Trinity scholarship. And the baby of the family, Edward Bulwer Lytton, "little Plorn," had recently (1868) sailed for Australia – a heartbreak for his father – to join his brother Alfred.

There at Gad's Hill he worked out the rest of his time, with an occasional public dinner in London to attend. It cheered him that the first monthly number of *Edwin Drood* ran straight to fifty thousand copies. There was no failing there.

Just in this closing evening of Dickens's life a little touch of royal recognition came his way. Dickens had not seen Queen

Oliver Twist
Cruikshank's illustration
for Dickens's
Oliver Twist

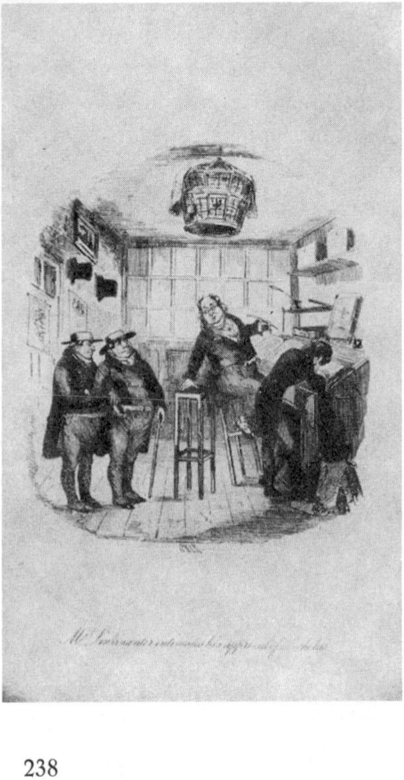

Nicholas Nickleby
Illustration by
Phiz
(Hablôt K. Browne)

Victoria for the thirteen years that had elapsed since his presence in the royal box at his amateur theatricals. For her, as for him, the world had changed. Her marriage, too, had ended in a separation, that left her widowed and secluded forever. She found a gracious pretext for sending for Charles Dickens, who waited upon her at Buckingham Palace. She gave him, humbly enough, a signed copy of her own little book on her *Life in the Highlands*, a work whose origin disarms criticism; told him how the Fenians in New York had insulted her travelling son Prince Arthur; was delighted to learn from Mr. Dickens that not all New Yorkers were Fenians; and so dismissed him with an invitation for himself to the next levee and for his daughter to the next drawing room.

A little later, at a royal request, Dickens dined in company with the Prince of Wales and the King of the Belgians. But these little sunset gleams of favour passed without further consequences. After Dickens was gone, it was stated in the press that "The Queen was ready to confer any distinction which Mr. Dickens's known views and tastes would permit him to accept" and that "more than one title of honour had been declined." The item was repeated and enlarged in various ways, but John Forster, who must have known, says that it is absurd.

When Dickens first planned his *Edwin Drood*, it was to centre round the idea of a "boy and girl pledged to be married and going apart." But to this he had added, as he told John Forster in a letter, "a very curious and new idea," which, however, he explained was not a "communicable one." But he was now undertaking to communicate it. The long days of early summer found him in his little chalet, bent over his writing table. The pen hurried across the page. He had much to do. It was later than he thought.

And beside him, as he wrote, stood the shrouded figure that never left him, peering over his shoulder at the manuscript – waiting to beckon him away.

The summons came.

It was on the afternoon of June 8, 1870. Dickens had spent a long day working in his chalet on his new book, with a brief interval – cheerful enough – for a light lunch. At about five o'clock he rose from his work. In front of him was the unfinished twenty-third chapter of *Edwin Drood* with its closing words: "and then falls to with an appetite." What happened after that may be told in the words of his daughter Mamie.

"When he came again to the house, about an hour before the time fixed for an early dinner, he was tired, silent and abstracted, but as this was a mood very usual to him after a day of engrossing work, it caused no alarm nor surprise to my aunt, who happened to be the only member of the family at home. While awaiting dinner he wrote some letters in the library and arranged some trifling business matters, with a view to his departure for London the following morning.

"It was not until they were seated at the dinner-table that a striking change in the colour and expression of his face startled my aunt. Upon her asking him if he were ill, he answered, 'Yes, very ill; I have been very ill for the last hour.' But when she said that she would send for a physician he stopped her, saying that he would go on with dinner, and afterward to London.

"He made an earnest effort to struggle against the seizure which was fast coming over him, and continued to talk, but incoherently and very indistinctly. It being now evident that he was in a serious condition, my aunt begged him to go to his room before she sent for medical aid. 'Come and lie down.' she entreated. 'Yes, on the ground,' he answered indistinctly. These were the last words that he uttered. As he spoke, he fell to the floor. A couch was brought into the dining-room, on which he was laid, a messenger was dispatched for the local physician, telegrams were sent to all of us and to Mr. Beard. This was at a few minutes after six o'clock. I was dining at a house some little distance from my sister's home. Dinner was half over when I received a message that she wished to speak to me. I found her in the hall with a change of dress for me and a cab in waiting. Quickly I changed my gown, and we began the short journey which brought us to our so sadly-altered home. Our dear aunt was waiting for us at the open door, and when I saw her face I think the last faint hope died within me.

"All through the night we watched him – my sister on one side of the couch, my aunt on the other, and I keeping hot bricks to the feet which nothing could warm, hoping and praying that he might open his eyes and look at us, and know us once again. But he never moved, never opened his eyes, never showed a sign of consciousness through all the long night. On the afternoon of the ninth the celebrated London physician, Dr. Russell Reynolds [recently deceased], was summoned to a consultation by the two medical men in attendance, but he could only confirm their hopeless verdict. Later, in the evening of this day, at ten minutes past six, we saw a shudder pass over our dear father, he heaved a deep sigh, a large tear rolled down his face and at that instant his spirit left us. As we saw the dark shadow pass from his face, leaving it so calm and beautiful in the peace and majesty of death, I think there was not one of us who would have wished, could we have had the power, to recall his spirit to earth."

Chapter Thirteen

THE MYSTERY OF MORE THAN "EDWIN DROOD"

Edwin Drood Still Alive – Joyful Resurrections at Last Certain

THE SHOCK OCCASIONED BY DICKENS'S DEATH AND the sense of loss which it brought were so great that minor considerations connected with it were for the time forgotten. The fact that Dickens had left behind him an unfinished book was of no consequence as beside his unfinished life. Presently it became known that Dickens's current serial story, the *Mystery of Edwin Drood*, was not only unfinished, but that it never could be finished. When attention was turned to the matter it was found that beyond the last words written in his little chalet at Gad's Hill on June 8, 1870, there was scarcely a note, scarcely a scrap of real evidence to indicate how the story was intended to move onward to its close. There was little or nothing, and there remains little or nothing, beyond internal and subjective evidence. With the lapse of years the *Mystery of Edwin Drood* has but become more mysterious still. Two generations of readers have pondered, with increasing interest, as to whether Edwin Drood is alive or dead. Quite a literature of books and articles has arisen around the problem. On the occasion of Dickens's centenary in 1912 it was made the subject of a mock trial of the supposed murderer. Two opposing schools of thought have arisen between which no compromise is possible.

The greater weight of authority, perhaps, inclines to the theory that Edwin is dead. But one may also – with an optimism proper to the memory of Dickens – insist on holding that Edwin Drood is still alive. The verb is in the present tense. For unless Charles Dickens killed Edwin Drood in 1870, he is alive today. He is just as much alive as Mr. Pickwick, still living quite unchanged in his little villa – if only one could find it – or Mr. Micawber on his sheep range, absolutely unaltered, somewhere in the wilds of Australia.

The only question is whether or not Edwin Drood was done to death by his creator.

At the time of Dickens's death, as already said, the story was appearing, after the fashion of the time, in serial parts. Judging by the length of the other books, similarly published, and by the unfolding of the plot itself, the story was about half completed. The fortunes of Edwin Drood and his mysterious disappearance, surrounded with every circumstance of tragedy, even of horror, had been followed by tens of thousands of interested readers. The unravelling of the mystery was a subject of eager expectation. But as time passed, and the papers and notes of Dickens were collected and examined, the strange truth was revealed that the mystery of Edwin Drood was destined to remain a mystery forever.

Of written testimony as to the dénouement of the story but little remained; there were a few scraps of dialogue, apparently for minor characters in a later connection; a scribbled page of possible titles that Dickens had prepared, after his custom, and from which he had finally settled upon the title as it stands; these and a cover design that had appeared on the serial numbers, with little pictures to illustrate the plot – themselves destined to be mysteries – were all that was ever found.

It is, of course, impossible here to recite at length the outline of the unfinished story. But even those who know it best will not object to be reminded for a moment of its salient features.

With true artistic instinct for contrast, Dickens had laid the scene of the mystery, and of the horror that attends it, in the drowsy cathedral town of Cloisterham (Rochester) and centred it in the gloomy and resonant cathedral and in the dark, ancient crypt that lay beneath its floor. Here moves the strange figure of Durdles, the drunken stonemason, who prowls in the great crypt at night, tapping with his little hammer to find where the hollow sound of the ancient walls marks the resting-places of the dead. In the gloom of the cathedral and in the darkness of the crypt we feel that the stage is being set for the completion, or at least the attempt, of a crime. There is the crypt itself. There is the winding stairway that leads upwards from the crypt to the dizzy heights of the great tower where the wind at night howls through the yawning openings of the stone. Around the cathedral is the graveyard, shadowed by ancient trees, with the monuments of the dead, and beside one of them a great heap of quicklime that, as Durdles is made to tell us, will in a few hours burn a dead body, once laid in it, into nothingness.

Even a child, in reading the story, feels that the introduction of this heap of lime is ominous with meaning.

And who are to be the actors in the scene? Of this, too, there is no doubt. Here is Edwin Drood, gay and high-spirited, on the threshold of life, a bright future before him, a favoured child of fortune; overfavoured, it seems, for his plighted engagement to his sweet fiancée Rosa – a thing arranged from their childhood – fails to please him. Here also is the obvious villain of the piece, Jasper, uncle of Drood, though not much older than he, by profession organist of the cathedral: dark, saturnine, repellent; a man of a double life and of dark vice, who makes mysterious visits to London, where he lies in the squalor of an opium den, stupefied and murmuring of the crime he means to commit. In his hideous fashion, Jasper is in love with Rosa, to whom he teaches music and in whom, in a mesmeric way, he seems to inspire a species of terror. As the time for the pre-arranged marriage between Drood and Rosa approaches, Jasper plans to do away with Drood, to kill him in some strange and awful way, evidently connected with the cathedral and the crypt, most probably by enticing him to the tower in the dead of night and hurling him over the railing of the stairs, to be dashed to pieces on the floor below. From there, it seems, he means to carry Drood's body to a vault in the churchyard of which he has stolen a key, and to shovel in upon his lifeless body the lime that lay heaped beside the vault.

All this, except only the conjectured details of the crime, is plain and evident to every reader. No one doubts that Jasper is the villain. No one doubts that he means to kill Drood. No one doubts his motive for meaning to kill him. And no one doubts that the cathedral of Cloisterham is to be the scene of the crime. The only question is. Did Jasper succeed in his fell purpose?

This essential background already exists before the secondary characters of the story enter into the lives of the three described. Their introduction prevents the plot from being too simple and direct, and supplies a means, in the narrative, of turning suspicion toward someone else than Jasper, when Drood disappears. For this purpose we have the introduction of a brother and sister – Neville and Helena Landless – who come to reside in Cloisterham. The sister is to enter the "finishing school" at which Rosa, who is an orphan, still has her home. The brother is to be taken in as a resident pupil by the Rev. Mr. Crisparkle, a canon of the cathedral, a central figure of the story – the friend and confidant of everybody. Neville and his sister are a strange pair – twins – united by an intense and almost occult sympathy, reared (in the East) in adversity and ill-treatment, and with an almost Oriental tendency to passionate love and hatred. Helena is at once captivated with the gentle and shrinking Rosa. Neville, too, quite evidently falls in love with her, and is then led to conceive an intense dislike for Edwin Drood, whose offhand treatment of his little fiancée arouses Neville's contempt. Jasper foments the quarrel. At his rooms one night he drugs the wine of the young men. There is a violent scene, in which they come to blows. Next day it is whispered in the town that young Landless has tried to kill Edwin Drood. Jasper lays plans. He invites Drood and Landless to dine with him, by way of reconciliation, on Christmas Eve. The night is wild with rain and storm. "No such power of wind has blown for many a winter night. Chimneys topple in the street, and people hold to posts and corners and to one another to keep themselves upon their feet. The violent rushes abate not, but increase in frequency and fury until at midnight, when the streets are empty, the storm goes thundering along them, rattling at all the latches and tearing at all the shutters."

Such a night, indeed, as Dickens loved to depict, fit time for crime and mystery.

On the night of the storm Drood disappears. The morning after it Jasper, disheveled and wild with excitement, comes to Mr. Crisparkle's house to say that his nephew can nowhere be found. He had left Jasper at midnight alone with young Landless. He is, as far as the story reaches, never seen again. The problem is, What happened to him?

In the novel, as Dickens wrote it, there are twenty-three chapters. Drood disappears at the end of chapter XIV, and the narrative is carried some six months further, but with no solution of the mystery. Landless is arrested on suspicion, but released. Jasper learns, with evident consternation, that his crime, or attempted crime, was needless, for Drood and Rosa, on the very day of it, had already agreed to break their engagement; they were not in love with one another and had come to know it. Each relinquished the engagement with a certain sorrow, but with relief. Henceforth they were to be brother and sister to one another.

All this is told to Jasper by Mr. Grewgious, the queer, shrewd old lawyer, such as Dickens loved to paint, who is Rosa's guardian, and who had, long years ago, been deeply and hopelessly in love with Rosa's mother – a memory that still lies close to his solitary heart. Jasper, at this disclosure, falls into a hideous fit of hysteria, half unconscious, his face leaden, his hands clutching at his hair. Grewgious watches him with cold, disdainful scrutiny, as from one who knows.

The plot moves on. Jasper attempts to make love to Rosa. He is fierce and maniacal. She is terrified. She runs away from Cloisterham and takes up her abode in London under the protection of her guardian. There she meets a new character in the story, a retired naval lieutenant, Mr. Tartar, as vigorous and sunburned and as wholesome as Jasper is sallow and repulsive. They fall in love at once. There is no doubt, even in the half-finished story, of *their* destiny.

Neville, a victim of public suspicion, with nothing but his sister's love and the friendship of Crisparkle to sustain him, leaves Cloisterham and goes also to London. His love for Rosa is as evident in the narrative as it is hopeless.

Meantime, as the written chapters close, there appears in Cloisterham another character, a certain Mr. Datchery, a strange gentleman with a great mop of white hair (obviously a wig), who prowls about picking up information, under the guise of being an idle fellow, with nothing better to do than to occupy lodgings near Jasper's home, talk with Durdles, the mason, and Tope, the verger, and Mr. Sapsea, the chuckle-headed mayor of the town.

Datchery is evidently someone in disguise, some character already known in the story, acting as a detective to trace out the murder, or attempted murder, of Drood. But who is he? Is he, as some people have guessed, the lawyer, Mr. Grewgious? Is he, perhaps, the peculiar personage, Bazzard, Mr. Grewgious's law clerk, who somewhat mysteriously is granted a vacation from his work at this very juncture? Or is he – boldest guess of all – Helena Landless, anxious to vindicate her brother's honour by fixing the crime upon Jasper? Or is he – most fascinating of possibilities – Edwin Drood himself?

Whoever he is, Datchery busily investigates; is evidently making progress; is gathering the threads of the mystery; gets, by good fortune, into touch with the ancient and evil hag who conducts the opium den that is the scene of Jasper's periodic debauches; adds mark by mark to the strange score which he keeps, done in chalk, on his cupboard door; and so, coming home to his supper of a certain night, well satisfied with his work, adds a final score mark – "and then falls to with an appetite."

These were the last words that Dickens wrote, on June 8, 1870, when he was stricken. He died on the day following.

There, then, is the outline of the mystery, enough, perhaps, to recall to readers who already know the book the salient features of the unfinished story.

The years that have passed since *Edwin Drood* was penned have in no way abated interest in the unsolved problem. Quite a library of literature has grown up about it.

Presumptuous writers have even dared to complete the story. An American writer, Henry Mitford, published a sequel to it in 1872. A three-volume sequel by Gillan Vase appeared in London in 1878. A still more authoritative sequel was written by no less a being than "The Spirit of Charles Dickens," as interpreted by an obliging medium of Brattleboro, Vermont. Andrew Lang was never tired of writing articles on the mystery. The subject had been approached by a hundred authors – historically, analytically, evidentially, psychologically, and in every other known fashion. Yet the interested public is apparently, and perhaps rightly, never tired of it. More "Drood" articles and "Drood" books appeared in the decade just before the war than in the thirty-five years preceding. Apart from casual comments and current discussion, there have been put forth, in all, eight complete books on the mystery, and eighty formal articles in the leading magazines, in addition to which it has been made the theme of five dramas, in which various conclusions are given, and became, as everybody remembers, the subject of a sort of mock trial or judicial investigation, by the literary wits of London, in the year of the Dickens centenary.

What, then, is the consensus of opinion of all those writers? There is none, in the complete sense, but the most reputable opinion – regret it though one may – appears to be that Drood is dead; that he was killed by Jasper; that Datchery hunted Jasper down; that he was arrested and condemned to die, and that in prison, before his execution, he confessed and fully explained the details of his crime.

To the true lover of Dickens this is a sad conclusion, accepted at best with reluctance. To one who loves to think of Mr. Pickwick as still alive and well in his little villa, of Mark Tapley as still jolly, and of the Cheeryble Brothers as still as cheery as ever, it is almost impossible to acquiesce in the untimely death of so bright and promising a youth as Edwin, the title-page hero of a Dickens book.

Is the conclusion necessary?

Let us see, then, what is the evidence that Drood is dead. In the first place, we have the statement of John Forster, who was Dickens's lifelong friend and biographer. "I have a very curious and new idea for a story," wrote Dickens to Forster on August 6, 1869, just before he began writing *Edwin Drood*, "not a very communicable idea (or the interest of the book would be gone), but a very strong one, though difficult to work." The words, be it noted, are the actual words of Dickens himself. In so far as they point either way, it would be more easy to interpret them as suggesting that Drood, through some miraculous chain of circumstances, is alive; for a mere murder is not a "very curious and new idea," even when done in the gloom of a cathedral crypt. But Forster, after quoting this passage from the letter, follows it up by saying: "The story, I learned immediately afterwards, was to be that of the murder of a nephew by his uncle, the originality of which was to consist in the review of the murderer's career by himself at the close. The last chapters were to be written in the condemned cell."

To this we must add the testimony of Madame Perugini (formerly Miss Kate Dickens, daughter of the novelist). In an article on the Drood mystery (*Pall Mall Magazine*, 1906), after quoting Mr. Forster as above, she adds, "We know also that my eldest brother, Charles, positively declared that he had heard from his father's lips that Drood was dead."

Another piece of evidence comes from a written statement of the celebrated artist, Sir Luke Fildes, who as a young man had drawn the illustrations for the book, under the directions from the author. Dickens told the artist that Jasper must have a necktie of double length, and not of single length, as Fildes had first drawn it. "I asked him," writes the artist, "if he had any special reasons. After a short silence, cogitating, he suddenly said, 'Can you keep a secret?' I assured him he could rely upon me. He then said, 'I must have a double necktie. It is necessary, for Jasper strangles Edwin Drood with it.'"

This is all the testimony that there is purporting to come direct from Dickens – other than the revelations of the Brattleboro spirit.

At first sight it sounds convincing to the point of certainty, but on examination it falls far short of it. It is mere hearsay evidence. Kate Dickens understood her brother to say that he understood his father to say that Drood was dead. This is nothing. There is too much room for error or misunderstanding. Dickens may have spoken playfully, or evasively, or ironically, or mumblingly, or – as is indeed likely – ambiguously, on purpose, and Charles Dickens Junior may have received an impression contrary to fact.

Compare, for example, the answer which Dickens is reported to have given to his sister-in-law, Miss Hogarth. "My aunt" (it is still Kate Dickens speaking) "said that she knew absolutely nothing, but she told me that shortly before my father's death, and after he had been speaking of some difficulty he was in with his work, without explaining what it was, she found it impossible to refrain from asking him, 'I hope you haven't really killed poor Edwin Drood?' To which he gravely replied, 'I call my book the Mystery, not the History, of Edwin Drood.'" This is as cryptic as the book itself. But, at least, it shows, as does the remark to Fildes about keeping a secret, how jealously Dickens guarded his mystery till the moment should come to reveal it in due course. Thus there is no doubt that John Forster understood Dickens to imply that Jasper killed Edwin, but whether Dickens really said so, or merely said something that sounded like it, is another matter. As to Fildes's testimony about the scarf, it is neither here nor there; everybody knows that Jasper meant to try to kill Edwin, and to say that "Jasper strangles Drood with it" is not necessarily to say "Jasper kills Drood with it."

Here ends all oral and direct testimony in the matter. To some people, and to some of the best critics, it seems strong enough to be final. Others may have the hardihood to feel that it seems far from being so.

One turns then to the evidence offered by the notes, headings, and memoranda prepared for the book, including the cover designed by C.A. Collins for the wrapper in which the serial parts of *Edwin Drood* appeared. There were left among Dickens's papers the little headings which be used for each of the twenty-two written chapters – not to be printed in the book, but as guides for himself in writing – the stakes, so to speak, driven into the ground in advance to mark his path. Two at least of them seem to point to Edwin's death. The notes for chapter II include the jotting, "Uncle and Nephew. Murder very far off." Those for chapter XII include the direction, "Lay the ground for the manner of the murder to come out at last."

Now this looks at first like strong evidence. If there was no murder, why should Dickens, writing only for himself, call it a "murder"? But again, on examination, the evidence loses a good deal of its finality. Suppose that Dickens really meant the direction to "Lay the ground for the manner of the attempted-murder-which-apparently-is-a-murder-till-the-sequel-discloses-it-not-to-be-one, to come out at last," by what word would he have indicated it? It is quite clear that he might have written "the assault" or "the crime," etc. But as he was writing only for his own eye, with no question of the honesty or dishonesty of the term used, one can well believe that he might simply call the thing "the murder." A certain supposition as to what really happened, if well founded, would give strong reason for his doing so.

This is all that can be found in the notes to support the idea that Drood is dead. On the other hand, there is very strong evidence in them pointing the other way: indicating, that is, that Jasper failed in his attempt and that Drood is alive. It is as follows: There has been preserved a list of titles which, as shown by Dickens's notes, were those among which he finally selected, with the aid of which he finally constructed, the title as it stands. They read as follows:

THE EDWIN DROOD TITLES

The Loss of James Wakefield
James's Disappearance
Flight and Pursuit
Sworn to Avenge It
One Object in Life
A Kinsman's Devotion
The Two Kinsmen
The Loss of Edwin Brood
The Loss of Edwin Brude
The Mystery in the Drood Family
The Loss of Edwin Drood
The Flight of Edwin Drood
Edwin Drood in Hiding
The Loss of Edwin Drude
The Disappearance of Edwin Drood
The Mystery of Edwin Drood
Dead? or Alive?

Dickens very often wrote down lists of possible titles for his stories. The above were found among his notes as titles of the book ultimately called *The Mystery of Edwin Drood.*

The reader will observe at once that this list of titles is very difficult to reconcile with the idea that Drood was to be murdered and never to reappear. Such words as "Loss" and "Mystery" and "Disappearance" are colourless, while two of the titles are almost incompatible with the idea of Drood being dead. *The Flight of Edwin Drood* and *Edwin Drood in Hiding* are only consistent with the murder theory on the supposition that Dickens in writing them planned the title as a misleading lie. From an ingenuous mind with the knowledge already in it as to what Drood's fate was, such titles could hardly have come. On the other hand, supposing that Dickens knew that Drood was not dead but was in hiding, he would quite naturally frame such titles as these and then reject them on the ground that they gave too much away, and would substitute for them a neutral title such as the one selected.

But when all of the above evidence has been duly tested in either direction, many will doubt that it has the same value as what is called the "subjective evidence" drawn from the book itself; by which is meant the idea that every reader must form for himself as to how the story ought, as a matter of art and in the manner of Charles Dickens, to continue and to end. Up to a certain point, proof of this sort is absolutely convincing. Thus, if one half of Leonardo da Vinci's picture of The Last Supper had been torn off and lost and had not been completed, we should have a very positive idea of what the other half probably was, and an absolute certainty of many things which it was not; if, for instance, we were told that the other half consisted of a comic picture of the six missing apostles standing on their heads, we should have asserted that it simply was not so. And even if a friend of Da Vinci's had said that Da Vinci had confided to him before his death that the part of the picture still to be completed was to be made comic, we should have preferred to think that Da Vinci's friend had misunderstood him. This example is, of course, extreme, but it is at least illustrative of what is meant.

Now which ending fits into the book best – Drood alive or Drood dead? Call up the two or three hundred million readers of Dickens's books, past and present, and ask them without giving them time for second thought, and the answer will be an overwhelming shout of "Alive!" Surely it is a poor kind of story (speaking generally) which bears the title *Alive or Dead? A Mystery?* and ends up with the answer, Dead. Death is too easy. There is no "curious and new idea" – alas! – about being dead. But the real ingenuity of the problem that fascinates every writer of mystery fiction is how to bring the "dead" back, alive and hearty, in the concluding chapters. We have but to remember the joyful resurrection of Red Riding Hood's Grandmother, and The White Cat, to realize that this dénouement is as old as fiction itself.

So much for generalities. Unfortunately, when we turn to the Drood story itself, many critics are found who tell us that the story points to Drood's death. What has he to come back to? His engagement with Rosa is ended. She has fallen in love with and will certainly marry Lieutenant Tartar, R.N. – a genuine Dickens marriage, that would be rounded off at the end of the book with the mention of the various little Tartars who resulted from it, as merry and sunburned as the jolly lieutenant himself. One fears, indeed, that Dickens would even have called one of them, the gentlest, Edwin. Helen Landless, too, say the critics, is paired off with that muscular Christian, the Rev. Septimus Crisparkle. Neville Landless is no friend of Drood. The rest of the characters are not connected with him. What can Drood come back to? they ask. There is no place left for him.

Moreover, so they tell us, the machinery of the plot, the mechanism of the murder, is such that it is hard to see how Drood can escape it. Jasper means (no one doubts this) to put Drood's body into quicklime, either in the crypt of the cathedral or in a vault in the churchyard outside. He has stolen the keys (or the wax impression of them) that give him the needed access. He has been particular to remember that Drood's watch and chain and scarf pin must not be thrown into the lime with him, as they cannot be corroded and might reveal the murder. This is thrown into a high light in the story, with obvious intent. The reader is meant to think about it; he is invited to think about it. More than this, things are so arranged that on the night of the crime Drood carries in his pocket a gold ring, a fact which Jasper does not know. This ring was given to Edwin by Mr. Grewgious to hand on to Rosa; it was the ring of Rosa's mother, taken from her hand long years ago when she was drowned, and later given by her husband at his death to Grewgious, the guardian, to keep till the girl should marry. When Drood and Rosa part, Drood keeps the ring in his pocket, having said nothing of it to Rosa, meaning to restore it to her guardian. He has it with him when he dines with his evil uncle on the night of the tragedy.

The ring is set in a high light by Dickens. It is, and is meant to be, the great clue to the unravelling of the plot. And the best, at least the most reputable, critics concur in saying that it is the link by which the chain of evidence is completed. Found in the heap of quicklime, it proves, they say, that Drood was killed, and it proves the manner of his death. On the other hand, they argue, if Drood was not killed, the whole business of the ring seems to lose its significance. Why should Dickens say (in chapter XIII when Edwin decides not to give the ring to Rosa and keeps it in his pocket): "Among the mighty store of wonderful chains that are forever forging, day and night, in the vast iron-works of time and circumstance, there was one chain forged in the moment of that small conclusion, riveted to the foundations of heaven and earth and gifted with invincible force to hold and drag"? What holding and dragging does it do, after all, if the dead body of Edwin is not thrown, ring and all, into the quicklime?

More than this. If it is argued that Drood is not strangled to death (there is, of course, no doubt that the assault was made), why in the name of common sense does he not have Jasper arrested? Why does he not tell what has happened? Why disappear? Why hide? What is Datchery, whoever he is, prying round for, if Drood was not killed after all? There is, they say, no point to it all.

These are the arguments, or the main ones, which have convinced most students of the problem that Drood is certainly and finally dead.

Now in a subjective matter of this sort no one must dare to dogmatize. Too much depends upon the feeling or idea which the work conveys to the individual mind. But one may at least say, in all humility, that he cannot bring his mind to the idea of Edwin's death. If Dickens killed him, then the story is, in its essence, commonplace. The mystery is merely a mystery as to where a dead body is hid. Dickens has indicated Jasper as the murderer as clearly as if he had written it on a placard. The motive is there, the method is there, everything. If it turns out that Drood is murdered, then it turns out that every reader knew it all along, and that the only mystery lies in the fact that the other characters did not know it. Surely this is but a poor sort of art. Say what one will, or rather what John Forster will, about the originality and interest of Jasper's confession, one cannot but feel that the story, with its pre-conceived conclusion, would run lamely to its end.

No, no, Dickens meant something better than that; and what is more, we (that is, all the readers of the right school) know that he did.

What, then, was to be the sequel? Let us first clear our minds of the idea mentioned above that there is no place left for Drood to come back to. This is wrong. Drood falls in love with Helena Landless. Dickens practically says so. In chapter VII he tells us that "Edwin Drood is *already* enough impressed by Helena to feel indignant that Helena's brother should dispose of him so coolly, and put him out of the way so entirely."

Will the reader please note the word *already* which is set in italics above? It seems to come, consciously or unconsciously, straight out of Dickens's knowledge of the conclusion.

And notice what follows in chapter XIII, where Edwin and Rosa are breaking their engagement:

"And yet there was one reservation on each side: on hers that she intended through her guardian to withdraw herself immediately from the tuition of her music master; on his, that he did already entertain some wandering speculations whether it might ever come to pass that he would know more of Miss Landless." And again, in the next chapter, in describing Edwin Drood's last day on earth – his last day, that is, according to the murder theory:

"Though the image of Miss Landless still hovers in the background of his mind, the pretty, little, affectionate creature [Rosa], so much firmer and wiser than he had supposed, occupies its stronghold. It is with some misgivings of his own unworthiness that he thinks of her, and of what they might have been to one another, if he had been more in earnest some time ago.... And still, for all this, and though there is a sharp heartache in all this, the vanity and caprice of youth sustain that handsome figure of Miss Landless in the background of his mind."

Now if Edwin Drood is really and truly to be murdered that very night, if this is really the last of him on earth, can anything be more inharmonious, more inartistic, more repellent than this introduction of Helena Landless? It is not only pointless, but it is execrable.

But if Drood is not to die, if he escapes from Jasper's hands, to play his part in running Jasper down, and if in the sequel a "place" is needed for Drood, here it is already prepared.

It is said by some of the critics that Helena marries Crisparkle. But is this so? Of Helena's esteem and admiration for the clergyman (about sixteen years older than herself) there is no doubt, nor of her gratitude for his kindness to her brother. And Crisparkle may, or he may not, fall in love with Helena. But if so, he is destined to step aside in self-forgetting sacrifice; his is the part assigned in *Bleak House* to Mr. Jarndyce in his love for Esther: a part dear to Dickens's heart. A marriage between Crisparkle and Helena does not seem fitted for the needs of romance. The clergy (be it said in all reverence) are too "tame" to make the kind of marriages that novelists must use.

Drood, then, as we see it, was not murdered, but lived to marry Helena, and to be great friends, undoubtedly, with Mr. and Mrs. Tartar – the Rev. Mr. Crisparkle and his delightful old mother being always welcome guests at both establishments.

How, then, did Drood escape? What happened? And why did he not declare himself?

Here we come to the "murder" itself, and here, of course, one must remind the reader we are stepping out on the open ground of conjecture with absolute certainty left behind.

Now the trouble with the Drood murder is that there is too much of it. It is too well prepared. Jasper is a man of evil hatreds and is in love with Rosa. That is enough of itself to make him kill Drood. Jasper is also an opium fiend, a man of disturbed brain, who lies in an opium den, with a homicidal dream in his heart, rehearsing a hundred times his crime. That is enough to make him kill anybody.

As to the mechanism of the murder, there is too much of it again. Every critic has found here an *embarras de richesse* in the material prepared. We can never know just how the killing of Drood was planned or done, because there was enough mechanism ready to kill him two or three times. Jasper can strangle him to death with the scarf, either drugged or not drugged (for we know that Jasper is by way of drugging his friends); he can throw him off the stairway of the tower to the stone floor of the crypt below, or he can kill him, either drugged or not, in the crypt itself. Then he can dispose of the body in lime in the crypt, or drag it out to the vault in the graveyard of which he has the key, and there bury it in lime. With such a wealth of material, no one can say just what Jasper did.

To this will the reader please add that Jasper may be, and is, at any moment in the book, taken with a strange maniacal seizure due to his opium, in which a film comes over his eyes, his brain reels, and his consciousness of what he does is lost.

Here, then, as many of us see it, comes in the "curious and new idea" that Dickens wished to work out.

Jasper takes Drood at midnight to the crypt and up the stair. There he drugs and strangles him and, as he thinks (he has rehearsed the thing in his opium dreams a thousand times), hurls him over the railing of the stair to the stone floor below. He drags the body (so he thinks) to the vault, and with hideous maniacal eagerness shovels in the lime upon it, the storm howling about the madman as he works. But at some point Drood has escaped his hands: drugged, half-conscious, unknowing what is happening, unable to believe that Jasper has attacked him, Drood has escaped death. There is no need to ask at what precise point, for a half-dozen points would do; nor to ask whether Jasper drags an empty coat, or merely empty air – for Jasper is mad. No need to ask why Drood does not arrest Jasper. He recovers consciousness. He makes his way from the scene. He cannot believe that his clouded memory of Jasper's sudden attack is true; he has a dim memory, as he clings to the rail of the stairway, of Jasper looking into the abyss below, shaking his fists in frenzied rage at something that he seems to see lying there. Jasper descends the stair. He does not come back; in his insane fancy he is burying Drood in the vault. Drood escapes, either at once or after hours of unconsciousness: it does not matter. What is he to do? He hardly knows what has happened.

He sees no one. He goes at once to Mr. Grewgious in London for advice and help. Grewgious is in no doubt as to what has happened, but he tells Drood that they must wait. There is no proof – no evidence. Drood is to remain in hiding and a watch must be set on Jasper till they gather the details that will convict him of his murderous assault and intended crime.

Let the reader, if he will, turn to the chapter where Grewgious comes from London and interviews Jasper, and see how intensely full of meaning it becomes, if we can believe that Grewgious has meantime seen Drood, and that he knows.

A watch is set on Jasper – and the watch is Datchery, who is perhaps Drood himself, or perhaps Grewgious's clerk Bazzard, though this is an independent and secondary matter.

How, then, does the ring enter into the story? Why, under the supposition above, it becomes the vital clue by which Jasper's guilt is fastened upon him. In the hands of Grewgious, Drood, Landless, Bazzard, and the group of associates who are on Jasper's trail – and of whom we may think Helena Landless is certainly one, as this brings her into close connection with Drood – the evidence accumulates. At this stage, be it observed, it is not murder which they hope to fasten upon Jasper, but only a maniacal attempt on Drood's life. Owing to Drood's uncertainty as to what has happened, they have no exact proof. But they piece the facts together. The street urchin who figures in the story under the nickname of "Deputy," and who haunts the cathedral grounds at night, has certainly, so every reader of the novel admits, seen something of what happened on the night of the crime. The little note that Dickens wrote for himself – "Keep the boy suspended" – would, of itself, indicate this. Probably what Deputy saw was Jasper coming from the crypt and going to the vault, opening its door with furtive glances and maniacal mutterings, and then shovelling in the lime. His testimony makes clear to the confederates Jasper's plan for the disposal of the body. They know now why the watch and chain were taken from Drood while he was unconscious.

Jasper does not know about the ring. The confederates let him know that Drood carried it on the fatal night. This means, to Jasper, that the ring must be lying still uncorroded in the lime. He must secure it. He does just as they suspect. He visits the vault at night. Lantern in hand, he opens the door. To his horror he sees before him the figure of Edwin Drood. So has Dickens planned it with his characteristic love of the extreme of melodramatic sensation, and here is the explanation of the picture at the foot of the wrapper which has puzzled every student of the problem.

Jasper, insane with horror, rushes upon Drood. But Landless, who has followed close behind, is too quick for him and seizes him. There is a desperate struggle, and in the struggle Landless is killed. John Forster, in his recollections of what Dickens told him, said that he thought he recalled the statement that Landless is killed by Jasper in the attempt to apprehend him. He was quite right. And here, too, is the explanation of the mystic sentence, "When shall we three meet again?" with which Dickens headed the chapter where Drood, Landless, and Jasper dine together on the night of the crime. They do meet again. They meet in the vault where Jasper thought to find only the charred bones and the dust of Edwin Drood.

Jasper is tried for the murder and for the homicidal attempt on his nephew's life. He is condemned. From his cell is given his confession. But the confession is not "the new and curious idea." This phrase refers to the idea that an opium fiend who has rehearsed his crime a thousand times may be hallucinated with the idea that he is committing it.

The story ends, as Dickens loves, with wedding bells and children's faces in the perspective of the future. Drood marries Helena. Tartar marries Rosa. The Rev. Mr. Crisparkle stands aside, disregarding his own feelings, as becomes a well bred clergyman. No one dances more gaily at the weddings than he. Nor is there any merrier friend and playmate of the little Droods and the little Tartars than the cheery Crisparkle, a little gray about the temples, but as ruddy and as much addicted to cold water and long walks as ever: no merrier playmate, unless perhaps it be an odd, angular man of the name of Grewgious, who —

But there, the ending has now become too easy. There is nothing to do but to call up the Brattleboro Spirit and ask it how the matter stands.

EPILOGUE

At Rest in Westminster Abbey – Dickens's Will – His Family – First Editions and Manuscripts – His Place in Literature

THE NEWS OF THE DEATH OF CHARLES DICKENS came to the people of England with something like the shock of a national disaster. It was without warning. Those immediately associated with him knew under what a great strain he had been living and were aware of the dangers that it might imply. But for the world at large, Dickens at fifty-eight years of age was still at the height of his energy and activity. His elastic step, his keen eye, his well knit figure – steel and whipcord as someone called it at the time – showed to the casual eye no sign of the ravages of age.

The blow when it fell came with the added weight of the unexpected. All London was affected by it as by some grave national calamity. "The crowds," wrote an American visitor, "seemed to walk the streets with muffled feet." The London *Times* chronicled the death of Dickens in a noble tribute to the genius and his place in the heart of the people. "Charles Dickens is no more. The loss of such a man makes the ordinary expression of regret seem cold and conventional. It will be felt by millions as nothing less than a personal bereavement."

The wish was universally expressed that Dickens should be laid in Westminster Abbey. The Dean of Westminster, Dean

Stanley, whose office carried with it the necessary authority, offered to the son Charles Dickens Junior the privilege of burying his father's body among England's greatest dead. But a difficulty arose in that such a burial was directly contrary to the views that Dickens himself had repeatedly expressed, and which he had embodied in his will. He had a horror of the trappings and the pageantry of death, the false pomp that mocks the silent reality. Years before, he had written in *Household Words* (1852) an article on "Trading in Death" denouncing the repulsive finery and display of the undertaker. The summer before his death he had refused, on grounds of opinion, to deliver a graveyard speech at the inauguration of a monument.

A compromise, however, was made by the extreme simplicity with which the remains of Charles Dickens were borne to the grave – without pomp and with no other ceremonial than the plain ritual of the burial service. The grave, left open that the thousands of his admirers might pay a last tribute to his memory, was filled with the flowers cast into it.

Charles Dickens left behind him a very considerable family, for all of whose wants his means were ample to provide. To his wife, as indicated already, he left an annuity of £300. To his sister-in-law Miss Hogarth he left £8,000, together with all his papers, and he made John Forster the executor and administrator of the estate. Apart from a special legacy of £1,000 to his daughter Mary and various small benefactions, his estate by his will was to be divided among his children as they attained their majority. The entire estate was valued at about £93,000.

All of Dickens's ten children survived him except two: Dora Annie, who had died as an infant and Walter, the soldier son, who died at Calcutta, December 31, 1863.

The eldest son, Charles, continued the publication of *All the Year Round.* But the magazine was the work of Dickens, his father, and of Dickens alone. After it came to an end, Charles Dickens Junior conducted the printing firm of Dickens & Evans and was afterwards, as a reader, connected with the Macmillans. In 1887 he made a tour of the United States reading, with no little success, from his father's books. He edited a complete edition of his father's works in 1892-93 and died in 1896. His sister Mary, who died only a few days later, left behind her a little volume of reminiscences – *My Father* – to which reference has already been made. Kate Dickens, after the death of her first husband, Charles Collins, married again and became Mrs. Perugini. She died in 1929.

Francis Dickens, the third son, went to the Northwest of Canada, became an officer in the Mounted Police. He was at Battleford during the rebellion of 1885; a diary written by him at the time has since been published. Alfred Tennyson Dickens returned from Australia and visited America early in the present century. The sailor son, the little admiral of the wistful eyes, did not long survive his father. He was taken ill, was invalided home, and died at sea on the way to England in 1872. Harry Dickens, the Cambridge scholar, had a distinguished career at the bar, was knighted in 1922. He published in 1929 a little memorial, *Memories of My Father,* a charming reminiscence and tribute. He was the only child of Charles Dickens surviving in 1933.

No writer in the world's history has had so wide a public as Charles Dickens. His books have penetrated where Shakespeare is unknown and where the Bible is not accepted. We are told, by those who know, that the works of Charles Dickens are at the present time the "best sellers" in the world.

In the United States and in the British colonies the name of Dickens became and remained the same household word as in his mother country. For all the English-speaking world Pickwick and Mrs. Gamp and such are as real as the people next door – and better known.

The prices paid for first editions are no real evidence of the value of a book or the eminence of the author. Indeed the "first edition" hobby is one of the minor forms of mental derangement, seldom ending in homicide, and outside the scope of the law. But it may be noted for what it is worth that among the treasures of that market are the first editions of Dickens – especially in the form of the monthly instalments in which most of the books appeared. In 1927 a copy of *Pickwick* in this form was sold for $16,300, and a still higher figure was reached in 1929 when the Kern copy of *Pickwick* was sold for $28,000.

Still more valuable, of course, are the manuscripts of Dickens's works, which would represent, if valued in their entirety, a colossal fortune. But the great bulk of them have passed into the national and other institutions, where they are not for sale. The great bulk of these manuscripts passed into the hands of John Forster, some in Dickens's lifetime and the rest by the terms of his will. On Forster's death in 1876 they were left to the Victoria and Albert Museum at South Kensington, where they still are. But the list does not include *Pickwick Papers, Nicholas Nickleby, The Uncommercial Traveller, Great Expectations,* or *Our Mutual Friend.* Of *Pickwick* there exist thirty-seven pages of manuscript. Dr. Rosenbach of Philadelphia bought the pages of the *Pickwick* manuscript in separate lots. For a lot of five pages sold at auction in London in 1928 he paid £7,000. A few days before, a page and a half was sold in Philadelphia for $9,000. The rest of the *Pickwick* manuscript is still outstanding – destroyed or lying unknown in a lumber room. Dr. Rosenbach also acquired one hundred and sixty-one pages of *Nicholas Nickleby, The Uncommercial Traveller* manuscript is lost from sight. The *Great Expectations* manuscript was given as a present by Dickens to a friend and is now in the Wisbeck Museum in England. It came to it as a gift of Chauncey Townsend of the "Religious Opinions" mentioned in a previous chapter. Dickens presumably gave it to him. The manuscript of *Our Mutual Friend* came into the possession of G.W.C. Drexel, editor of the Philadelphia *Ledger,* who gave it to the Drexel Institute. Its preceding migrations are not accurately known. Of the lesser pieces, outside of the novels, the Pierpont Morgan collection has *A Christmas Carol*, *The Cricket on the Hearth*, and *The Battle of Life*.

Few stock exchange booms show a better rise in value than that of the thirty-two pages of *Pickwick*, sold for $775 in 1895 and $35,000 in 1928.

The fact is that, when all is said and done, Charles Dickens has still not been measured up to the real height of his genius. Starting as a humorist, one might almost say, as a comic writer, and writing of the ordinary people, he was handicapped at the start, as far as academic rank goes. It is difficult to be funny and great at the same time. Aristophanes and Molière and Mark Twain must sit below Aristotle and Bossuet and Emerson.

The result is that in all schools and colleges where literature is taught as a study and not read as a diversion the name of Dickens has not yet been put where it belongs. Whole courses are devoted to Shakespeare, a man – or a collection of men – of far lesser genius. But Shakespeare wrote about kings, at the time a great advance from writing about giants. Milton seems to the colleges profound because he wrote of hell, a great place, and is dead. In short, the whole college estimate is based on theme, on scholarship, and on deadness. Dickens is too recent, too ordinary, too easy to understand.

Transitory popularity is not a proof of genius. But permanent popularity is. People of the adolescent generation of today may have the impression that Dickens is passed by in favour of a rising group of newer men. This is not so. These newer men come and go, rise and fall, and are forgotten. Dickens stays. Forty years ago newer writers were replacing Dickens; and thirty years ago; and twenty. The world today does not know their names.

In due time it will be known that the works of Charles Dickens represent the highest reach of the world's imaginative literature. This at its lowest is a poor thing, a tale told by an idiot. At its highest – the world's supreme achievement in art.

FINIS

CHRONOLOGY

EVENTS

1812 – Feb. 7. Charles John Huffham Dickens born at Landport, Portsea.
1814 – 1816. Family in lodgings in London.
1816 – 1821. Family in Chatham.
1821 – Moved to London.
1822 – Dickens went to work in a blacking warehouse. Father in Marshalsea prison.
1823 – 27. At school in London.
1827 – Clerk in an attorney's office.
1829 – 31. Reporter in Doctors' Commons.
1831 – Entered Reporters' Gallery in the House of Commons as a reporter for the *True Sun*, then for the *Mirror of Parliament*, and then (1834-36) for the *Morning Chronicle*.

WORKS

1833 – First published article ("A Dinner at Poplar Walk," afterwards called "Mr. Minns and his Cousin") in Dec. no. of *Old Monthly Magazine*.
1833-35 – Sketches in *Old Monthly Magazine* and in *Evening Chronicle* (first signed *Boz* in August, 1834).
1836 – Feb. *Sketches by Boz*, 2 vols., illustrated by George Cruikshank.
The Posthumous Papers of the Pickwick Club, edited by Boz, illustrated by H. Seymour and Hablôt Browne (Phiz) in April-Dec. (monthly nos.).
Sunday under Three Heads, by Timothy Sparks (*nom de plume*), illustrated by Phiz.

1836 – April 2. Married Catherine Hogarth.
1837 – Jan. 6. Birth of Charles Dickens, Junior.
Death of Mary Hogarth.
1837 – July. Ten-day tour on the Continent.
1838 – March 6. Mary (Mamie) Dickens born.
1839 – July. Cottage at Petersham.
Oct. Birth of Kate Macready Dickens.
Moved from Doughty Street to Devonshire Terrace.
1841 – Feb. 8. Birth of Walter Landor Dickens.
1842 – Jan. 4. Dickens and his wife left Liverpool on a tour to the United States and Canada: left New York June 7, 1842.
Holiday Trip to Cornwall with Stanfield, Forster, and Maclise.
1843 – Summer at Broadstairs.
Oct. Presided at the opening of the Manchester Athenaeum.
1844 – Left with his family for a year on the Continent – France, Italy.
1845 – Returned in summer from Italy to Devonshire Terrace.
Aug. Amateur theatricals at Kelly's Theatre.
Oct. Birth of Alfred Tennyson Dickens (6th child; 4th son).
1846 – Jan. 21. Editor of *Daily News.*
Feb. 9. Resigned editorship.
May 31. Left England for the

The Strange Gentleman (play in 2 acts, St. James's Theatre, 29 Sept., 1836. Published 1837).
The Village Coquette. Comic Opera. Sketches by Boz. Second series. One vol. Dec.
1837 – *Pickwick Papers* continues from Jan. till Nov., then published as a book by Charles Dickens.
Oliver Twist began as a serial by Boz, Jan., 1837.
1838 – *Oliver Twist.* Three vols. Charles Dickens. Illustrations by George Cruikshank.
Memoirs of Joseph Grimaldi, Edited by Boz.
Sketches of Young Gentlemen – Illustrated by Phiz.
Nicholas Nickleby. In monthly parts, began in April, 1838. Illustrated by Phiz.
1839 – *Sketches by Boz.* First complete edition, in monthly parts, Nov., 1837-June, 1839. Illustrated by George Cruikshank.
1840 – *Sketches of Young Couples.* Illustrated by Phiz.
1841 – *Master Humphrey's Clock.* Three vols. Illustrated by George Cattermole and Hablôt Browne. Included *Old Curiosity Shop* and *Barnaby Rudge.*
The Picnic Papers. A Symposium to which Dickens contributed the preface and the opening story, *The Lamplighter.*

Continent. Summer at Lausanne.
Nov. Paris. 48 Rue de Courcelle.
Dec. 15-23. Visit to London. Back to Paris.
1847 – Back to London.
Temporarily at Chester Place.
April 18. Sydney Smith Haldinand Dickens born (7th child; 5th son).
Summer at Brighton and Broadstairs.
Dec. 1. Presided at Opening of Leeds Mechanics Institute.
Dec. 28. Presided at Opening of Glasgow Athenæum.
1848 – Jan. Visit to Edinburgh.
1849 – Jan. 16. Birth of Henry Fielding Dickens (8th child; 6th son).
Feb. Visit to Brighton.
Back in Devonshire Terrace.
Summer at Bonchurch, I. W.
1850 – June. Trip to Paris and Rouen.
Aug. 15. Birth of Dora Annie Dickens (9th child; 3d daughter).
Nov. Private theatricals at Knebworth. *Every Man in His Humour.*
1851 – Feb. To Paris with J. Leech.
March 31. Death of John Dickens.
April 14. Death of Dora Annie Dickens.
May 16. Private theatricals at Devonshire House, before the

1842 – Oct. *American Notes for General Circulation.* Two vols.
1843 – *Martin Chuzzlewit.* Illustrations by Hablôt Browne. Monthly nos., Jan.-Dec.
A Christmas Carol in Prose. Illustrated by John Leech.
1844 – *Martin Chuzzlewit* finished and published as a book in July. Illustrated by Hablôt Browne.
Preface to Evenings of a Working Man (J. Overn).
The Chimes. Illustrated by Maclise, Stanfield, Doyle, and Leech.
1845 – *The Cricket on the Hearth.* Illustrated by Maclise, Stanfield, Landsen, Doyle, and Leech.
1846 – Pictures from Italy. (*Daily News,* Jan.-March. Later in the year in book.)
Dombey and Son. Began in monthly nos. Illustrated by Hablôt Browne.
The Battle of Life. Illustrated by Maclise, Stanfield, Doyle, and Leech.
1848 – April. *Dombey and Son* in book form.
The Haunted Man. Illustrated by Stanfield, John Tenniel, Frank Stone, and J. Leech.
1849 – *David Copperfield* began in monthly parts in May, 1848. Illustrated by Hablôt Browne.
1850 – March 30. First no. of

Queen and the Prince Consort.

1852 – March 13. Birth of Edward Bulwer Lytton Dickens (l0th child; 7th son).

1858 – Back in Tavistock House.
Feb. 9. Dinner for Hospital for Sick Children.
Apr. 29. First public reading (St. Martin's Hall), for profit.
May. Dickens separates from his wife.
July 1. Nominated (but not elected) for Rector at Glasgow University.

1859 – Sept. At Broadstairs for a fortnight.
Oct. Second part of the first series of readings.

1859-60 – Last winter at Tavistock House.

1860 – Permanent residence at Gad's Hill.
Kate Dickens married to Charles Collins.

1861 – Took a house in London (3 Hanover Square) for the spring.
March. Began second series of Readings (ended April, 1862).
Charles Dickens, Junior, married Miss Evans.

1862 – Feb. Exchanged Gad's Hill for 16 Hyde Park Gate for the Spring Readings in London till end of June.
Oct.-Dec. Two months in Paris.

1863 – Visited Paris in January.

Household Words.
Nov. *David Copperfield* in book form. Illustrated by Hablôt Browne.
Christmas. Being the first Christmas no. of *Household Words.*

1851 – *What Christmas Is.* Second Christmas no. of Household Words.

1852 – *Bleak House* began in monthly parts in March, 1852. Illustrated by Hablôt Browne.
Stories for Christmas. Third Christmas no. of *Household Words.*

1858 – *A House to Let.* Ninth Christmas no. of *Household Words.*

1859- April 30. First no. of *All the Year Round.*
May 28. Last no. of *Household Words.*
A Tale of Two Cities. Weekly serial in *All the Year Round*; also in monthly parts. In book form in Dec., 1859. Illustrated by Hablôt Browne.
The Haunted House. First Christmas no. of *All the Year Round.*

1860 – *Hunted Down.* New York *Ledger*, also reprinted in *All the Year Round.*
The Uncommercial Traveller. Serial papers in *All the Year Round*; in book form in Dec., 1860.
Great Expectations. Began as a

Readings at the British Embassy. Readings in London.
Sept. Dickens's mother died.
Dec. 24. Death of Thackeray (Christmas Eve). Walter Dickens died in India (New Year's Eve).

1864 – New Year's at Gad's Hill.
Feb.-June. A house in London, 57 Gloucester Place.

1865 – In London at 16 Somers Place.
June 9. In a railway accident at Staplehurst.
Swiss chalet set up at Gad's Hill.

1866 – Third Series of Readings. (Managed by Dolby in 1866-67 and resumed 1868-70 after the American tour.)

1867 – June 5. Presided at the Annual Festival of the Railway Benevolent Society.
Nov. 9. Sailed for America. Landed Boston, Nov. 19.
Lecture tour in U.S., Dec. 2, 1867-April 20, 1868.

1868 – April 18. Farewell dinner at Delmonico's, New York.
Sailed for England, April, 1868. Oct. Resumed public readings.

1869 – Jan. Began second part of series of readings.
Health failing, readings broken off.
April. Public Dinner at Liverpool.

serial in *All the Year Round* in Dec., 1860.
A Message from the Sea. Second Christmas no. of *All the Year Round.*

1861 – *Great Expectations* in book form in three vols.; in 186l in one vol., illustrated by Marcus Stone.
Tom Tiddler's Ground. Third Christmas no. of *All the Year Round.*

1862 – *Somebody's Luggage.* Fourth Christmas no. of *All the Year Round.*

1863 – *Mrs. Lirriper's Lodgings.* Fifth Christmas no. of *All the Year Round.*

1864 – *Our Mutual Friend.* Began in monthly nos. in May, 1864.
Mrs. Lirriper's Legacy. Sixth Christmas no. of *All the Year Round.*
Our Mutual Friend. In book form in two vols. in Nov., 1865.
Dr. Marigold's Prescriptions. Seventh Christmas no. of *All the Year Round.*

1866 – *Mugby Junction.* Eighth Christmas no. of *All the Year Round.*

1867 – *No Thoroughfare.* Ninth Christmas no. of *All the Year Round.*

1868 – *A Holiday Romance.* Written for a child's magazine.
George Silverman's Explanation. Written for the *Atlantic*

1870 – Jan.-March. Twelve Farewell Readings in London.
March 9. Received by the Queen at Buckingham Palace.
April 5. Presided at a dinner in aid of the News Vendors' Institution.
March 7. Royal Academy Dinner (last public appearance).
May. Returned to Gad's Hill.
June 8. Stricken.
June 9. Died.

Monthly (both pieces reprinted in *All the Year Round*).

1870 – *The Mystery of Edwin Drood.* Sixth monthly nos. were issued.
Illustrated by S.L. Fildes.

INDEX